WOMEN DEFYING HITLER

WOMEN DEFYING HITLER

RESCUE AND RESISTANCE UNDER THE NAZIS

Edited by Nathan Stoltzfus, Mordecai Paldiel, and Judy Baumel-Schwartz

BLOOMSBURY ACADEMIC

LONDON • NEW YORK • OXFORD • NEW DELHI • SYDNEY

BLOOMSBURY ACADEMIC
Bloomsbury Publishing Plc
50 Bedford Square, London, WC1B 3DP, UK
1385 Broadway, New York, NY 10018, USA
29 Earlsfort Terrace, Dublin 2, Ireland

BLOOMSBURY, BLOOMSBURY ACADEMIC and the Diana logo are trademarks
of Bloomsbury Publishing Plc

First published in Great Britain 2021

A catalogue record for this book is available from the British Library.

A catalog record for this book is available from the Library of Congress.

ISBN: PB: 978-1-3502-0154-5
HB: 978-1-3502-0155-2
ePDF: 978-1-3502-0156-9
eBook: 978-1-3502-0157-6

Typeset by Deanta Global Publishing Services, Chennai, India
Printed and bound in Great Britain

To find out more about our authors and books visit www.bloomsbury.com and
sign up for our newsletters.

CONTENTS

Contents

ACKNOWLEDGEMENT

To begin, special thanks is due to Volker Berghahn, emeritus historian of German and modern European history at Columbia University, for opening up space at Columbia University for our conference in October 2018 on the occasion of the seventy-fifth anniversary of the Rosenstrasse Protest. He genially put his time, resources, and organizational skills to the service of academic inquiry and discussion. We are also deeply grateful to Dorothy and Jonathan Rintels for endowing the Professorship in Holocaust studies in the Arts and Sciences and History Department which co-sponsored the conference with the Columbia History Department.

We are also deeply grateful to the German Consulate in New York, which sponsored an event in commemoration of the Rosenstrasse Protest on February 27, 2018, where we met survivors and descendants of the protest and the idea for a conference came to life with the invaluable support of German Consul David Gill. The German Consul granted crucial financial support in support of the conference and Mr. Gill generously attended the conference to give the opening address. Not to miss out our appreciation to the Columbia University Jewish Studies, and in particular the German Department with Mark Anderson, who was very helpful with opening Deutsches Haus for the conference at a minimum cost.

Thanks are also due to all the persons who attended our 2018 Columbia conference, some of whom followed this up with articles in this book. We mention them all in alphabetical order: Mark Anderson, Volker Berghahn, Renate Bridenthal, Elisheva Carlebach, David Gill, Susanne Heim, Marion Kaplan, Anne Nelson, Stanlee Stahl, and William Weitzer—and yours truly, Nathan Stoltzfus and Mordecai Paldiel. Not to forget Judy Baumel-Schwartz, who accepted our invitation to co-edit this book, so that with her extensive scholarship, bolstered the emphasis on the role of gender in resisting the Nazi phenomenon.

We express heartfelt thanks to Danielle Wirsansky for applying some of her boundless energy to the project, in carefully reading all the articles for composition and style, before submitting them to the publisher.

Finally, speaking of the publisher, Rhodri Mogford and Laura Reeves, of Bloomsbury, stand out for their diligence, patience and understanding. Thanks to them, the production of this book proceeded along smooth lines and friendly cooperation, and they too deserve all of our thanks.

FOREWORD
German Consul General David Gill

Confronting the Nazis

It is so crucial that we remember and that we illustrate how courageous people resist and how resistance is possible even in the darkest chapters of human history. It is particularly important in times when civil courage and the advocacy for freedom and individual rights worldwide are necessary.

Before I moved to New York a year ago I lived for almost 30 years in the borough of "Mitte" in the center of Berlin, a neighborhood which is shaped by the former, but to some extent also by returning, Jewish life in Berlin. A neighborhood where the signs of the happy times and the most terrible times of Jewry in Berlin can be seen everywhere. In the years when my children were much younger I used to take them to school. And every morning I walked by a rather unimpressive little dead end street between huge buildings of socialist architecture from the 60ies. Not much is left from the time before Berlin was destroyed on this little street which is called Rosenstrasse and only a few people recognize the monument in this little street. For today you will see a photo of this monument, if you open the program or invitation. And even less people know what it stands for. What courageous, fearless women achieved at this very place 75 years ago in the middle of the Nazis' Reich. That is why conferences like yours are so important.

When the women went out on the streets shouting "Give us our husbands back!" they risked everything. We know confronting the Nazi-Regime could have resulted in prison and death. Nevertheless, those women never gave up. They expressed their anger and disagreement in a protest. It continued for days until the police, eventually, released their husbands. No one had believed that they would see their loved ones ever again, but the courage they showed in risking their own lives helped them to succeed in their goal.

This act of courage shows the power of love and the strength of solidarity. It also shows that never losing hope and standing together in difficult times can make unimaginable things happen.

What happened 75 years ago at the Rosenstrasse can inspire people all over the world, also in our respective countries. It should encourage us to stand up against racism, xenophobia, antisemitism and against those who advocate hatred in our societies. In doing so we risk so much less than the courageous women in Berlin.

Looking at the Rosenstrasse protests should also be a reminder and incentive for civil society and governments or multinational organizations to support brave people worldwide who stand up against injustice, the abuse of power and the denial of democracy, human rights and the rule of law. It is important that we show solidarity to those who risk their personal freedom and sometimes their life when they fight for justice and freedom.

Therefore, I am very grateful when you focus on the persecution, resistance and rescue of Jews and other minorities. And I am interested to hear more about recent research on the risks and dilemmas of resistance against the Nazi occupation in Europe.

It is the look back which often can guide us to do the right thing. To be able to focus clearly, we need research, scientific publication and teaching of our history, we need dedicated historians and scientists from other disciplines.

WOMEN DEFYING HITLER

AN INTRODUCTION

Nathan Stoltzfus, Mordecai Paldiel, and Judy Baumel-Schwartz

This book was conceived as a commemoration on its seventy-fifth anniversary of the German women's Rosenstrasse Protests in Berlin in early 1943, and the subsequent release of their husbands, upward of 2,000 German Jews. As Hitler's Reich crumbled, intermarried Jews comprised 11,150 of the 11,359 German "full Jews" still surviving who were not in hiding or had not been deported.[1] The escalation of popular protests against authoritarian repression in recent decades illustrates the continuing timeliness of that protest. To find a much broader context for this event the book identifies resistance and rescue in which women became involved both inside Germany under the Hitler dictatorship after 1933 and from 1938–9 in Nazi-occupied Europe. It does not survey all the ways people, especially women, found to defy Hitler but identifies some prominent case stories from among the many others who knew from the start that they were against what Hitler stood for.

The array of examples we characterize here, from open, largely spontaneous protests to organized, clandestine resistance, also reveals consequential differences in the ways the regime responded to different forms of opposition. Although many women did defy Nazism unobtrusively, while others frustrated Nazi plans by standing their ground, some were actively involved in attempts to undermine the Hitler dictatorship. If unable to conceal their defiance while focusing on resistance and rescue within their grasp, many of the women in this book were willing to openly identify themselves in acts of defiance, rather than remaining in a conspiratorial underground.

Women's protests in France and Germany show that open collective opposition that made limited demands within certain circumstances could be effective. The most critical intervention in the rescue of "full" German Jews was the Rosenstrasse Protest. In 1943, starting during the last days of February, the Berlin Gestapo's Final Roundup seized up to 2,000 Jews married to non-Jews and imprisoned them in an administrative building in the heart of Berlin at Rosenstrasse 2–4, around the corner from Gestapo headquarters. The imprisoned Jews were almost all men married to non-Jewish women, who hurried to Rosenstrasse and began a protest that lasted a week, despite repeated orders from guards that they "clear the streets or be shot." Heinrich Himmler's men knew this arrest as part of the "elimination of Jews from Reich territory," which coincided with Berlin Gauleiter Joseph Goebbels' resolve to clear the Reich capital of Jews by mid- or late-March, and the urgent demand from industries at Auschwitz for a quota of skilled workers that could be met only with intermarried Jews. But the women who set out to make a scene drew the attention of Joseph Goebbels, who wrote on March 6, 1943, that he had released the intermarried Jews because of the "unpleasant scenes" of those siding with the Jews.

Individual Contributions

The first chapter by Nathan Stoltzfus argues that the regime's response to the Rosenstrasse Protest can be understood within the context of its series of concessions to intermarried defiance. Furthermore, it offers insights on the central question of how Hitler centralized power and ruled his own "race," indicated by the restraints intermarried Jews imposed on "cumulative radicalization," a spiraling ruthlessness to cleanse the Reich itself, above all, of every trace of "Jewish blood." Hitler wanted intermarried Jews gone at the earliest moment that this did not draw attention to them or the fate of Jews generally. Himmler and the Central Economic Administrative Office had the additional incentive of wanting Berlin's intermarried Jews for their Auschwitz slave mills in early 1943. The competing power centers Hitler established, permitting tactical adjustments as circumstances changed, agreed on working toward the supposed historic mission of clearing the Reich of Jews until the Rosenstrasse protesters introduced open dissension. Public protests were rare exceptions although the question of whether further protests in similar circumstances would have resulted in a crackdown is one that Goebbels considered following a possibly organized protest in the Ruhr in October 1943 by 300 women. He fretted that Germans had become aware that they could achieve specific goals by organizing street protests to pressure the regime's "pliant spot."[2] An enormous difference separated protesting Germans who went along with the regime overall and the defiant women on Rosenstrasse, who tied their own fate to their Jewish partners from the beginning of Hitler's rule until the end.

Judy Baumel-Schwartz introduces historians' reflections on rescue by tracing the development of women's Holocaust studies beginning in the later 1970s and the evolution of a gendered understanding of female Jewish experiences. This development illustrates important, but initially overlooked, histories, and what she calls women's "double jeopardy," targeted simultaneously as Jews and also as women. One of the arguments leveled against studying women in the Holocaust as a separate topic was that it focused on the minutia, ignoring what scholars then termed the "major topics" in contemporary Holocaust research: leadership, resistance, and the like. However, as she shows in her article, women played a major role in different forms of armed and unarmed resistance. The most common form of women's resistance, she argues, typically illustrated *amida bashoa*—"day-to-day stand"—which became instrumental in the acceptance of this form of resistance in scholarship.

Volker Berghahn, while also concerned with defiance and resistance to the Hitler dictatorship by women inside Germany and in Nazi-occupied Europe, not only adds further case studies but also raises the question of whether these women and also the men with whom they cooperated, should be differentiated by socioeconomic class and generation. There are also differences in the time frame, with the Communist and Social

2

Democrat working-class opposition being the first to organize, but also the first to be wiped out by the Gestapo. The conservative resistance, civilian and military, did not mobilize until the late 1930s. This was also the time when most women of middle-class background, many of them belonging to a younger generation, decided to defy Hitler in many clandestine ways up to the very end of the war, knowing that, if caught, they would be tried and executed by a regime that had become ever more lethal.

Anne Nelson compares events in occupied France with operations by women in a parallel movement in Berlin, examining the theme of resisting another double peril, first the physical obliteration of the Holocaust, then the obliteration of women's stories in this field following the war. Suzanne Spaak, who came from a prominent family in Brussels, moved to Paris in 1940, where she organized and financed one of the most extensive and effective rescue networks in France, for Jewish children scheduled for deportation from Drancy to Auschwitz. Nelson examines how these networks of women operated in the midst of censorship, surveillance, and terror. Suzanne Spaak was executed and those who did survive the war were almost forgotten, as research focused on the French Résistance run by men. The Righteous Among the Nations Program by Yad Vashem has recognized some fourteen members of Spaak's rescue network, of which ten are women. Spaak was remembered by a colleague as "belong[ing] to those idealists who jettison their private lives, personal wishes, and material concerns as soon as a great ideal enters their hearts."[3]

Paula Schwartz's contribution revolves around food, challenging the notion that women's food protests were apolitical. She evaluates the women's underground press, memoirs, interviews, and police reports to show that women's protests, forbidden actions by dozens to hundreds in all zones of the occupation, disturbed the peace and stability of the regime. These protests were characteristically confrontational and public but for practical and tactical reasons not violent. Women demonstrated and marched in delegations with petitions to officials in town halls, prefects' offices, and food warehouses. By May 1942, it had become clear to officials that women's demonstration in Paris targeted the regime itself and scores of protesters were arrested, facing detention and imprisonment in camps. By protesting, French women acted like political subjects before gaining exercise of full citizenship, following the liberation of France.

Mordecai Paldiel contributes two chapters to this volume of women who dedicated themselves to save Jews from apprehension; first non-Jewish rescuers and then Jewish women ones. Motivated to stand up for mistreated victims out of feelings for common humanity, women took a lead in helping Jews escape apprehension and death. The honoring of non-Jewish rescuers of Jews is grounded in a 1953 Israeli law creating Yad Vashem, which called upon the Jewish people, represented by the state of Israel, to honor those among non-Jews who were prepared to risk their lives to rescue Jews, and thus resist the Nazis in what they considered one of their most principal goals—the physical annihilation of all living Jews, including children, as a pseudo-religious undertaking. Yad Vashem, under a special program created in 1962, has honored over 27,000 men and women as Righteous Among the Nations for risking their lives to save Jews from the Nazis. These include persons from different walks of life: intellectuals and noneducated, blue-and white-collar, clergy and secular; in short, persons from various professions, including diplomats.[4] Overall, women played a slightly greater role than men, and their contribution to the rescue of fellow Jews is what Paldiel tried to bring out in his two articles.[5]

Paldiel's selection of histories covers a wide range of countries: from occupied Netherlands to the Warsaw Ghetto, and to Auschwitz. While the honoring non-Jewish rescuers of Jews has been lauded by Yad Vashem for many years, the position with regard to Jewish women rescuers has, up to recently, been largely dismissed as having little significance, on the claim that Jews were obligated to help each other in times of stress. What was overlooked was that Jewish rescuers operated under a two-edged sword: the danger to themselves as Jews targeted by the Nazis and as rescuers of other Jews, considered a capital offense under Nazi law. Recently, more stories have come to light of help to Jews by fellow Jews on a grand scale, such as the story of Recha Freier, in Berlin, who created, in the first months of the Nazi takeover in 1933, an escape route for Jewish youth to Palestine—a project affecting thousands of youth, later known as Youth Aliyah. Coupled with the rise of public demands to honor Jews who through self-sacrifice created clandestine rescue operations in various parts of Europe to save not just a handful but numerous Jews, and worked in tandem with non-Jewish rescuers, who Yad Vashem declared to be Righteous Among the Nations, it is now felt that major Jewish rescuers also deserve special praise, in recognition of initiatives by individuals and group rescue networks, spanning many occupied European countries, who rescued hundreds, and sometimes thousands, of fellow Jews on the run, as, for instance, the Jewish Defense Committee in Belgium, and the Oeuvre de Secours aux Enfants in France.

One such heroine, Marianne Cohen, a German-born Jewish rescuer, who had escaped to France before the war, volunteered to lead many children across the border into Switzerland. On one of these secret crossings, in 1944, she was captured and tortured to disclose her underground confederates, but she kept silent and was murdered. Shortly before her execution, she penned a message from her French jail, which included the words: "Tear out my nails today, I will not betray. You don't know how long I can hold out but I know."[6] The dozens of children who made it safely across into Switzerland (and those arrested with Marianne Cohn who survived while interned) would certainly expect their heroine publicly acclaimed, by more than mere a few words of thanks.[7]

Like Schwartz, Susanne Heim, addresses the important issue of the character of women's protest and its impact. She examines debates about the Rosenstrasse Protest from the mid-1980s to the mid-2000s, among scholars in online platforms, meetings, and publications, and the temptation to see the survival of intermarried Jews as a miracle. She discusses how German society has commemorated or forgotten the protest and finds that in German Memorials and Museums a trace of the protest can be found. Beginning in the late 1990s, Wolf Gruner mounted a challenge to the standard interpretation that the protest had rescued Jews, using as the "centerpiece" of his challenge a document from the Frankfurt/Oder Gestapo of February 26, 1943, to argue that the regime had always planned on sending Berlin's intermarried Jews back home. Heim concludes, however, that the regime's intentions were not clear regarding the fate of the intermarried Jews it had imprisoned on Rosenstrasse, and none of the power centers with interest in the fate of those Jews was certain that it would conceivably prevail. She concludes that since we will never know with certainty what the protest's impact was, we should abandon that inquiry for more productive ones, with greater points of consensus.

Chris Osmar and Nathan Stoltzfus consider the overall context of the regime's decision-making processes during late 1942 and early 1943 and agree with scholars since the 1960s who have found that the Rosenstrasse Protest did rescue Jewish family members from the slaughter. If the protest's history is to be determined by consensus, that consensus should deal openly with all contrary arguments and sources, not to mention all the troubling questions that remain if we posit that the regime did not intend to deport intermarried Jews at this point regardless of the women's protest. Intermarried Jews were the thorniest of the "enemy race," openly perpetrating Rassenschande ("racial treason"), begetting "half-breed children," and stirring dissension about race ideology, featuring non-Jews defending Jewish family members with their lives. Examining the Frankfurt/Oder document the authors find that it supports rather than undermines arguments about the protest's importance.

Gabriele Nissim's chapter discusses his philosophy of honoring rescuers and how he has put his vision into practice by establishing the Committee for the Gardens of the Righteous Worldwide (GARIWO). Devoted to preserving the memory of rescuers of victims who became the targets of mass exterminations and genocides throughout history, GARIWO worked in coalition with the Union of Italian Jewish Communities and the City of Milan, to select the Rosenstrasse protesters as its annual honorees for the year 2020 on the European Day of Remembrance. History shows that rescuers were not paragons of virtue so much as flawed human beings who, despite misgivings, began with smaller acts that worked up incrementally to extraordinary life-saving deeds, through practice and often compromises.

Carolyn Enger descends from German Jews who survived in intermarriage, traces the journeys of her father and godmother as they navigated the complexities of being recognized as neither German nor Jewish in Nazi Germany and after. Starting with her grandmother's conversion from Judaism to Christianity, she examines her grandmother's subsequent marriage to her grandfather and her father's identification as a Mischling ("half-Jew"). There is then his marriage to Enger's Christian mother, with her chapter ending with her own conversion from Christianity to Judaism. She concludes with a discussion of her Mischlinge Exposé, a project in which she situates the historical context of the existence of Mischlinge as part of her work as a pianist and documentation of her family's history.

The final contribution goes back to the Rosenstrasse Protests in which Rita Kuhn, one of the last living eye-witnesses, describes the experience of imprisonment in her chapter, including the Gestapo guard who greeted her with seeming regard for the protesters: "your relatives are protesting for you out there; that is German loyalty!" Her daughter Ruth Wiseman then reflects on the differences between what her stories meant for her and what her mother remembered once she began to relate these events in public during the 1980s. Like Enger, she converted to Judaism.

Do Defiant Women Reform Models of Resistance?

"Well behaved women seldom make history," wrote historian Laurel Ulrich about colonial New England.[8] Centuries later, as the Second World War erupted across Europe, gender norms still confined women mostly to the private sphere, quiet and subservient. This gender disparity held particularly under Hitler's rule, although the regime did see its famous women enablers like Leni Riefenstahl as very well behaved indeed; crimes followed conformity and obedience.

Generally, the Second World War helped women wrest their way beyond the usual support capacity assigned to them, whether by traditions, governments, or organizations. Judith Baumel-Schwartz writes that following years of struggle Jewish women's resistance can now be found in standard histories. But it took time until that happened. The record of women's defiance has lagged behind that of men during postwar decades when standards of rescue and resistance were established, as Anne Nelson writes.

For generations, dominant models identified resistance with military operations, a battle of arms against arms that the regime inevitably won. It has been doubly challenging to bring women's resistance into standard works, because they are not men but also because they frequently use nonviolent means to resist. Scholars have developed an expansive vocabulary for militarized resistance but none that applies to women's networks of defiance. A primarily militarized vision of resistance obstructs a view of the range of resistance actions as well as the range of regime responses.

One possible gender difference identified here for further exploration is integration by women of defiance into their everyday life activities, a day-to-day stand for what they thought was right. Personal integrity sometimes required noncompliance with totalitarian rule and its conformers so as not to "live within the lie," as illustrated by the refusal to divorce by Gentile women married to Jews of Nazi Germany. To protect their family members, they decided time after time what compromises to make with propaganda, regulations, or neighbors and society. Other women organized their defiance, sometimes clandestinely.

The emphasis in women's defiance not on doing away with Hitler but on rescuing lives suggests that their motivations were humanitarian, driven by respect for human life and a drive to show the way toward a decent human civilization. A frequently identified motivation of men's resistance was to honor their country, a motivation seen as "political" and illustrated by statements of the heroic resister about the "men of the German Resistance," by Major General Henning von Tresckow.[9] Intimately related to the differences that gender made were the careers of men and the concomitant responsibility for the economic life of the family, which is often identified as a rationale and motivation for collaboration. Not having access to bombs and guns, women were more likely to resort to collective, public actions such as protest. Suzanne Spaak had principled reasons as well, joining a pacifist organization and rescuing hundreds of lives without arms. Women's defiance of maintaining habits of integrity from before the regime did not depend on whether the regime's winning hand would hold or any territory gained in the war could be saved for Germany.

Much of this can be understood if we examine the concept of perspective. Through what lens are we looking at the Holocaust that allows women and their activities to become more visible? If we are examining the topic through the lens of the Auschwitz chimneys, in other words, the Final Solution, then the ultimate fate of all Jews, at least in Nazi eyes, was supposed to be the same. However, the moment one begins to examine life during the Holocaust and not just death, the different gender narratives become clearer. Baumel-Schwartz writes that the differences gender made in the camps become visible only when studying everyday social experience. Seeing Auschwitz solely as a site of death and murder, on the other hand, obscures the elemental perspective about how people lived there.[10] Her work reveals some ways that men and women's defiance differed: men in the camp tended to favor physical forms of sabotage while women chose psychological subversion.[11] In occupied France, women were expected to eat last if there was not enough food to go around. This points to the expectation that the challenge of living in crises under extreme stress was dumped on women: specifically the challenge of sharing privation that often brings out the worst—some are happy to hoard supplies as others around them are starving.

Within the Reich and regarding Hitler's chosen "race," Nazism's racist worldview and perhaps it's notions of gender differences could also provide something of a resistance foothold, in case circumstances motivated persons to show highly uncommon courage. The so-called "German-blooded" women like those married to Jews had far greater possibilities for defiance. Even in camps some found that traditional gender norms sometimes granted strong women a strong hand. Vladka Meed, incarcerated with other Jews in the Warsaw Ghetto, became a secret courier, helping Jews find safe hiding places while supplying them with false documents, and found that it was easier for women to stroll the streets than for men, with telltale circumcision to give them away. A woman in a super-masculine culture might have advantages, as Schwartz also writes. During sudden document checks, women with small children were more likely to be allowed to pass by. Children accompanying French women protesters also provided some protection against arrest, Schwartz writes.

Women might also be granted a swifter death, as Nelson illustrates. Of the forty-five Red Orchestra members sentenced to death, many men were slowly strangled from meat hooks, while women died by guillotine. Authorities also met the Rosenstrasse protesters less harshly because they were women, Walter Laqueur argued.[12] French and German authorities sometimes made limited concessions to women protesters, fearing the consequences otherwise. In Germany, Goebbels worried following a women's protest over food rations in October 1943 that the regime must stop conciliating protesters since each time it did, this cost the regime a measure of authority.[13] Consider the dramatic food protests of women in Witten and nearby cities of the Ruhr in October 1943, for example. Although they are recounted in detail by the SD, the Nazi secret intelligence force, this protest has been noted by historians of East Germany while overlooked by those in the West, even though the SD reported that these women protesters verbally scorned the regime, while they declared their willingness to give their lives on the spot for their cause.

Histories of marginalized women's resistance is a building block for a fuller sense of defiance. If active female resisters as discussed in this book are largely excluded from models of politically motivated and centrally organized attempts to bring down Hitler's Germany, do women's histories show that standard models might be reformed successfully? If the military represents a brotherhood model of resistance, is there a sisterhood type of defiance that emerges with women's history as it is being written? Nelson sees this in networks of assembled women, sometimes informally and openly, in social connections through day-care centers, charity lunches, book clubs, and church circles.

Arguably according to one historian the 1943 Berlin Rosenstrasse Protest has also been overlooked and minimized precisely because it was the work of women.[14] The women put their lives at risk in protest for a matter of fundamental significance, their Jewish partners with whom they had tied their fate every day they refused enormous pressures to divorce, from society and regime, according to the 2000 conclusion of a German court.[15] Their clear self-interest was in divorce, but their resistance illustrated the day-to-day stand.

For decades reputable historians of Hitler and the Holocaust found that the Rosenstrasse Protest, as Goebbels wrote and other contemporaneous documents back, caused the regime to release rather than deport intermarried Jews, during the days it sent off some 8,000 other Berlin "full Jews." Raul Hilberg and Uwe Adam both concluded that the RSHA was making preparations for the deportation of Jews in mixed marriages in late 1942 and early 1943. In fact, hundreds of intermarried Jews wearing the star were arrested and killed before the Rosenstrasse Protest, despite guidelines temporarily exempting them. H. G. Adler wrote that protest "by a courageous demonstration of women caused the Gestapo, in an exception, to give in, and the husbands were released." Sybil Milton, who like Hilberg was a founding historian of the US Holocaust Historical Museum and fought for the "legitimacy" of gendered Holocaust history, as Baumel-Schwartz wrote, concluded that 200–300 wives had protested, with the result that "the Gestapo released those men married to German non-Jews." Among others, German historian Wolfgang Scheffler, who served as expert witness in the 1969 trial of the chief of the former head of the Berlin Gestapo Otto Bovensiepen, concluded that the protest changed the fate of the Jews imprisoned on Rosenstrasse, as did German attorneys in the case.[16] As an expert in the trial against David Irving for Holocaust denial in 2000, Richard J. Evans also agreed: "a large crowd of 'Aryan' German women successfully staged a public demonstration to force the release of some two thousand of their arrested Jewish husbands."[17]

Resistance, Rescue, Primo Levi's "Gray Zone"

Few debates yield more incongruities than resistance and the nature of Hitler's rule, and here we consider both from the perspective of how women's history might change both. No doubt the use of force for Hitler's rule within the Reich did not mirror Nazi brutality in occupied territories not to mention the camps. Armed rebellion did goad the regime to mobilize its greater firepower, but women's resistance was characteristically different. Resistance was sometimes possible even in the death camps, although the perspective of those who weren't there is hardly suited for perceiving it.[18] The persons we write about could not be expected to have seen what we now perceive to be the possibilities for resistance, from our perspective of years of research.

These women, some sent to Nazi camps, illustrated not only fundamental opposition to Nazism but also self-sacrifice without gaining advantage for themselves, despite what the survivor Primo Levi described as the "gray zone" world inside Auschwitz, with its extreme conditions of privilege and collaboration, master and servant, that forced many desperate inmates to compromise morally in order to buy a bit of bread or time. Chaim Rumkowski, who as the leader of the Łódź ghetto, identified with the oppressor's power, did "courageously" defend his councilmen when they were threatened by the Gestapo, if only perhaps because he "progressively convinced himself that he *was* a messiah," with real power.[19] According to some, Rumkowski is undoubtedly guilty although judgment is not as easy as black and white, Levi cautions. In the "gray zone" of Nazi camps, biological and cultural traits characteristic of all human societies turned lethal: privilege protected privilege, the power of a few oppressed the many, and the burden of oppression was passed down to those with less. Collaborators hardened by their betrayal begot collaborators, "burden[ing] them with guilt, cover[ing] them with blood, compromis[ing] them as much as possible, thus establishing a bond of complicity so that they can no longer turn back."[20]

Acts of Rescuers as a Tool for a Different Understanding of Human Behavior

Returning to persons who acted, not as resisters, but as preservers of life, Paldiel underlines that while the Holocaust displayed human behavior at its worst, it also manifested a most laudable type of altruistic behavior that preserved innocent human life, as evidenced by the acts of the rescuers of Jews. This draws into questioning some views in Western philosophical thoughts that human beings may be reduced as mostly aggressive creatures, concerned only with their own welfare, who exploit others to advance their own good. However, the men and women who saved Jews, some they may have known from before but were not family related, and stood the risk of losing their lives if apprehended, is clear proof that altruism is as a powerful constituent human behavioral mode, and inherently as strong as the negative components that have been highly magnified by some philosophers and social scientists who propounded Darwinist theories and reduced human behavior to simply self-centered egoism. These rescuers provide striking refutations to the Freudian idea of *homo homini lupus;* of man as a wolf to fellow man.[21] That negative type of behavior, admittedly, cannot unfortunately be ruled out among the many, but it does not necessarily comprehend all that we know of human behavior at a deep level, and including all living persons.

Paldiel points out the idea of the French-Jewish philosopher Emmanuel Levinas of the impact of proximity between two persons that arouses in one to see the other as part of one's own self. Levinas terms that face-to-face encounter, the springboard where one sees the Other (*autrui*, in French) the locus of one's self obligation toward that other person. In Levinas's opinion, I am a self, not as Heidegger claimed that the sole existential value is one's self-centered being, to the disregard of others. On the contrary, Levinas states: I carry the alterity of the Other in myself. I question myself in light of the Other. Given that the Other is the source of my questioning, my answering is a responding to the Other, and that is the birth of ethics.[22] This idea by Levinas may explain the sudden urge of the would-be rescuer to help the person facing him/her as the Holocaust went into high gear, as most rescue stories to emerge from that horrific period have their source in special encounters, of proximity and face-to-face situations, and where the survival of one of the two parties facing each other is almost exclusively contingent on the response of the other party. Most rescue stories to come out of the Holocaust, indeed, originated in face-to-face encounters.

Whatever theory explains best the rescuer's dominant motivation, conscious or subconscious, the thousands of Righteous Among the Nations honored by Yad Vashem, who come from different walks of life, have taught us that the respect of the life of fellow human beings is a powerful inborn force among many, going so far as to risk one's own life to ensure the existence of the other person. In the words of Irena Sendler, who saved hundreds of children from the Warsaw Ghetto: "As long as I live and as long as I have the strength I shall always say that the most important thing in the world and in life is Goodness."[23] That is a significant statement to come from the mouth of a person, tortured and almost executed to force her to reveal her rescue confederates, and such a person and her message can serve as a role model and educational tool for a more beneficial type of human relations.

Understanding Women's Defiance

All this brings back to the beginning. What do we ultimately mean by Women Defying Hitler? Are we only targeting "rescue" and "resistance" as expressions of that defiance? Are demonstrations the only public expression of this phenomenon? What about social interaction and cohesion of women under the Nazis, in ghettos, areas without ghettos, and camps? How do self-help and mutual assistance enter into the equation?

A closer look at the chapters included in this volume shows that in practice, all of these topics are discussed one way or another. Even among the women demonstrating at the Rosenstrasse Protest one can note gendered tones of cohesion and social interaction. Rescue activities initiated or carried out by women often utilized gendered forms of mutual assistance. A broader definition of "resistance," as seen in several articles in this collection, also includes acts that in normal times could be seen as part and parcel of daily life. The difference is rooted in timing, location, and perspective. A woman reading a book about democracy with the words "Free Speech for All" on its cover while riding on a tramcar in a major city in peacetime is a form of recreation. That same woman, reading that same book, on that same tramcar in that same city becomes an act of defiance when it takes place in a Nazi-occupied country during the Second World War.

Then there is the question of gendered behavior. If a woman and a man are carrying out the same act of defiance is there a gendered component involved? Take sabotage, for example. How does men's sabotage of Nazi installations, programs, and practices differ from that of women? In an interview given in the mid-1980s, Auschwitz survivor Zipporah Goldstein described the difference between gendered forms of sabotage that she witnessed while working as a slave laborer at the so-called "Kanada" sorting barracks in the camp. When coming across fur coats originally worn by the victims on their deportation to the camp, before wrapping them up to be sent back to Germany for use by the local population, male prisoners would unravel the seams, leaving only the lining intact. Thus, within a few moments of wear, the coat would fall apart, leaving its new German owner clothed in a thin lining during the cold winter. As opposed to physical sabotage, women prisoners utilized a psychological tactic, placing a note in the coat pocket that read: "German woman: know that you are wearing a fur coat that belonged to a Jewish woman gassed to death in Auschwitz." Different genders, different tactics. Both, however, were acts of sabotage carrying the same punishment. Flogging and death.

Even when utilizing the same resistance tactics, the social expectations from each gender caused them to be interpreted differently, particularly in a world that was still divided into "men's society" and "women's society." A man in his late teens or early twenties travelling from the countryside to the city in wartime Poland holding a basket or sack would immediately arouse suspicion. If he was a city dweller what was he doing out of the city? Why was he not at work? And if he lived in the countryside what reason could he have to be travelling to the city? A young woman of the same age, carrying the same basket, and travelling to the same city aroused less raised eyebrows. In the gendered society of that time, country women in wartime were likely to be travelling to the city in order to try and sell home-grown foodstuffs. Thus, women were more likely to act as couriers carrying baskets containing clandestine ammunition hidden under the eggs or potatoes, as the very presence of men, long before discovering that they were circumcised, aroused suspicion. Different genders, similar tactics, different level of danger based on the norms of a gendered society.

Let us conclude this introduction with a caveat. Unlike early studies of gender and the Holocaust, which at times posited women's suffering as being worse, sacrifices as being greater, and social bonds as being stronger than those of men, studies of women and the Holocaust today speak about differences between the genders: diverse activities, divergent responses, disparate tactics, and distinct models of behavior. The nature of these differences, particularly in how women defied Hitler, is the crux of this volume, which will focus on the "how" in the hope of ultimately better understanding the "why."

Notes

1. Raul Hilberg, *The Destruction of the European Jews* (New Haven: Yale University Press, 2003), Vol. II, 487.

2. "The Volk knows perfectly well where the pliant spot of the leadership is, and will always know how to exploit it. . . . The state must never, against its own best interests, give way to the pressure of the street." Elke Fröhlich, ed., *Die Tagebücher von Joseph Goebbels*, part II, Vol. 10 (Munich: K. G. Sauer, 1997–2001), entry for November 2, 1943.

3. Quote from B. Aronson in "Suzanne Spaak," entry in Yad Vashem's "Women of Valor: Stories of Women Who Rescued Jews During the Holocaust." https://www.yadvashem.org/yv/en/exhibitions/righteous-women/spaak.asp (accessed May 6, 2020).

4. Paldiel headed Yad Vashem's Righteous among the Nations operation from 1982 to 2007, and is credited for having added thousands of names to the honorary Righteous roster.

5. For more on rescuers honored by Yad Vashem, consult the following by Mordecai Paldiel, *The Righteous Among the Nations* (New York: HarperCollins, 2007); *Saving the Jews* (Rockville: Schreiber Publishing, 2000); *Churches and the Holocaust* (Jersey City: Ktav, 2006); *The Path of the Righteous* (Hoboken: Ktav, 1993); *German Rescuers of Jews* (Seattle: Amazon Publication, 2017); and *Es Gab Auch Gerechte* (Konstanz: Hartung-Gorre, 1999).

6. Mordecai Paldiel, *Saving One's Own* (Philadelphia: Jewish Publishing Society, 2017).

7. She has indeed been honored by the Israel office of the International B'nai B'rith organization, under the leadership of Alan Schneider, under its Jewish Rescuers Program.

8. Quoted in Laurel Ulrich, *Well-Behaved Women Seldom Make History* (New York: Alfred Knopf, 2007), xiii.

9. Francis R. Nicosia, "Introduction: Resistance to National Socialism in the Work of Peter Hoffmann," in *Germans Against Nazism: Nonconformity, Opposition, and Resistance in the Third Reich*, eds. Francis R. Nicosia and Lawrence D. Stokes (New York: Berghahn, 2015), 4: "Through a love of Germany [the resistance] committed treason" in order to "redeem the honor of their nation." Christopher R. Browning, "Who Resisted the Nazis?" *The New York Review of Books*, July 2, 2020.

10. Judith Baumel-Schwartz, *Double Jeopardy: Gender and the Holocaust* (Ann Arbor: University of Michigan Press, 1998); Judith Baumel-Schwartz, chapter three.

11. Judith Baumel Schwartz, "Auschwitz: Women used Different Survival and Sabotage Strategies than Men at Nazi Death Camp," *The Conversation*, March 27, 2020. https://bit.ly/2z2KQWj (accessed May 16, 2020).

12. Walter Laqueur, "Foreword," in *Resistance of the Heart: Intermarriage and the Rosenstrasse Protest in Nazi Germany*, ed. Nathan Stoltzfus (New Brunswick: Rutgers University Press, 2001 [1996]), x.

13. Elke Frölich, *Tägebucher*, 222.

14. Katharina von Kellenbach, "The 'Legend' of Women's Resistance in the Rosenstrasse," in Nathan Stoltzfus and Birgit Maier-Katkin, eds. *Protest in Hitler's "National Community": Popular Unrest and the Regime's Response* (New York: Berghahn Books, 2015), 106–24.

15. https://lexetius.com/2000,2144 (accessed May 21, 2020), citing *BVerwG, Urteil vom 13. 9. 2000 – 8 C 21.99; VG Meiningen (lexetius.com/2000,2144)* (BGH, op. Cit., P. 111), which repealed a judgment of 7. Oktober 1998.

16. Adam, Judenpolitik im dritten Reich, 17, 29, 316. Hans Günther Adler, *Der verwaltete Mensch: Studien zur Deportation der Juden aus Deutschland* (Tübingen: J.C.B. Mohr, 1974), 202. Sybil Milton, "Women and the Holocaust: The Case of German and German-Jewish Women," in *When Biology Became Destiny: Women in Weimar and Nazi Germany*, eds. Renate Bridenthal, Atina Grossmann, and Marion A. Kaplan (New York: Monthly Review Press, 1984), 319; Raul Hilberg, *Perpetrators, Victims, Bystanders: The Jewish Catastrophe,*

1933-1945 (New York: Aaron Asher Books, 1992), 132; Wolfgang Scheffler, *Judenverfolgung im Dritten Reich* (Berlin: Colloquium Verlag, 1960), 44. *Urteilsgründe*, trial against Kurt Venter and Max Graustueck [(500) 1 Ks 2/69 (10/69)], 79, 80. Trial against Otto Bovensiepen et al., B Rep 058, 1 Js 9/65, Landesarchiv Berlin.

17. Professor Richard J. Evans stated that: "Hitler was apparently not prepared simply to brush aside the criticisms uttered by the Ministry of the Interior and the Ministry of Justice and follow the demands by the party radicals to include most 'half-Jews' and Jews in 'mixed marriages' in the extermination ('expulsion') program. There are numerous possible reasons for this. Hitler repeatedly chose not to interfere with internal conflicts between different agencies of the Nazi dictatorship in an attempt to avoid association 'with possible unpopular policy options'. This may have been an instance of such a refusal. He also probably wanted to avoid causing unrest among the non-Jewish relatives or partners of the Jews involved. . . . That these 'Aryan' Germans would not necessarily allow deportations to go ahead without resistance was powerfully confirmed in the famous Rosenstrasse incident in February 1943 when a large crowd of 'Aryan' German women successfully staged a public demonstration to force the release of some two thousand of their arrested Jewish husbands and even the return of a handful who had already been sent to Auschwitz." Expert Report by Professor Richard J. Evans (2000) Irving vs. Lipstadt, https://phdn.org/negation/irving/EvansReport.pdf. Cf. Nathan Stoltzfus, *Hitler's Compromises: Coercion and Consensus in Nazi Germany* (New Haven: Yale, 2016), 276; Richard J. Evans, *The Third Reich at War* (New York: Penguin, 2009), 271–3.

18. Peter Hayes wrote that opposition within the Reich only "goaded the Reich into more radical action" and in support cites only a general strike in Holland in 1941 Peter Hayes, *Why: Explaining the Holocaust* (New York: W.W. Norton, 2017), 159, 353. Claudia Card, "Women, Evil, and Grey Zones," *Metaphilosophy* 31, no. 5 (2003). doi: 10.1111/1467-9973.00166.

19. Primo Levi, *The Drowned and the Saved* (New York: Simon and Schuster, 1988 [1986]), 51.

20. Ibid., 31–2.

21. Thomas Hobbes, in *Leviathan*, in Chapter 13, describes human existence without a supreme authority to contain man's inborn lusts as, "solitary, poor, nasty, brutish, and short." Sigmund Freud, *Civilization and Its Discontents* (New York: W.W. Norton, 1961), 5, 19, also sees the need of authority to restrain man's natural aggressiveness; man's inborn instinctual feelings toward others is, "to gratify their aggressiveness on him, . . . to use him sexually without his consent, to seize his possessions, to humiliate him, to cause him pain, to torture and kill him. *Homo homini* lupus [Man is a wolf to man]."

22. Emmanuel Levinas, *Totality and Infinity* (The Hague and Boston: M. Nijhoff, 1979).

23. Sendler, Yad Vashem Archives 31.2/153. Also, Anna Mieszczkowska, *Irena Sendler: Mother of the Children of the Holocaust* (Santa Barbara: Praeger, 2011), 74–81.

CHAPTER 1
CUMULATIVE RADICALIZATION
"MIXED-RACE" MARRIAGES UNDER HITLER AND REMEMBRANCE
Nathan Stoltzfus

I declare that in the year 1943 I also took part in the demonstrations on Rosenstrasse. . . . After we demonstrators were threatened with pistols by the Gestapo, we first quickly dispersed but then a short while later gathered together again and protested more.

> —Gertrud Blumenthal, March 6, 1955, in response to German-Jewish Leader Heinz Galinski's call for "participants in the Demonstration March on Rosenstrasse" to register for reparations.[1]

Sepp Dietrich . . . offers to put a company of the Leibstandarte [elite SS Troops serving Hitler] at my disposal so that I can reach my goal with brute force, which at the moment, given the current state of affairs, would not be the appropriate means to get my way.

> —Joseph Goebbels, Diary entry for February 2, 1943[2]

Ruling the people in conquered territories is a psychological problem. One cannot rule them by force alone. True, force is decisive, but it is equally important to have that psychological something which the animal trainer needs to master his beasts. They must be convinced that we are the victors.

> —Adolf Hitler, Address to Higher Leaders of the Eastern Army, evening of July 1, 1943[3]

Following his order to release the intermarried Jews imprisoned at Berlin's Rosenstrasse 2–4 recorded on March 6, 1943, Joseph Goebbels retreated to Hitler's lair to make sure the Führer had his back. Goebbels knew ways to get Hitler's approval and wrote on March 9 report that "the Führer has the greatest understanding for the psychological questions of the war. . . . In the Jewish question [Hitler] approves of my actions and specifically gives me the mandate to render Berlin free of Jews . . . I describe my actions to the Führer as generous toward the people, hard toward the wrong doers. The Führer also considers this completely correct." Capitalizing on this smaller victory to receive absolute power over his Gau, greater Berlin, Goebbels continued: "He confirmed to me once again that in such cases only I lead the command of the Reich Capital. Here as well the ministries must obey my mandate. The entire public life is subordinate to me. In catastrophes only one person can give orders." Already in 1926, at the outset of Goebbels' ascent to power as Gauleiter of greater Berlin, Hitler's "absolute trust" in Goebbels gave him a degree of control which "no other Gauleiter" possessed.[4]

German intermarriages of Jews and non-Jews and their protest illustrate characteristics of Hitler's rule that are difficult to reconcile with common images, and have opened debates about the way the regime made decisions within the Reich. There is general agreement that Hitler was responsible for the Holocaust but disagreements about how Hitler got what he wanted. Agreement that the protesting women were totally vulnerable is also common by now. Without their protest it would be easier to believe that open opposition inevitably led to punishment.

Historians who view the Rosenstrasse Protest as an act of rescue have argued that Nazi genocide planners were trying to remove as many intermarried Jews who wore the yellow badge as possible during Himmler's "Elimination of Jews from the Reich" arrests, which triggered the Rosenstrasse Protest. (The postwar neologism for this massive wave of arrests which the Berlin Gestapo knew as the "Final Roundup" of Jews is "Factory Action"). As the regime reached toward its self-assigned historic mission of removing all Jews from German soil along with Goebbels' resolve as Berlin's Gauleiter to declare the city "free of Jews" by March 1943, it proved willing to temporarily defer fulfilling this ideological goal in order to sustain Hitler's image and increase German commitment across the Reich to the war. Defiance in the form of a street protest reveals regime strategies for keeping Germans fully committed to war while protecting Hitler's popular prestige at the expense for the moment of banishing some Jews marked with the yellow badge. Critical for the women's rescue of family members was the regime's experience of their defiance over the previous decade. Given their refusal to cooperate from the beginning with regime propaganda and demands, the regime knew these women had tied their fate to that of their husbands, illustrated by their continued protest on Rosenstrasse in the face of repeated threats from armed guards to "clear the streets or we will shoot."

In this perspective, the Nazi ideology of power, grounded in German popular perceptions, sometimes conflicted for the moment with the Nazi ideology of "racial cleansing." Governing required balancing the two in order to reach Nazi goals quickly. Attending to popular backing was especially crucial when the regime undertook policies that would alienate many Germans and thus had to be done in secret (i.e., genocide and "euthanasia"). Preserving secrecy itself added vulnerability to the demands of maintaining Hitler's image since secrecy had to be guarded from public scrutiny as well as the controversial program it was hiding.[5]

The cult of personality—the Hitler myth—was a cornerstone of the Führer's power operating inside the Reich, an imperative for sustaining basic mechanisms of Nazi rule. This included "working towards the Führer," the radicalizing process of satraps competing with each other to write Hitler's vaguely stated ideas into policy. In the face of conflicting imperatives, when sustaining the Hitler myth conflicted with Nazi policies, Hitler, Goebbels, and others were willing to make temporary, strategic compromises. The history of intermarried couples and their Rosenstrasse Protest, as they temporarily reversed plans to deport at least the Jews from Rosenstrasse, reveals these compromises particularly well.

Hans Mommsen's oft-cited concept of cumulative radicalization posits that Nazi authorities competed for Hitler's approval by radicalizing the persecution of Jews, in a metaphorical ratcheting effect that escalated persecution into the genocide of Jews across Europe.[6] The concept works better to explain the murder of the Jews East of the Reich than it does to explain processes in the belly of the beast. Deporting Jews from the Reich required managing German perceptions by secrecy and camouflage. In the East, non-Jews married to Jews were deported with the Jews if they refused to divorce. But within the Reich, the Gestapo hesitated to deport intermarried Jews until their non-Jewish partners abandoned them (when an "Aryan" partner divorced, the Gestapo assumed they could deport the divorced Jew without causing objections).[7]

Authorities seeking Hitler's approval within the Reich were constrained to accomplish Hitler's ideological goals *and* at the same time to promote Hitler's popular image and the forward momentum of his mass movement. Within the Reich, his lieutenants not only had to do what Hitler wanted but also do it in the way that did not arouse notable popular opposition. Their policies and programs had to protect the Führer's image, in all its camouflage, the glue that held popular consensus in place. Inside the Reich and among Hitler's own race the processes of "cumulative radicalization" were tempered by these specifically domestic conditions. The theory becomes less persuasive as an explanation for the regime's decision-making regarding cases further toward the margin, at the edge. This edge occurred where Hitler's ideology of mass movement power conflicted with the ideology of race, relevant only inside the Reich. This edge, where one ideological imperative conflicted with another, emerged with cases that interrupted the ideologically driven flow of processes with concerns about how they played in the popular mood.[8]

The defiance of Jewish-"Aryan" couples that culminated after ten years in the Rosenstrasse Protest brought the conflict between the imperative for governing and the imperative for "racial purification" to its apogee and shows in sharp relief some contours of decision-making in Hitler's regime that are less apparent elsewhere. Was the regime a monolithic machine carrying out hide-bound orders flawlessly from Berlin to the farthermost peripheries over which Hitler ruled with an eagle eye, crushing any opposition in his predetermined course? Or did Hitler lead more by controlling his image than dictating, bent on changing German attitudes which in turn influenced the way he responded to defiance at home, as he presided over a flexible decision-making process that made room for his influence in the wide range of matters that show his fingerprints? Germany could not rule even the inferior races of the eastern occupied territories "by force alone," Hitler told military leaders.[9] The same axiom held for Hitler in other domains: inside the Reich, with a goal of forging a society that thought as he did, Hitler used targeted force to crush opposition but sought to "educate" Germans and draw them into his mass movement with positive incentives.

The view here is that Hitler identified goals in basic terms and waited for opportune circumstances to move toward them, much as the Nazi Party was organized to take advantage of a crisis when the Great Depression struck.[10] It was easy for Nazi leaders to agree on black and white cases, especially when this proceeded smoothly. The half "Aryan," half-Jewish "mongrels" (Mischlinge) of intermarried children ruffled the exacting bureaucrats converting categorical ideology into political policy. Their intermarried parents, however, one "Aryan" and the other a "full Jew," posed a different problem and defined a sharper edge of what happened when a fringe group, publicly visible, refused to fall in line. The history of intermarriage is especially well positioned to disclose facts and patterns. The one charge Goebbels leveled against operations managers when he intervened to order the release of Jews from Rosenstrasse was that they were working slavishly according to orders rather than adjusting to the unplanned circumstances of the protest.[11]

The response of the regime to the rare popular protests of Nazi Germany does not fit the common conceptions that the regime set its course strictly according to its ideology and crushed anyone in its way. Persons who hid Jews are rightly honored but survival in intermarriage doesn't fit the common model that open rescue was impossible and severely punished (even the military failed to kill Hitler). For a country that can pride itself in dealing with its reprehensible past Germany has certainly made the Rosenstrasse protesters fight for their commemoration, as discussed here later. After decades of overlooking intermarried Germans—their protest and their decisive influence on the survival of German Jews—German commemorations and histories have now reached a consensus that the women protesting were courageous, historian Suzanne Heim argues in these pages, and we should rest on this certainty of agreement, commemorating their courage without delving into the matter of rescue since we will never know for sure how the regime responded to the Rosenstrasse protests.

There is power in consensus although the quest for certainty does stand out brilliantly against the grueling day-to-day uncertainty the regime forced upon the intermarried "Aryans" as a terrible punishment for not choosing the certainty of divorce; divorce and the comfort of conformity appeared to be in their self-interest, not loyalty to Jewish partners. The historian might also wish to know why the women were not punished for open defiance. How did the Gestapo respond differently to different forms of rescue? We want to know where the protesters got the courage to stand out against the common social pattern, in their day-to-day stand. But we also want to know how Hitler concentrated so much power in his own hands and convinced so many that he really was a very great man. The fate of intermarriages offers a basis for judgment. Even if tomorrow we unearthed a recording of Hitler mumbling that the Jews at Rosenstrasse were released because of the protest, *we would still want to know how and why*. We would want to know what it said about Hitler's power and the way that the regime made decisions. The history of intermarriages offers valuable insights.

The Hitler Myth and Discontinuous "Cumulative Radicalization" Inside the Reich

There are several critical contexts for examining the impact of the Rosenstrasse Protest and this open form of rescue by women, beginning with the strategic side of Hitler's rule that led him to make compromises to masses of Germans who were openly upset when Nazi policies curtailed traditions.[12] Consider the phase-by-phase, case-by-case method characterizing decision-making regarding the deportation of German Jews. This indefinite "system" maximized the genocide as Hitler's agents "worked towards the Führer," making decisions to imitate how they imagined Hitler would act. Within the Reich, however, quickly evolving challenges such as an unwelcome gathering of women on the street that took the side of Jews during a massive deportation to clear all Jews from the Reich, set otherwise united authorities against each other, with some pushing toward goals of racial ideology while others erred—for the moment—on the side of preserving the Führer's image.

A second key context for evaluating the protest from this perspective is the impact of the Reich's early 1943 military debacles on the loose assemblage of agencies working toward National Socialism's "historic mission" of murdering the Jews. Controlling the eastern territories for the longer term, now that rapid Blitzkrieg conquest had failed and German occupiers were greatly outnumbered, was an elevated concern for Nazi leaders.[13] The bombing of German cities and defeat at Stalingrad led to Goebbels' initial efforts to establish his Total War regimen, which ran concurrent with the Rosenstrasse Protest as he faced opposition from a trinity of heavy weight associates of Hitler. These Total War measures depended essentially on new levels of popular will power and self-sacrifice, rendering Propaganda Minister Goebbels yet more attentive to popular morale and signs of public dissent. The third critical context for understanding the regime's response to the protest is the series of temporary compromises the regime had made with intermarried couples due to their continuous noncompliance over the previous decade since Hitler had taken power.[14]

Two cornerstones of interpretation are foundational for the perspective that cumulative radicalization could be limited—within the Reich only—by the dictatorship's recognition that it relied on the "Aryan" people for realizing its goals: the Hitler myth and the related mechanism of working towards the Führer, both delineated by Ian Kershaw.[15] The dictatorship's perceived dependency on the people was intensified by the war, and Hitler's resolve to avoid the social unrest he blamed for Germany's loss in the previous world war. He moved toward achieving his overall goal of convincing the people to internalize and pass along the Nazi worldview by spectacles and feats demonstrating that his sociopolitical order would fulfill their own aspirations better than their previous leaders.

Along with the "cumulative radicalization" model, the transition from Nazism's program of centralized "euthanasia" to the "wild euthanasia" organized around willing accomplices following Hitler's "halt" of euthanasia in August 1941, is instructive for understanding the fate of intermarried Jews. Despite Reich regulations to the contrary, regional leaders found ways to deport intermarried Jews and were rewarded rather than punished if this did not stir rumors and unrest. But the real lynchpin was the question of whether intermarried "Aryans" would divorce, entrusting their Jewish partners to the Gestapo.

"Cumulative radicalization" illustrated the general principle of "working towards the Führer," a mechanism to explain the development of policy without direct orders from Hitler. Party activists took "for granted (usually on grounds of self-interest) that [Hitler] approved of measures aimed at the 'removal' of the Jews, measures seen as plainly furthering his long-term goals," Ian Kershaw wrote. While his agents took the initiative, Hitler "had to do little or nothing" to escalate the persecution of the Jews.[16] Within a Reich seething with competing centers of power, "Hitler did not have to devise a blueprint, timetable, or grand design for solving the 'Jewish question,'" Christopher Browning wrote. "He merely had to proclaim its continuing existence and reward those who vied in bringing forth various solutions. . . . The combination of Hitler's anti-Semitism as ideological imperative and the competitive polycracy of the Nazi regime created immense pressures for the escalation of Nazi Jewish policy even without broad public support in that direction." The broad public did its part by recognizing Jews as "the other," illustrated by society's quick isolation of German Jews and a common drive to prove which Germans had no Jewish ancestry, an effort achieved with church records that prelates might have declared private and off limits for such purposes. As Browning writes, having articulated the ideological imperative of antisemitism, Hitler could depend on party leaders and bureaucrats for an "escalating search for an ultimate or final solution." [17]

Here it is important to note that intermarriages, families fusing Jews and Gentiles, caused dissension rather than a steadily spiraling escalation, exhibited by bureaucratic squabbles over whether to forcibly annul these marriages and the racial identity of their Mischlinge children, illustrated by the Wannsee Conference and follow-up meetings in March and October of 1942. Structurally, the flexibility of this system of "working toward the Führer" is well represented by the independent authority of regional Nazi Party bosses, the Gauleiters, which also served to protect Hitler's plausible deniability, keeping any marks of his finger prints out of controversies that divided the German people.

Gauleiters were directly responsible to Hitler but charged with independently transforming Germans into Nazis as adroitly as possible. The Führer prized the plasticity of this structure of regional governance, in light of Germany's diverse regional identities. Gauleiters were not a mere structure of administrators who received and passed along orders down the flow chart. Rather, they set up their own laboratories of fascism, competing over the most effective tactics and timing to meet common Nazi goals within their own regions ahead of the others. They moved independently of national directives, particularly on sensitive issues, the ones most likely to place the ideological imperatives of policy in competition with the imperative of burnishing the Hitler myth. They did compete to make their regions "free of Jews" although the general process of removing Jews family by family did not bring ideological imperatives into conflict with governing imperatives nearly so much as seizing a Jewish partner from a mixed marriage, or deporting Aryans with their Jewish partners.

The system of satraps competing to reach Hitler's goals displaced responsibility for the controversies that inevitably erupted as Nazi policies violated social habits. Managing the conflicts that arose as new policies conflicted with sustaining the Hitler myth, however, were the essence of the Nazi leadership principle. Nazi leaders were supposed to avoid such frictions, but in certain cases no one but the top Nazi leader, the Führer himself, could determine how to resolve a conflict between Hitler's popular prestige and alien programs for realizing Nazi ideology.[18]

Some Gauleiters earned Hitler's tribute by removing crucifixes from public Catholic schools in their regions but those whose efforts caused disruptive unrest were charged with misjudging their region. Gauleiters Carl Röver of Weser-Ems and Adolf Wagner of München-Oberbayern received crippling attacks for incompetent clumsiness when their crucifix removals aroused ongoing scenes of noncompliance and protest. Wagner, once one of Hitler's closest associates, never recovered from the ongoing tumults his removal of crucifixes caused in the spring of 1941. Hitler as well as regional leaders were livid about this badly timed disturbance of the people when Gauleiters were supposed to be focusing popular energy on winning the war. Protests caused Wagner as well as Röver to rescind their crucifix decrees and reconfigure their approaches.[19]

Occasionally Hitler weighed in, behind the scenes when possible, not to promote but to prevent cumulative radicalization inside the Reich. Even into the final phase of the war, Hitler continued to curb his Gauleiter's wishes to escalate the use of force to just the level of soft coercion in order to enforce regulations restraining German masses from traveling back and forth between evacuation sites and their homes in cities under attack in allied bombing raids. In January 1944, in a Führer decision procured by Goebbels on behalf of all the Gauleiter and affirmed as late as October of that year, Hitler said the Gauleiters must educate the people so they saw that Nazi regulations were in their own best interests, rather than using force. Of course, the Nazis wanted a people who would grit their teeth and redouble their efforts under the strains of war. But to protect his image as the leader they should follow unquestioningly, building a totalitarian state on a totalitarian society so it would last a millennium, and also to avoid rebellions like those during the First World War, Hitler tried to solicit popular cooperation, which worked more readily while Germany was winning the war.[20]

Cumulative radicalization had limits inside the Reich, whether regarding "racial cleansing" or constraining Germans whose full energy the Nazis needed to win the war. This is indicated by the Nazi "euthanasia" program for killing Germans identified as incurable. A staunch Nazi illustrated this in her letter to the SS and Police Leader Heinrich Himmler, which caused him to close the "euthanasia" center at Grafeneck. Else von Löwis urgently pinpointed the widespread trust across the Reich that Hitler would surely intervene to stop the slaughter if only he knew of it. Around Grafeneck where the people could continuously observe the smoke ascending from the crematoria burning the bodies of "euthanasia's" victims, this critical belief was fraying, Löwis wrote, importuning that "the people are still clinging to the hope that the Führer does not know about these things otherwise he would intervene. . . . We must preserve this weapon [of belief in Hitler] untarnished, like no other." Shortly thereafter in December 1940 Himmler wrote that "the worst public mood has set in [around Grafeneck] and in my opinion there remains only one option: discontinue the use of the ['euthanasia'] institution."

Further evidence that the regime operated to maximize loyalty rather than merely crushing resistance at every turn, Hitler reversed the Gestapo's call to send Judge Lothar Kreyssig to a camp for maligning Nazi Euthanasia and accusing the Justice Minister of murder. Instead, Hitler complied with Kreyssig's request to retire with his pension.[21]

Also instructive for understanding the fate of intermarried Jews is the transition from Nazism's program of centralized euthanasia to the "wild euthanasia" organized around willing accomplices following Hitler's "halt" of euthanasia in August 1941. The point of interest here is not how "euthanasia" was introduced by a subordinate to push toward Hitler's goals with well-timed policy proposals but rather what happened when the absolute of racial hygiene conflicted with the absolute of maintaining Hitler's image. From "euthanasia" the regime learned that the most persistent unrest arose from families of euthanasia victims, and proceeded to deport German Jews in family units. The management of the particularly offensive and odious intermarried Jews, in Nazi sight, is foreshadowed by the movement from a more visible, centralized process of Nazi "euthanasia" murders to the "wild" mechanism for carrying out these murders that took measures to avoid impacting German-blooded persons specifically. Euthanasia measures moved behind the scenes after so many Germans rose up in anguished unrest, which Bishop August von Galen then articulated from his pulpit in August 1941, causing Hitler to halt the program. The subsequent phase of euthanasia was known officially as "wild euthanasia" because it relied on willing regional doctors and nurses in more than on specific directives from Berlin. Wild euthanasia was "actually decentralized and chaotic," murders that were folded into the "normal hospital routine" depending on those who were willing.[22]

The Führer needed to maintain his authority based in popular acclaim, although he also needed to banish all persons with Jewish blood. Thus the Gauleiters were put in charge of the timing and even to some extent the definition of "racial cleansing" of their territories, which they were supposed to know well enough to work at speeds and use tactics that did not cause scenes of unrest. Gauleiters tried to deport their region's Jews ahead of others while also circumventing spectacles that stirred dissent.[23] This way of handling a touchy matter also served to maintain Hitler's plausible deniability, given that deporting Jews and stealing their property might cause dissent, rumors, and questions about the ultimate fate of the Jews. Indicating his status, Goebbels informally served as the access point to Hitler for the other Gauleiters.

Hitler's initial authorization of deportations of German was met with "a whole range of new initiatives from numerous local and regional Nazi leaders."[24] Pomerania Gauleiter Franz Schwede sending more than 1,000 Jews including non-Jewish partners who refused to divorce, from Stettin and Schneidemühl to Lublin already in February 1940. The problem of intermarried Jews was deferred repeatedly because they were the most touchy of the sensitive tasks of "racial cleansing." Officials around the Reich looked for ways to solve their intermarried Jewish problems, some with small Jewish populations shoving intermarried Jews onto trains with the other full Jews headed for Auschwitz. Non-Jews from nonprivileged marriages like Eva Klemperer made this difficult by moving into a Jewish House with her husband, and refusing to agree to save herself should the Gestapo deport her husband.[25]

Intermarried Jews represented yet a higher level of image management than other German full Jews, another level of delicacy, as Goebbels saw it. Throughout the Holocaust, the regime regularly took into custody intermarried Jews whose partners had abandoned them one by one (whether by divorce or death), while it waited for an opportune moment, such as great acclaim for military victory, to deport as many intermarried Jews as possible en masse, without advertising the genocide and the presence of intermarried couples. Mass deportations of intermarried Jews were not merely determined by directives from the top but by regional authorities, established to deal with such delicate matters with territory-specific finesse, in ways that did not cast doubt on propaganda's image of consensus.[26] The Rosenstrasse Protest came at a crucial moment in the war as fortunes turned and Goebbels was embroiled in a battle for Total War measures, aligned with Speer and Göring against the bitter opposition of the Committee of Three-- the "Three Kings," Keitel, Lammers, and Bormann.[27] It illustrates the improvised nature of the way the regime worked, particularly when dealing with difficult questions it had hoped to put off until a moment of great triumph would please the masses, giving Hitler a sense of increased leeway to impose sacrifices.[28]

While intermarried German Jews were "temporarily" (*vorerst, vorläufig*) held back from deportations, individual Gauleiters improvised ways to draw these hypersensitive cases into the Holocaust without drawing attention to the embarrassing existence of intermarried couples. Hundreds of intermarried Jews were drawn into the Holocaust in ways that avoided the appearance that all such Jews were being killed. Some were sent to work camps and then if they survived to death camps. Gauleiter Jakob Sprenger of Hesse-Nassau was the most high profile of officials who invented ways to draw intermarried Jews into the Holocaust stealthily, and he was able to get away with it by falsely criminalizing them as long as this did not "attract any additional attention."[29] In Berlin by late 1942, the notorious deportation expert Alois Brunner began deporting some intermarried Jews along with others. Brunner deported at least one "half-Jew," covering his tracks by changing that persons papers to identify him as a "full" Jew. Brunner understood his job as getting the rest of Berlin's Jews out, bending the guidelines to suit that purpose. His tactics, however, led to open protests in the neighborhoods where he was active and he was sent to Greece to deport Thessaloniki's Jews.[30]

Nazi policy, not only in the matter of Jewish policy, "was flexible and always determined by tactical necessity," wrote Guenter Lewy.[31] Goebbels fumed that in the case of intermarriages this resulted in piecemeal arrangements awarding special status not only to the Jewish partners but also to their "Aryan" partners, a difficult challenge for public image. He fumed about this in October 1942 as he began to think more about how to deal with both partners in these marriages. Intermarriages led to an "intolerable situation" (*Übelstand*), with "Aryans" welcoming their marriage to Jews as a "contribution to a more comfortable life" (exemption from military service for example). Some still found refuge as artists within his Reich Chamber of Culture.[32] In early October 1942, Hitler's personal secretary and head of the Party Chancellory Martin Bormann wrote to Goebbels that Jews in privileged intermarriages must be deported like those in nonprivileged marriages, and Goebbels suggested to Hitler that they too be ordered to wear the star, but Hitler would not hear of it.[33]

The rubbery system of rule illustrated well by Gauleiter independence in their region has a direct bearing on Gauleiter Goebbels' decision to release rather than deport the intermarried Jews at Rosenstrasse. Goebbels modeled working towards the Führer as well as anyone, which was especially important in the task of removing Jews from the Reich capital, not only because the eyes of so many including foreign diplomats and journalists were on that city but because Berlin was home to about half of Germany's intermarriages. The agents who had wanted to deport intermarried Jews from the Rosenstrasse had blindly following orders rather than adjusting their sights to fit circumstances as they evolved, he complained, which required shifting the balance of concern from deporting intermarried Jews at the moment toward protecting the public mood and sense of solidarity for the sake of 'total war'.[34] The release was not a major defeat for Goebbels but another adjustment like the series of exceptions for intermarried Jews the regime had already made as their non-Jewish partners continued to refuse to divorce.

Intermarried Defiance Increased the Restraints on Cumulative Radicalization

Restraints on cumulative radicalization held "full" intermarried German Jews back not only during the Rosenstrasse Protest but from being the very first herded into Nazi death mills. They were figures of loathing for the regime and the community, heretics marrying their fate to Jews while scorning the magnificence of Hitler's national community. Their treason of *Rassenschande* was not only continuous but open. They were public, if unpunished, violators of the law banning friendly relations between "Aryans" and Jews, and the progenitors of mixed-race children that caused dissension about how to classify them. It was easy for Nazi leaders to agree on open and shut cases, especially when the translation of ideology into policy proceeded smoothly. "Half-breeds" ruffled the exacting bureaucrats changing categorical ideology into policy. Their intermarried parents, however, one undoubtedly German blooded and the other a "full Jew," posed a completely different problem, and a different edge.

Intermarried Jews who were "full Jews" according to the 1935 Nuremberg Laws, represented yet another level of remove from the cases most readily explained by cumulative radicalization. Combining Jews and non-Jews in families, they delineated heightened and more delicate challenges to the appearance of consensus behind Hitler and Nazi ideology, as well as to the general secrecy of the Holocaust itself. Nevertheless, step by step, the regime created exemptions for them to protect Hitler's image and his authority. The history of intermarried noncompliance and the regime's subsequent concessions is a key context for explaining the release of Rosenstrasse's intermarried Jews and their survival. Regime leaders expected intermarried "Aryans" to divorce under social and official pressures but as they instead continued to protect their Jewish partners the regime made a series of exceptions for intermarried "full Jews." Hitler's secret order of December 28, 1938, which followed complaints about the treatment of Jews during the Crystal Night Pogrom, divided intermarried Jews into privileged and nonprivileged groups. It followed Göring's statements that National Socialism would solve Jewish question "one way or another," while shortly preceding Hitler's infamous prophecy in January 1939 that war would lead to the "destruction of the Jewish race in Europe."[35] Bormann identified Hitler's order to divide intermarried Jews into two groups as a "fundamental decision on the Jewish Question." The decision was made so that the Gestapo could more purposely persecute intermarried Jews, reducing the volume of concurrent protest by moving against them one group at a time. But there is no significance to these developments at all—nor do they make sense—if the regime merely achieved by force whatever it wanted to do at any point.[36]

By 1942, Goebbels and others looked to close out the job of deporting anyone identified by the star as a Jew—which included the full Jews in nonprivileged mixed marriages but not those in privileged mixed marriages. How was it that precisely intermarried Jews, including those in nonprivileged marriages who wore the yellow star, were rescued?

There was no final and definitive decision from the Wannsee Conference or elsewhere about how to handle the Reich's intermarried Jews. The Wannsee Conference of January 20, 1942, was not a decision-making body and not the final word.[37] The conference itself was succeeded in March and October of 1942, by similar conferences dominated by Himmler's RSHA (Reich Security Main Office) dealing with similar issues, in particular intermarriages, which had already taken up much time at Wannsee. On October 27, conferees opted to annul intermarriages and according to Otto Hünsche, Eichmann's deputy and leading conference participant, it further produced agreement that all intermarried Jews who wore the star should be deported.[38] Both of these decisions are reflected in Goebbels' diary of December 6, 1942: "I am presented with a new proposal for the liquidation of Jewish marriages: proceed by compelling divorce and otherwise resort to evacuation"—inclusion in mass deportations. These were the plans of Himmler and his men. Goebbels recorded his responses to this plan after he procured Hitler's agreements. He rejected the plan for compelling divorce and intermarriages, fearing social unrest. But at the same meeting Goebbels received Hitler's authorization for the second part of the October 27 plan which called for the deportation of intermarried Jews wearing the star. "The Führer commissioned me with first ensuring that the unprivileged "full Jews" are taken out of Germany. Once they are all gone, we can approach the remaining remnants of the Jewish problem." The careful way that Goebbels at this time used the word "privileged" in only in relationship to intermarried Jews indicates his intention to deport intermarried Jews wearing the star but not those who did not.[39]

Goebbels, who like Hitler was committed to removing all traces of Jewish blood, had ranted against the grotesquery of "full Jews" and full "Aryans" in intermarried couples, and advocated treating gentiles who refused to divorce their Jewish partners as Jews rather than temporarily exempting their Jewish partners from genocide. Now, as he wrote on February 18, Goebbels in coordination with Himmler and the SS had his eye on deporting anyone in Berlin wearing the star by March of 1943, in a determination to finally render his Berlin Gau free of Jews. This desire to push Jews from Berlin, as Joachim Neander has written, was abetted by the pull exerted by the Auschwitz war industry's demand for labor. The RSHA had promised and the SS Main Economic and Administrative Office at Auschwitz was expecting a number of Berlin workers "of such magnitude" that "could only have been reached by deporting a significant portion of the Berlin Jews" from intermarriages. "Thus these authorities had consciously decided to end the 'temporary' exemption of intermarried Jews from deportations" at least to the extent necessary to supply the promised number of skilled slave laborers.[40]

Like Hitler on a smaller scale, Goebbels protected his own prestige, starting with the recognition that the Berlin region under his command as Gauleiter was the vanguard marker for the other regional Nazi leaders. "The ruthlessness that [Hitler] recommends to all Gauleiter in the face of Jewry is already a political imperative in Berlin," he boasted in February 1943.[41] On June 23, 1943, Goebbels evoked rivalry between himself and his closest rival, Vienna Gauleiter Baldur von Schirach, by praising the achievements in his Berlin Gau and sneering at those in Vienna, which Hitler settled by publicly humiliating Schirach.[42] Goebbels' was likely thinking that until he was successful in removing intermarried Jews from his Gau, others would have to wait. This prestige thinking is reflected in orders to authorities in France, who inquired about deporting their intermarried Jews: until this was done within the Reich it was not to be done elsewhere.[43]

Goebbels and Hitler saw ridding Germany of all Jews as an imperative, as a parasite "race" and because as a "fifth column" they spread sedition. At the same time, Goebbels' Total War measures depended more than ever on the people's willingness to put their energies fully into the war, heightening the concern about drawing attention to the fate of German Jews and above all to the existence of intermarried couples. Considering these conflicting imperatives, Goebbels opted for scenes of intimidation to suppress any acts of defiance. On February 2, several weeks in advance of the Elimination of Jews from the Reich arrests in Berlin, Goebbels arranged for the help of the most elite SS corps, the *Leibstandarte Adolf Hitler*. This would help him achieve his goal, he wrote, although he worried that the moment, as Germany was losing rather than winning its battles, was not the right moment for the use of "brute force."[44] Hitler signaled the particular need for attention to morale during the first week of war with an order banning all "unnecessary" provocations of the churches, and Goebbels told his fellow Gauleiters after Germany's stunning defeat of France that such moments of triumph when the regime was living up to its promises expanded their leeway for using force to achieve their ends.[45] Hitler regarded the people collectively as the engine for accomplishing his goals and Nazi leaders closest to him like Goebbels made decisions within the context of circumstances, looking for the opportune moment to press forward or let up in driving toward their goals.

Beginning February 27, in what the Berlin Gestapo called the final roundup of Berlin's Jews, uniformed police along with a detachment from the Leibstandarte SS swept across the Reich capital, signaling repression of dissent with the most brutal arrest of German Jews. The deployment of SS-men from its most elite division and the unusual and open brutality of these arrests, are noted by an SS-man who was so concerned he published his observations in the SS newspaper *Das Schwarze Korp*.[46] This deployment of the SS in the evidently brutal arrest of Berlin's Jews was one more in an escalating series of efforts by the regime to terrorize intermarried Germans into letting the Gestapo take their Jewish family members, after various other efforts over the course of a decade had failed. Goebbels does not mention that these "Aryans" he wished to intimidate were women, wives of husbands marked with the yellow badge, and whose houses were also publicly marked as Jewish. A Frankfurt/Oder decree said to show that the Gestapo always intended to send the imprisoned Jews from Rosenstrasse home, Osmar and Stoltzfus demonstrate that it encouraged the Gestapo to deport intermarried Jews.

That order does outline what a real "factory action" (a postwar invention for the massive arrests in Berlin) would look like—the arrest of Jews from factories.[47] In contrast, the arrests in Berlin beginning February 27 were much more broadly in line with Goebbels' mandate to clear Berlin of Jews than the Frankfurt/Oder "factory action." In Berlin, Jewish authorities received notice that "every person on the street wearing the star must expect to be arrested," except employees of the Jewish Community who wore a red Gestapo-stamped armband to mark their exception. Every person wearing the yellow badge without this red armband was arrested as they arrived at the distribution center to pick up their new ration cards, including Rita Kuhn's father as she writes here. Trucks carrying arrested Jews lurched to a stop when someone on the street was spotted wearing the star, as Gestapo agents leaped out and gave chase. Jews were also arrested from their homes. This was not a scene proceeding according to regulations for arrests outside of Berlin, but one showing an effort to clear Berlin of Jews, accompanied by brutal scenes of terror, of broken limbs and victims thrown onto trucks streaming blood, by SS-men wearing medals of valor in war. The roughly 2,000 intermarried Jews caught up in the operation were concentrated in the Jewish Community building in the heart of Berlin at Rosenstrasse 2–4.[48]

Before the end of the first day of arrests, a crowd began to develop on the Rosenstrasse, a sizable contingent of "Aryan" women come in pursuit of their Jewish husbands that would develop into a protest of hundreds in the coming days. The women's own escalation of resistance in continued open protest, despite demands from guards that they clear the streets or be shot, persuaded Goebbels that the best way toward deporting intermarried Jews once and for all was to turn again to the "temporary" reprieve given intermarried Jews. The hundreds of determined and desperate women intended to make scenes the regime could not ignore, and they did in fact draw the attention of none other than Joseph Goebbels, creator and guardian of the Hitler myth, who pushed the protests off the stage by releasing the Jews saying it would allow him to make a cleaner sweep later. While citing Joseph Goebbels' diaries freely elsewhere when it suits their argument, those who deny the protesting women any agency, readily dismiss Goebbels' diary regarding the Rosenstrasse events.

But contemporary sources corroborate Goebbels' statement that the protest rescued the Jews from deportation, including an American intelligence report "considered trustworthy" from the OSS dated April 1, 1943, not to mention others from within Germany at the time.[49] Martha Mosse, the first woman to work as a lawyer advising the

Berlin Police Department, who was a top level authority from 1934 to 1943 at the Reich Association of German Jews, wrote that "of the special action against Jewish partners in mixed marriages, who were quartered by the *Leibstandarte* in a [Jewish Community] building on Rosenstrasse, I know only the deportation of this group was prevented by the intervention for their Aryan partners and that the transit camp had to be vacated again."[50] Some have dismissed this as "too vague" to be taken into consideration.[51] But it confirms the testimonies of other witnesses, including the Gestapo agent Herbert Titze, who declared to the court that "mixed marriage partners sent to the Rosenstrasse Camp were released again. The 'Aryan' wives of these Jews had gathered together for a protest action in front of the camp."[52] In December 1945, Georg Zivier, whose wife demonstrated for his release, gave details of the protest with the same conclusion while reprimanding the German public for not joining in. The exacting Jewish lawyer, sociologist, and statistician Bruno Blau, shortly after the war, wrote that the protesting women "demanded the release of their husbands without regard for themselves, demonstrated throughout the day until the police drove them off. Through their courageous behavior, their willingness to make sacrifices and their persistence, they finally managed to get the Gestapo to give in and release those arrested." Blau makes the discomfiting conclusion, in relation to common and understandable beliefs, that open opposition was futile: "the women showed that it was not impossible to successfully oppose the Nazis."[53] Other Jews married to Gentile Germans sang praises to their partners for rescuing their lives.

While not granting credibility to the sources mentioned earlier, those who say that the intermarried Jews wearing the yellow star were not rescued by their partners at Rosenstrasse have not taken into account the important documents that Joachim Neander uses to demonstrate that there was not only a "push" from Berlin to deport these Jews but a "pull" from Auschwitz for their labor. At Auschwitz, where war industry factories demanded more workers to meet the quota Himmler had said he could deliver, a telegram written during the fourth day of the Rosenstrasse protests from the SS Main Economic and Administrative Office (WVHA) shows unmistakably that the entrepreneurs were expecting a number of skilled Jewish workers from Berlin. That number could not be met without the inclusion of intermarried Jews, already rounded up and waiting to be transported.[54]

As for arguments from the other side, the documents indicating that the fraction of the Jews imprisoned at Rosenstrasse who immediately received jobs does not indicate that deportation was not the Gestapo's plan. There is no indication that these assignments were planned in advance of the arrests; they bear merely a chronological relationship to the protest rather than an indication of a plan, and may well show how officials improvised in the face of protest. The Gestapo did not imprison children of intermarried couples so they would not be separated from their parents.[55] The Wannsee Conference of January 20, 1942, did not decide once and for all that intermarried Jews would not be deported, and Goebbels did have the authority to determine the timing of the fate of Berlin's Jews.[56] The Jews who survived in intermarriage have their partners "to thank," not a Gestapo deportation directive of February 20, 1943. If intermarried Jews survived due to "exemptions applicable to them" or "existing regulations" who put the exemptions there and why? Not every intermarried Jews survived, but those who did thanked their partners, not "fortune" in the abstract, as though the intermarried couples had not crafted that fortune by refusing to divorce.[57] The link between protest and the release of the Jews was not invented only after Hitler's Reich collapsed. The release of Jews following the Rosenstrasse Protest does not suggest that all "Jews" in intermarriage survived.[58]

Who rescued the intermarried Jews? Without documentation of certainty, Heim suggests consensus among historians instead. But this leaves important questions unanswered, and scholars have their own methods of finding the facts, which is supposed to allow the inspection of an unorthodox interpretation among historians who are secure in consensus.[59] If all historians did was provide yes or no answers to this or that question, the demise of history as a scholarly discipline should follow. The suggestion that we honor the Rosenstrasse protesters for courage but not rescue might seem miserly considering that, in the words of a German Federal Administrative Court ruling from 2000:

> Aryan spouses were repeatedly advised to separate from their Jewish spouses if they did not wish to share their persecution measures. . . . It is clear from their legal measures and actual procedures that the National Socialist rulers regarded everyone who was associated with Jews and refused to part with them as an opponent of the German government.[60]

Debates About Hitler's Rule Reflected in Debates on Intermarried Jews and Methodology

Today, when Hitler is adduced more than ever to describe or explain events, it is more important than ever to make sure our understanding of his power reflects the past well. The Rosenstrasse history seems to question common images of the bigger picture, and could be welcome as an opportunity to consider central, vexing matters, the work of intellectuals. There is no more reason to abandon the commemoration of intermarried Germans and their Rosenstrasse Protest because of disputes about how the regime responded than there is for abandoning the honoring of other events of defiance, also disputed. The question of whether we can know for sure is no less daunting in the case of this Rosenstrasse Protest than it is, for example, in the case of Hitler's responsibility for the Holocaust, which also cannot be nailed down in black and white by Nazi documents. One reason we have so little evidence on the protest is also due to Hitler and his circle's demand for plausible deniability, efforts to control their image. Nazi deceit extended to deception in the orders of the Gestapo, which are treated as completely trustworthy in order to deny the protesters the status of rescuers, even as eyewitness testimony of reputable persons who deserve the benefit of the doubt are freely discarded as unreliable. Gestapo directives, by contrast, are cited without so much as a note that deceptions are to be expected in such sources, particularly regarding the "embarrassing" cases of intermarried Jews.

Historians who deny the protesters a place as rescuers have searched for a specific document that makes an open and closed case that the regime never intended to deport intermarried Jews held on Rosenstrasse, a document certified with a Gestapo stamp (Antonia Leugers has pointed out ways they misunderstand these documents).[61] Seeking definitive evidence from Gestapo orders they portray the regime as an exact system with Berlin distributing the same order to every Gestapo office which was carried out exactly, regardless of rivaling power centers and players.[62] This precludes arguments like Neander's about influence from peripheries. Looking to pin down proof in black and white on a specific event can lead to overlooking the bigger picture and thus important contexts for interpreting the events. Seriously as well, placing too much stock in a single document precludes the bigger picture that emerges from many sources, which should be a better indicator of historical truth.

The Frankfurt/Oder order of February 25, 1943, has been used by a historian to discredit the historians Konrad Kwiet and Helmut Eschwege, who wrote that the protest had changed Gestapo plans since in his reading of the source they cited, by Kurt Ball-Kaduri had to be wrong. Ball-Kaduri was an outstanding German lawyer, adviser to the Prussian government, and a Zionist who was active in collecting sources on Jewish-German history since "he knew very well that many activities were conducted without any documentation, especially after the Nazi rise to power."[63] Unimpressed by the argument that he had to scorn Ball-Kaduri's source, Kwiet continued to publish the same conclusion years later:

> The strongest form of public protest found its expression in a late, spectacular demonstration. In February 1943, in the Rosenstrasse in Berlin, a group of German women succeeded in securing the release of their Jewish husbands who had been rounded up as forced laborers in the course of the Fabrik-Aktion.[64]

It is in fact hard to conceive that any of the other historians of such a caliber as H. G. Adler or Raul Hilberg, who have also written that the protest changed the minds of the Gestapo, and whose sources are also dismissed one by one, would have changed their judgment based on any singular document like the Frankfurt/Oder decree (and it seems quite unlikely that Hilberg and others never read it).

The significance of the protest cannot be simply resolved by this or that document any more than the decision-making processes of the regime itself can be so easily deciphered. Scholars reaching the conclusion that the protest was an act of rescue—within the context of other forces—have researched the ways that the regime made decisions, particularly at this time and place regarding Germany's intermarried Jews. The search for smoking gun evidence risks overlooking important clarifying contexts and questions that follow. The protest itself is sometimes not mentioned at all in the history of Himmler's Elimination of Jews from the Reich arrests, raising the question of why a story of German opposition to Nazis is so unwelcome.[65]

Those who see the protest as having rescued intermarried Jews at Rosenstrasse from death certainly agree that Hitler relied on repressing defiance with violence to the extent he considered it the most effective tactic available. But in relationship to people he wanted to invite into the national community he recognized the importance of norms, values, and thus of law that predated Hitler: "habits of the heart, the cultural remains of governing by way of rules rather than rifles" continued, enlivened through maintaining traditional norms in everyday life, as Jens Meierhenrich wrote.[66]

One explanation of the variations in the Reich's treatment of intermarried Jews, from region to region, is that this was due to the lack of any order from the top within a rigid structure carrying out orders.[67] This is not a regime with a direction waiting for circumstances that allowed it to improvise solutions on the spot, rather than being pinned down by a plan within circumstances it did not foresee. It is more of a monolithic regime ruling from the top and crushing every obstacle. The departure point is that it was not possible that "such demonstrations could have hindered the deportation plans of the RSHA."[68] When the Rosenstrasse Protest appears rather abruptly in one recent history of the Holocaust the context is the claim that opposition only "goaded the Reich into more radical action." The context provided for judging the protest's impact is that the regime reacted with violence at whatever levels it needed in order to repress opposition. Proof of how the regime would respond to the Rosenstrasse Protest if it had actually really gotten in the way of Gestapo plans, he writes is the "classic example" of the Nazi response to the general strike in Amsterdam in February 1941, as though the regime acted the same in all circumstances, within or outside the Reich, and at all moments during the war.[69] The question, urgent for understanding the Holocaust and the regime's ideas about how to manage it, of why the Nazis did not deport "full" German Jews in intermarriage—why it did not send these most deplorables to their deaths first of all—remains unaddressed.[70]

Positing that the protest was futile leaves open questions: How for example, should we explain why the regime murdered the entire families of intermarried couples from the East who refused to divorce, in contrast to the exceptions it made for intermarried couples within the Reich, with the result that virtually all of the "full" German Jews who survived Hitler were married to a non-Jew who had refused to divorce.[71] Why would the regime prefer to return intermarried Jews to their homes in March 1943, only to start all over with the job again soon thereafter? Of German Jews surviving in the Jewish houses, established in 1939 to isolate German Jews from non-Jews, "almost all were Jews protected by a non-Jewish partner."[72] How is this to be explained, given that the regime also knew exactly where to find them when it wanted to deport them, if not for the protection provided by non-Jewish partners who had refused tremendous pressures and enticements to divorce? How is it preferable to say that the regime wished to have all intermarried Jews sent back to their homes, *in March of 1943*, rather than positing that intermarried Germans rescued them? Why is it desirable or acceptable to refuse tribute to intermarried persons for their rescue? Should we discredit rescue of this type because it was not a singular act but a nonstop daily struggle over the course of twelve years?

Historians who argue that the regime never intended to deport Jews from Rosenstrasse think that the regime wished to deport these intermarried Jews soon, in the near future.[73] But the evidence arguably points to the significance of the protest, where the struggle between the regime and the intermarried Germans over the fate of intermarried Jews reached its apex. Dozens of intermarried Jews who had been deported from Rosenstrasse to Auschwitz were released from Auschwitz and returned to work camps near Berlin where their wives visited them. Goebbels complained on April 18 that, contrary to his plans to deport everyone from Berlin wearing the star, there were still persons wearing the star who were "running about in the capital." Either they should take off the star or be carted out of the city, he wrote. Some employers began to tell Berlin Jews they could remove the star.[74] On May 19, Goebbels declared Berlin Judenrein without further deportations of intermarried Jews, including those who wore the star. Two days later, Eichmann's office got around to answering a request from German police in Paris wondering whether to deport French intermarried Jews. The response was that intermarried Jews in foreign areas must not be deported before the question of the treatment of intermarried Jews within the Reich is "clarified." Within the Reich, it arguably follows, Goebbels had to lead.

Rather than moving expeditiously toward the annihilation of intermarried German Jews following the Rosenstrasse Protest, the regime was moving away from it. On May 21, 1943, Ernst Kaltenbrunner, Himmler's deputy heading the RSHA, dispatched a memo. All German intermarried Jews were to be released immediately from concentration camps except those imprisoned on real rather than fake criminal charges. All intermarried German Jews imprisoned on false charges were to be released. After identifying four categories of Jews that had regularly been temporarily deferred from the deportations, including those working in armaments industries, Kaltenbrunner ordered that the first three categories were now to be deported. The fourth category, intermarried Jews, was not to be deported: "I order expressly that Jewish intermarriage partners are in no case to be sent . . . . Insofar as Jewish intermarriage partners have been deported on general grounds [along with other "full Jews"], they are to be successively released."[75]

Where Is the Remembrance of Women, Rescue, and Protest?

Historians have always discovered new histories as they reconfigure their set of questions to reflect the concerns of the day. At our point in history it has become increasingly awkward and counterproductive to ignore protest against any autocracy including Nazi Germany. The year 2019, hailed as a trend-setting "year of protest" and notably against authoritarianism, has educated millions of people in the political power of protest. Yet in German sites of official history there has been hardly a trace of the important forerunners to public, collective protests during the Nazi regime, including the Witten women's protest as well as that of intermarried women.

Few debates yield more incongruities than the nature of resistance to Hitler except for those related to how Hitler ruled, and introducing women and protest themes is hardly likely to bring harmony. Those who have argued that the protest was futile since the Jews would have been released anyway, emphasize a regime that used raw force to achieve and maintain power: to see a protest as influencing the regime dangerously misconstrues it, for if the Holocaust had been so easy to stop it would have never happened.[76] But "easy" hardly describes the lives of intermarried couples. If differences of interpretation have stifled commemorations of the story, as Heim suggests, they have not prevented The German Resistance Memorial and Topography of Terror, Germany's key institutions of public official history, from ignoring the protest for decade after decade when there was a consensus that the protest had prevailed.[77]

Germany invests wisely in remembering the Nazi past. To overlook the place of intermarried courage is also to overlook an important history of women in the fast-growing tapestry of protest, on the streets as well as in the pages of scholarship. Women turned to protest for suffrage because, barred from the halls of power, collective action on the street was the only place they could not be ignored. Protest has continued to be a domain and form of women's resistance, an open forum anyone can join. Men of Hitler's Germany turned for resistance to weapons of warfare while women necessarily did without these. The Rosenstrasse Protest has a place in the collected history of women's uprisings elsewhere such as the Argentine Mothers of the Plaza de Mayo beginning in 1977. Headlines today highlight not just public protests as a potent form of resistance to insistent government force, but about how women of the past century and mothers today have carved out a place for their concerns through open collective actions and protests.[78] Historians as well as officials commemorating Germany's past will want to place the intermarried couples and their Rosenstrasse Protest in the Nazis past and the growing global context of protest and women's history.

The early years of German unification showed signs that the protest would be recognized. On June 21, 1990, I gave a lecture on the Rosenstrasse Protest to a full house of hundreds at the invitation of the *Gedenkstätte deutscher Widerstand* (GDW). I had published an 8,000 word article in the German weekly *Die Zeit* on the anniversary of The German Resistance two years earlier, which led to a lot of interest, including from documentary film makers and well-versed Germans intensely interested in the Nazi past who had never heard of the protest. I had arrived as a Fulbright fellow to research the Rosenstrasse Protest in 1984 and within months made calls for eye-witnesses in German newspapers and radio programs, resulting in dozens of recorded testimonies from perpetrators and victims, all but one or two of whom had never been interviewed. But something apparently happened between the GDW invitation for a lecture on Rosenstrasse and its subsequent refusal to commemorate the protests, and a revelation of the discussions about this decision would be a good departure point for a broader discussion.

The Gerhard Schroeder-Joschka Fischer government's promotion of civil courage from 1998 to 2005 was a receptive era for recognizing protest as relevant for this century's political culture. Open, personal expressions as demonstrated in public protest became a model for the civil courage that was becoming a new national aspiration. German President Johannes Rau and Foreign Minister Joschka Fischer joined forces at the highest level to encourage a bottom up sense of responsibility for democracy, enjoining Germans to prompt each other in developing German democracy in civil society. Schools admonished students about their personal investment in democracy, sifting through Nazi history for examples of civil courage, including protest in Nazi Germany. In November 1999, remembering the Berlin Wall ten years after it crumbled,

Schroeder memorably called the East German demonstrations a lesson for all of the newly unified Republic, while Rau credited the East German "citizens' movement" with toppling the Wall, an elemental example of civil courage going forward.[79] The Schroeder-Fischer government's civil courage encouraged citizens to "show your face" for democracy, and local activists established memorials to brave Germans showing courage from town to town. In 2005, Joschka Fischer wrote in honor of intermarried Germans for their success at Rosenstrasse, lifting them up as "a special thorn in the flesh of those in power" that called out for "present and future action . . . today's message from these courageous women is never to give up and not to bow to the supposedly inevitable when faced with violence and oppression, no matter how hopeless a situation may seem."[80]

If it is possible to learn from Hitler's dictatorship about today's world it is also perhaps possible to learn from the current world about Hitler. Rarely has it been so obvious than today that dictatorships can take over democracies without a bloody revolution or coup d'état, a method Hitler concertedly rejected as a means to power after 1923 because he wanted to build up his authority based in the popular recognition that he was the Führer. Popular protest is an available and potentially powerful form of opposition to autocrats, also apparent in the priority autocrats give to preventing and crushing it, fearing it for reasons similar to those identified by Goebbels, wrote this about open collective protest following the women's demonstration in Witten on November 2, 1943: "The people know exactly where to find the leadership's pliant spot and will always exploit it. . . . The state may never, against its better insight, give in to the pressure of the street." "Giving in" to the people was more and more dangerous, wrote Goebbels, since each time it happened the state lost some of its authority—and in the end could lose all power.[81] Still to many what matters most about the Rosenstrasse Protest is somehow teaching the world that protest would have never had any impact in Nazi Germany.

Like intermarriages, the Holocaust itself defines an edge, the ultimate depravity that also defines the regime. We seek to know the contours through the shape of an extreme. The regime's response to the Rosenstrasse Protest shows the limits of the radicalization of terror and destruction that Hitler allowed to flourish outside the Reich. Other protests also defined edges of the regime's reliance on terror as Hitler strove to shape the German people after himself. Still today, the history of German street protests ask us to perceive Hitler's Reich from uncommon perspectives, which is particularly unusual for those who see Hitler as forcing his way through any opposition. Protests in Nazi Germany do provide an alternative German behavior toward the regime, opposition that would presumably be welcomed today.

Cumulative radicalization had limits within the Reich because Hitler's image mattered there, another reason that Hitler was opportunistic about choosing tactics for reaching his goals. Force and terror were always key tactics of Nazi rule, targeted against specific "Aryans" of Hitler's race so that most Germans knew exactly how to avoid the Gestapo and did not fear it.[82] The history of the struggle over the fate of intermarried Jews, culminating in the Rosenstrasse Protest, holds valuable evidence for this view of how the regime made critical decisions when conflicts between popular morale and policies erupted or threatened to erupt into unrest, during wartime. The women who chose day by day to share the fate of the Jews and thus gave the regime pause about deporting their Jewish relatives, could still be honored today. Their resistance and rescue was one of a kind, an outside group that reveals general characteristics of how Hitler gained and sustained power. The history of intermarried couples itself serves the idea that persons can and should try to make a difference. They were rare Germans but they help define what was possible within certain circumstances.

Notes

1. Wiener Library microfilms containing eyewitness statements and a list of women participants in the February demonstrations (AR 7187/Reel 600). Others among the hundreds of responses to Heinz Galinski's call also confirmed that guards threatened to shoot the protesters if they did not leave the streets and that the "numerous" (zahlreiche) protesters called out together "we want our husbands back." Bruno Blau's memoir *Vierzehn Jähre Not und Schrecken* also confirmed such details about the women protesting on Rosenstrasse.

2. Joseph Goebbels, diary entry for February 2, 1943, Bundesarchiv NL 118/95.

3. "Es ist nicht so, daß man sie nur mit der Gewalt allein beherrschen kann. Gewiß, die Gewalt ist das Entscheidende, aber ebenso wichtig ist, ich möchte sagen, dieses psychologische Etwas, das der Tierbändiger auch benötigt, um seiner Tiere Herr zu werden. Sie müssen die Überzeugung besitzen, daß wir Sieger sind." Hans Rothfels and T. Eschenburg, "Dokumentation," *Vierteljahrshefte für Zeitgeschichte* 3 (July 1954): 305–12, here 309. See https://www.ifz-muenchen.de/heftarchiv/1954_3_6_krausnick.pdf (accessed December 2, 2020). The quote was taken from files of the Wehrmacht leadership staff and included in the materials of the main Nuremberg trial as Document 739-PS," (p. 306).

4. Joseph Goebbels, *Die Tagebücher von Joseph Goebbels, Sämtliche Fragmente*, ed. Elke Fröhlich (Munich: Saur, 1987–2008), March 6, 1943, Vol. II/7, 487. Dietrich Orlow, *A Complete History of the Nazi Party, 1919-1945* (New York: Enigma Press, 2010), 65.

5. On conflicting imperatives and how a dual state (the prerogative state and the normative state consisting of two halves) such as Hitler's dictatorship, has "what Reinhard Bendix termed 'conflicting imperatives' . . . built into it," see Ernst Fraenkel with an introduction by Jens Meierhenrich, *The Dual State: A Contribution to the Theory of Dictatorship* (Oxford: Oxford University Press, 2017), ixx, xvii.

6. Hans Mommsen, "Cumulative Radicalization and Progressive Self-destruction as Structural Determinants of the Nazi Dictatorship," in *Stalinism and Nazism: Dictatorships in Comparison*, eds. Ian Kershaw and Moshe Lewin (Cambridge: Cambridge University Press, 1997), 26–52. Dan McMillan has written a brief summary of the Hitler Myth in *How Could This Happen: Explaining the Holocaust* (New York: Basic Books, 2014), 119–36.

7. "Aryan" is the Nazi term for ethnic Germans connoting racial superiority, those who would comprise the base of a racially defined German. In his dissertation on late war violence against foreign workers within Germany.

8. Christopher Osmar has argued that different standards of behavior held for security forces dealing with non-Germans in the East and in the Reich proper. Radical practices developed in the East were introduced into Germany through personnel transfers, but typically remained latent until activated by a crisis. A crisis could introduce a frame shift that could

apply norms from the radicalized east within Germany. Christopher Osmar, "'Now I am in Distant Germany, It Could be that I Will Die': Colonial Precedent, Wartime Contingency, and Crisis Mentality in the Transition from Subjugation to Decimation of Foreign Workers in the Nazi Ruhr" (PhD dissertation, Florida State University, 2018).

9. "Es ist nicht so, daß man sie nur mit der Gewalt allein beherrschen kann. Gewiß, die Gewalt ist das Entscheidende, aber ebenso wichtig ist, ich möchte sagen, dieses psychologische Etwas, das der Tierbändiger auch benötigt, um seiner Tiere Herr zu werden. Sie müssen die Überzeugung besitzen, daß wir Sieger sind." Rothfels and Eschenburg, "Dokumentation," 309. See also footnote 14.

10. "His political talent lay in defining goals in very broad terms and in his ability to wait for situations to emerge that would allow him to move closer to realizing those goals." Thomas Weber, *Becoming Hitler: The Making of a Nazi* (Oxford: Oxford University Press, 2017), 238.

11. "The fundamental evil of our leadership," he reflected, "and above all our administration is that everything is done by the book [nach Schema F]." Goebbels, *Die Tagebücher von Joseph Goebbels*, 487.

12. Harold Marcuse, on minimizing, in the 2004 H-German debate on the Rosenstrasse Protest, https://lists.h-net.org/cgi-bin/logbrowse.pl?trx=vx&list=H-German&month=0407&week=e&msg=gO43QNl7wetBjNmZQA0Oww&user=&pw=.

13. See the last two parts of Alexander Dallin, *German Rule in Russia 1941-1945: A Study of Occupation Policies* (London: MacMillan, 1957).

14. This is a central argument in Nathan Stoltzfus, *Resistance of the Heart: Intermarriage and the Rosenstrasse Protest in Nazi Germany* (New York: WW Norton, 1996) and in article form in Stoltzfus, "The Limits of Policy: Social Protection of Intermarried Jews in Nazi Germany," in *Social Outsiders in Nazi Germany*, eds. Robert Gellately and Nathan Stoltzfus (Princeton: Princeton University Press, 2001), 117–44.

15. Ian Kershaw, *The "Hitler Myth" "Image and Reality in the Third Reich"* (Oxford: Oxford University Press, 1987); Ian Kershaw, "Working Towards the Führer: Reflections on the Nature of the Hitler Dictatorship," *Contemporary European History* 2, no. 2 (July 1993): 103–18.

16. Ian Kershaw, *Hitler, 1939-45: Nemesis* (London: Allen Lane, 2000), 132, on survivors Raul Hilberg, *The Destruction of the European Jews* (New Haven: Yale University Press, 2003), Vol. II, 487.

17. Christopher R. Browning, *The Origins of the Final Solution: The Evolution of Nazi Jewish Policy, September 1939–March 1942*, with contributions by Jürgen Matthäus (Lincoln: University of Nebraska Press, and Jerusalem: Yad Vashem 2004), 10, 11.

18. Christiane Kuller, "The Demonstrations in Support of the Protestant Provincial Bishop Hans Meiser: A Successful Protest Against the Nazi Regime?," in *Protest in Hitler's "National Community": Popular Unrest and the Nazi Response*, eds. Nathan Stoltzfus and Birgit Maier-Katkin (New York: Berghahn Books, 2016), 38–54.

19. Nathan Stoltzfus, *Hitler's Compromises: Coercion and Consensus in Nazi Germany* (Yale: Yale University Press, 2016), 99.

20. On evacuations, Julia Torrie, "'If Only Family Unity Can Be Maintained': The Written Protest and German Civilian Evacuations," *German Studies Review* 29, no. 2 (May, 2006): 347-66, and *"For Their Own Good": Civilian Evacuations in Germany and France, 1939–1945* (New York: Berghahn Books, 2010), 94–127. See also Stoltzfus, *Hitler's Compromises*, particularly 207–43 on Hitler and the Gauleiters and 174–206 on Euthanasia/

21. Henry Friedlander, *Origins of Nazi Genocide* (Chapel Hill: University of North Carolina Press, 1995), 107–8, 121. Nuremberg Military Trial (NMT) Document NO-001, Else von Löwis to Frau Buch, Concerning the Treatment of Incurably Insane Persons, November 25, 1940; NMT, NO-002, Buch to Himmler, December 7, 1940 (Nuremberg trial document NO-002), Reichsführer-SS Heinrich Himmler to Oberdienstleiter Viktor Brack, December 19, 1940, Nuremberg trial document NO-018. Closing the euthanasia center was something of a shell game since the killings were moved to another location, as unrest continued to build up. Kreyssig excelled in Nazi *Menschensführung*, the power to sway the masses and their moods, and could perhaps prove useful after Germany won the war.

22. Friedlander, *Origins*, 110, 111, 152–62 (quote 153); E. Klee, ed., *Dokumente zur "Euthanasie"* (Frankfurt: Fischer, 1985), 231, 283; Christoph Heinzen, *Medizin und Gewissen- historische, systematische und aktuelle Perspektiven im Hinblick auf die Euthanasiegesetzgebung* (München und Ravensburg: Grin Verlag, 2003), 34, 35.

23. On racial cleansing as well as Gauleiter independence and the competition of "working toward the Führer" see Catherine Epstein, *Model Nazi: Arthur Greiser and the Occupation of Western Poland* (New York: Oxford University Press, 2010), 6, 94, 98, 208–11.

24. Kershaw, *Nemesis*, 481.

25. Ibid., 481, Klemperer, *I Will Bear Witness*, May 26, 1940, 339ff.

26. Cf. Karin Orth, *NS-Vertreibung der jüdischen Gelehrten. Die Politik der Deutschen Forschungsgemeinschaft und die Reaktionen der Betroffenen* (Göttingen: Wallstein, 2016), 272, note 13.

27. Kershaw, *Nemesis*, 450–1.

28. Hitler issued an order in September 1939 banning unnecessary provocations of the churches but vacillated on enforcing it during Germany's Blitzkrieg victories only to crack down on enforcement after Germany failed to take Moscow. Stoltzfus, *Hitler's Compromises*, 173, 182, 194–7.

29. This was the conclusion of the prosecutors in the conviction of Darmstadt Gestapo Agent Georg Dengler, Antonia Leugers, ed. *"Introduction," Berlin, Rosenstrasse 2–4: Protest in der NS-Diktatur* (Annweiler: Ploeger, 2005), 9–11, citing Anklageschrift gegen Dengler, May 11, 1950. IfZ, Gd 01.10. The prosecutors themselves concluded that these Jews were falsely criminalized in order to draw them into the Holocaust.

30. Hildegard Henschel, "Aus der Arbeit der jüdischen Gemeinde Berlins während der Jahre 1941–1943. Gemeindearbeit und Evakuierung von Berlin 16 Oktober 1941–16 Juni 1943," *Zeitschrift der Geschichte der Juden* 9, Nr. 1/2 (1972): 43–4; Mary Felstiner, "Alois Brunner: 'Eichmann's Best Tool,'" *Simon Wiesenthal Centre Annual* 3 (1986): 1–46.

31. Guenter Lewy, *The Catholic Church and Nazi Germany* (Cambridge: Da Capo Press, 1964); John S. Conway, *The Nazi Persecution of the Churches 1933-45* (Toronto: Ryerson Press, 1968), 225.

32. Goebbels, diary, October 2 and 3, 1942.

33. Goebbels, diary, October 4, 1942.

34. Goebbels, diary, March 6, 1943. See also the Osmar/Stoltzfus chapter in this book.

35. On Göring, see Browning, *Origins*, 11.

36. On the series of regime concessions to the defiance of intermarried couples, see Stoltzfus, "The Limits of Policy," 123–33. Hitler's "fundamental decisions" dividing intermarried Jews into privileged and nonprivileged is in Nuremberg Document 069-PS.

37. Cf. Meyer, 57: Meyer cites directives for withholding intermarried Jews from deportation as definite rather than "temporary," adding that Goebbels, "in his position as Gauleiter of Berlin, pushed action intended to include mixed marriage Jews in the policy of extermination—after the Wannsee Conference had declined to do this. Goebbels, not in position to accomplish this, was attempting to initiate policy 'from below.'" For years the US Holocaust Memorial Museum's description of the Rosenstrasse Protest reiterated that the Jews imprisoned at Rosenstrasse were not facing deportation because the Wannsee Conference had decided to exempt intermarried Jews, adding that the Gestapo—despite Himmler's November 1942 order to clear all camps of Jews including Mischlinge—"fully intended to incarcerate these [intermarried] Jews in forced-labor camps in the Reich." Another USHMM article, "The Wife who sent her Husband to Auschwitz," takes the protest more seriously, while stating that the Jews imprisoned at Rosenstrasse were "protected under 'privileged marriages' in the parlance of Nazi law." But these Jews were in *non-privileged* intermarriages—rather than privileged intermarriages—according to Hitler's regulation of December 1938 and wore the yellow star marking them as Jews to be deported. Abigail Hartley, https://us-holocaust-museum.medium.com/the-wife-who-sent-her-husband-to-auschwitz-e2a97ad02993 (accessed July 30, 2020). See note 59.

38. Peter Longerich, Wannseekonferenz: Der Weg zur "Endlösung," (Munich: Pantheon, 2017), 138; Stoltzfus, *Resistance of the Heart*, 193, 336.

39. Goebbels, diary, December 6, 1942 and April 18, 1943.

40. Joachim Neander, "Auschwitz, the 'Fabrikaktion,' Rosenstrasse: A Plea for a Change of Perspective in Protest," in *Protest in Hitler's "National Community,"* 125–42, here 132–3.

41. Goebbels, diary, February 8, 1943.

42. Kershaw, *Nemesis*, 590.

43. Stoltzfus, *Resistance of the Heart*, 255.

44. Goebbels, diary, February 2, 1943.

45. Goebbels was concerned that the Churches, by holding ceremonies for Germans who died on the war front, were winning converts. The Churches should not receive the credit since after all, "those who fell did not die for a Church but for Germany." Bundesarchiv, NS 18/112, to all Gauleiters, August 13, 1940. See also Guenter Lewy, *The Catholic Church and Nazi Germany* (Cambridge: Da Capo Press, 2000), 253.

46. Bundesarchiv Berlin, NS 19/3492, translated in Stoltzfus, *Resistance of the Heart*, 232–3.

47. Cf, Gruner in Antonia Leugers, "Widerstand gegen die Rosenstrasse. Kritische Anmerkungen zu einer Neuerscheinung von Wolf Gruner," *theologie.geschichte*, 1 (2006). http://universaar.uni-saarland.de/journals/index.php/tg/article/viewArticle/133/148.

48. Hildegard Henschel, "Aus der Arbeit der jüdischen Gemeinde Berlins während der Jahre 1941–1943. Gemeindearbeit und Evakuierung von Berlin 16 Oktober 1941–16 Juni 1943," *Zeitschrift der Geschichte der Juden* 9, Nr. 1/2 (1972): 33–52, here 47–9. Rita Kuhn's father was one who was arrested at the ration card distribution center on Friday, March 5, as she writes in her chapter.

49. "A source which is considered trustworthy has reported that action against Jewish wives and husbands on the part of the Gestapo had to be discontinued some time ago because of the protest which such action aroused." Harrison to Donovan, Office of Strategic Services, April 1, 1943, National Archives, Washington, DC, RG 226 (OSS) Entry 134: Washington Registry Office Radio & Cable Files, Box 171, Folder 1079 . Contemporaneous statements see 258ff. Leugers, "The 1943 Rosenstrasse Protest and the Churches," in *Protest in Hitler's 'National Community,'* 150, 182–3. See also Margarete Sommer's report (after August 5, 1942) in

Ludwig Volk, ed., *Akten deutscher Bischöfe über die Lage der Kirche, 1933-1945, vol. 5: 1940-1942* (Mainz: Matthias-Griinewald Verlag, 1983), 818.

50. Martha Mosse testimony to Wolfgang Scheffler, July 23 and 24, 1955 online at https://wiener.soutron.net/Portal/Default/en-GB/recordview/index/105300 and in H. G. Adler, *Theresienstadt 1941–1945*, trans. Belinda Cooper (Cambridge: Cambridge University Press, 2017), 719.

51. Dismissing Ms. Mosse's testimony as a "very vague source" is Wolf Gruner, *Widerstand in der Rosenstrasse: die Fabrik-Aktion und die Verfolgung der "Mischehen" 1943* (Frankfurt am Main: Fischer Taschenbuch Verlag, 2005), 24, without considering it together with all of the other relevant sources.

52. Statement of Berlin "Jewish Bureau" Gestapo agent Herbert Titze, August 1, 1966, Landesarchiv Berlin B Rep. 058, Nr. 22. This statement is removed from Titze's testimony in the Hörpol audio guide to Berlin Mitte, the site of the memorial to the Rosenstrasse protest. Hörpol self-identifies as a guide to Berlin's Jewish history concerned with antisemitism. See http://www.hoerpol.de/deutsch/Macht.pdf.

53. Germans "overlooked the sudden flare of a tiny torch which could have lit the fire of general resistance." Georg Zivier, "Aufstand der Frauen" *Sie: Frauenzeitung für Menschenrecht*, Dezember 1945. Bruno Blau, "Vierzehn Jahre Not und Schrecken" (ca. 1947), excerpted in Monika Richarz, *Judisches Leben in Deutschland: Selbstzeugnisse zur Sozialgeschichte* (New York: Leo Baeck Institute, 1982), Vol. 3, 466.

54. Neander, "Auschwitz, the 'Fabrikaktion,' Rosenstrasse: A Plea for a Change of Perspective" See also the chapter by Stoltzfus and Osmar in this book. On overlooking his argument see for example Maximilian Strnad, "The Fortune of Survival—Intermarried German Jews in the Dying Breath of the 'Thousand-Year Reich,'" *Dapim: Studies on the Holocaust* 29, no. 3 (2015): 173–96.

55. Gruner initially wrote that no Jew below the age of fourteen was imprisoned. Confronted with evidence in sources he had discounted that this was not the case, he explained that the Gestapo took children from their homes and locked them up at Rosenstrasse "so they would not be left alone at home when their parents were arrested." Gruner, *Widerstand in der Rosenstrasse*, 109.

56. Cf, Beate Meyer, »*Jüdische Mischlinge« Rassenpolitik und Verfolgungserfahrung 1933-1945* (Hamburg: Dölling und Galitz Verlag 2012), 57. Maria von der Heydt, "Wer fährt denn gerne mit dem Judenstern in der Straßenbahn?" in *Jüdisches Leben im Großdeutschen Reich 1941-1945*, eds. Andrea Löw et al. (Berlin: De Gruyter, 2013), 74.

57. Strnad, "Fortune of Survival," 174, 178.

58. Hartley, Wife who sent her Husband. https://us-holocaust-museum.medium.com/the-wife-who-sent-her-husband-to-auschwitz-e2a97ad02993, writes that "It's tempting to think . . . that every non-Jewish wife or mother resisted the arrest of her Jewish husband or son. But the truth is much more complex." The temptation could have been alleviated better with a few statistics than an anecdote: Marion Kaplan estimated that 99 percent of Jews who had not emigrated survived in mixed marriages. Emil Tuchmann of Vienna's Jewish Community's leadership, that 96 percent of that city's Jews survived in mixed marriages, which is similar to Evan Bukey's calculations of 5–7 percent. Ursula Büttner estimated that 7.2 percent of intermarried couples divorced during the Nazi years in Baden Württemberg while 9.9 percent divorced in Hamburg between 1942 and 1945. Evan Burr Bukey, *Jews and Intermarriage in Nazi Germany* (Cambridge: Cambridge University Press, 2011), 83 note 2, and 94 note 40.

59. What is the meaning of scholar-politician collaborations such as the recent article "There is no politics without history," jointly authored by the direct of the Institut für Zeitgeschichte

Prof. Andreas Wirsching, and German foreign minister Heiko Maas? Of course disagreement and thereby the refinement of our knowledge characterizes scholarship—if scholars contend fairly with opposing arguments. Andreas Wirsching and Heiko Maas, "There Is No Politics Without History," *Spiegel Politik*, May 7, 2020. https://www.spiegel.de/politik/deutschland/keine-politik-ohne-geschichte-a-d74deffe-c0f3-4ff7-a6af-dc713e74c6f3 (accessed July 3, 2020).

60. https://lexetius.com/2000,2144 (accessed May 21 2020), citing *BVerwG, Urteil vom 13. 9. 2000—8 C 21.99; VG Meiningen (lexetius.com/2000,2144)* (BGH, op. Cit., P. 111), which repealed a judgment of 7. Oktober 1998; On the problems intermarried couples encountered after the war see Ori Yehudai, "'Doubtful Cases': Intermarried Families in the Post-Holocaust Jewish World," *Immigrants & Minorities. Historical Studies in Ethnicity, Migration and Diaspora* 38 (2020): 27–53. doi: 10.1080/02619288.2020.1794839.

61. Antonia Leugers has pointed out the reasons to doubt Gruner's reading of Gestapo documents, including prominently a misreading of headers and the omission of significant parts of the Frankfurt/Oder decree that augur against his explanation of it. Leugers, "Widerstand gegen die Rosenstrasse," 177–8, 197–8.

62. Neander, "Auschwitz, the 'Fabrikaktion,' Rosenstrasse"; Nathan Stoltzfus, "Historical Evidence and Plausible History," *Central European History* 38, no. 3 (2005): 450–9, here 451–3.

63. Gruner, *Widerstand in der Rosenstrasse*, 23–4; Kurt Ball-Kaduri, EHRI Personalities. https://portal.ehri-project.eu/authorities/ehri_pers-000453.

64. Wolf Gruner, "The Factory Action and the Events at the Rosenstrasse in Berlin," *Central European History* 36, no. 2 (2003): 179–208, here 183; Konrad Kwiet rejected Gruner's analysis in "Without Neighbors: Daily Living in Judenhäuser," in *Jewish Life in Nazi Germany: Dilemmas and Responses*, eds. Francis R. Nicosia and David Scrase (New York: Berghahn, 2010), 134. See the response to Gruner's article, Stoltzfus, "Historical Evidence."

65. von der Heydt, "Wer fährt denn gerne," 74. Strnad, "Fortune," 74, overlooks the impact of noncompliance.

66. Jens Meierhenrich, *The Remnants of the Rechtsstaat: An Ethnography of Nazi Law* (Oxford: Oxford University Press, 2018), 11, 25–7, 151. It took generations for scholars to begin to see from the perspective of perpetrators, as seen by Harold Welzer: "die Tötungsmoral des Nationalsozialismus sowohl persönliche Skrupel als auch das leiden an der schweren Aufgabe des Tötens normative integriert hatte." National Socialism's ethic of killing had integrated both personal scruples and the suffering from the difficult task of killing, into normative experience.

67. Orth, *NS-Vertreibung der jüdischen Gelehrten*, citing Beate Meyer, 271, note 13. The Kaltenbrunner memo of May 21, 1943 is said to represent a decision by the RSHA to "shrink" the imprisonment of intermarried Jews by local Gestapo agents on "minor charges." But it is much more significant in its context.

68. Wolf Gruner, "Die Reichshauptstadt und die Verfolgung der Berliner Juden 1933-1945," in *Jüdische Geschichte in Berlin: Essays und Studien*, ed. Reinhard Rürup (Berlin: Edition Hentrich, 1995), 253. See also his statement in the H-German forum on Rosenstrasse.

69. Peter Hayes, *Why? Explaining the Holocaust* (New York: WW Norton, 2017), 353.

70. Ibid., xiv. claims to cite only the most reliable scholarship.

71. Kwiet, "Judenhäuser," 133–4. As Hitler's Reich fell, intermarried Jews were 11,150 of the 11,359 "full Jews" still surviving who had not been deported or gone into hiding *in the Old Reich*, according to Hilberg, *The Destruction of the European Jews*, Vol. II, 487. Of this count

of German "full Jews" from October 1944, seventy-two were foreign Jews. Of the 11,280 German Jews, there were in the city of Berlin alone some 200 Schutzjuden—Jews under the protection of the highest officials. Maximillian Strnad writes that "In September 1944, following the mass deportations, 12,206 of the 14,288 Jews still living in Germany proper (Altreich) were intermarried." Strnad, "Fortune of Survival," 173–96, here 174.

72. Kwiet, "Judenhäuser," 134.

73. Heim, chapter 5, 95.

74. Goebbels, Tagebücher, April 18, 1943.

75. Cf. Orth, *NS-Vertreibung der jüdischen Gelehrten*, 271, note 13.

76. Wolf Gruner and Beate Meyer in a 2004 H-German debate on the Rosenstrasse Protest, http://web.archive.org/web/20140311195627/http://www.h-net.org/~german/discuss/Rosen strasse/Rosenstrasse_index.htm.

77. See the Introduction, note 20.

78. Amanda Taub, "*Mothers' Power in U.S. Protests Echoes a Global Tradition*," New York Times, July 25, 2020, https://www.nytimes.com/2020/07/25/world/americas/protest-moms-power-police.html. Rosenstrasse's intermarried protesters were "Aryan" and thus privileged to protest.

79. Festansprache von Bundespräsident Johannes Rau, 10. November 1999 in Berlin, Bundesregierung Bulletin, 15 December 1999. https://www.bundesregierung.de/breg-de/s ervice/bulletin/festansprache-von-bundespraesident-johannes-rau-807998 (accessed May 26, 2008).

80. Joschka Fischer Vorwort, in Nathan Stoltzfus, *Widerstand des Herzens.: Der Aufstand der Berliner Frauen in der Rosenstraße—1943* (Hamburg: Deutscher Taschenbuch Verlag, 2002), i–iv.

81. Goebbels, Tagebücher, November 2, 1943.

82. Eric A. Johnson and Karl-Heinz Reuband, *What We Knew: Terror, Mass Murder, and Everyday Life in Nazi Germany* (New York: Basic Books: 2006), 355.

CHAPTER 2
WHOEVER SAVES ONE LIFE, SAVES AN ENTIRE WORLD[1]
WOMEN RESCUERS OF JEWS
Mordecai Paldiel

In this chapter, I deal with a special form of resistance; not joining a politically oriented anti-Nazi clandestine organization in order to help topple the Nazi regime, but of women who, mostly alone, decided that since Jews, as all other human beings, have a right to live, but were targeted for destruction by the Nazi regime, they were going to get personally involved to save as many lives as possible. This took various forms; from the life of a single child, to many others; and as many of the adult Jews on the run, that each of the rescuers were able to do singlehandedly—without in many cases the help of outsiders including, for reasons of security, of their own families.

For Jews, to avoid being consumed in the Nazi inferno, it meant desperately finding a helping hand, in some instances by fellow Jews equally on the run, and eventually by non-Jews, who were not targeted for extermination for simply being, as was the case of Jews. Help took many forms, such as being admitted for hiding in someone's home or farming barn, for a stay in total seclusion, or assist someone to move and escape to other safer havens with the help of fake identities, or finally, help in securing the lives of children whose parents could not take them along as they ran for their own lives. The stories mentioned here are of women honored as Righteous Among the Nations by the Yad Vashem Holocaust Institute in Jerusalem, under a special program launched in 1962, and still ongoing. While thousands of men and women have already been attributed the Righteous title (and I was privileged to have been intimately involved in that project for twenty-four years), in the present chapter I have selected a handful of stories that illustrate the great courage shown by these persons when challenged to counter what was an uppermost goal in Nazi designs—a world bereft of Jewish lives. All non-Jewish women rescuers mentioned here were awarded the Righteous title by Yad Vashem.

The twenty-eight stories selected here come from a larger repertoire of thousands of women rescuers, and these few stories describe rescue operations undertaken in various circumstances of danger to the rescuers. An additional factor in these stories is the extent of the existing social relationship between rescuers and those they saved. From the limited sample of only these twenty-eight stories, it turns out that in six of them, some lengthy prewar acquaintanceship existed between both sides; in seven stories, a relationship evolved during the early stages of the war years, but prior to the rescue operation; and in fifteen, that is over half of all stories, rescuers and rescued only met for the first time moments before the start of the rescue operation, such as persons who fled during a death march. This is also especially so where children were turned over to the hands of their benefactors, that in the case of nuns, the Jewish children had not known them from before, and we list ten stories of children rescue. Finally, two stories have their origin in romantic ties between both sides, and two stories are of women who openly protested against the regime's barbarities against the Jews, and were prepared to suffer the consequences of their open defiance. In the selection of stories, I also took care to diversify the nationalities of the women rescuers: eleven from Poland; nine from Germany; two from Netherlands; two from Hungary; and one each from Italy, Austria, Belgium, and France.

The reader is cautioned that this sample of twenty-eight stories, out of a larger repertoire of thousands of women rescuers recorded at Yad Vashem, is too small to draw any conclusions from sociological or psychological perspectives, such as the motivation of the rescuers. The sole exception is what I already indicated in the introduction; that of proximity and the face-to-face encounters between both sides, of rescuers and rescued, that in most stories prompted the rescue undertaking. That, in contrast to other forms of altruism that have their beginnings after a careful thinking process of one's preparedness to be of help to others, such as the story of Mother Teresa, in the stories of the Righteous, the decision-making comes abruptly and instantaneously; mostly instinctively, without the luxury of a prior lengthy reflection on whether to get involved or not.

Pre-war acquaintance. For Jews on the run, we start with a story where both sides knew each other from before. Such as Emma Richter, who, after the large roundup of Jews in Berlin on February 27, 1943, the so-called Fabrikaktion, sheltered her Jewish friend, Meta Sawady, first in her Berlin flat; then in a summer house on the outskirts of Berlin; constantly providing her friend with food and other necessities. The two had known each other for many years when they worked together as cashiers in a store.[2] In Vienna, 1941, stage actress Dorothea Neff hid in her home for over three years Lilli Wolff, her former costume designer. Neff continued her appearance in the prestigious Volkstheater, where she played leading roles, while keeping closeted in a back room of her home her longtime Jewish acquaintance. After the war, Lilli Wolff wrote: "The greater the darkness of a period, the brighter is the light of a single candle. God chose Dorothea Neff to save my life. . . . When she was born, the world became more bountiful, and part of that bounty was bestowed on me."[3]

In Przemyśl, Poland, Stefania Podgórska, born 1925, knew some of the people, but not all of the 13 people, she hid. Previous to the war, she worked half a day in the small grocery store of Max Diamant's parents, and half a day in the Diamant home helping out with domestic chores. In 1942, in the city ghetto, Max Diamant kept in touch with Stefania, asking her to find a place in the city where a large group of people could build for themselves a hideout. She chose a dilapidated home at the edge of the city, and she moved there with her younger sister Helena, born 1935. Max and friends stole out from the ghetto and began to build an identical double wall at one end of the attic that would serve as a hiding place behind it. Stefania and her sister Helena bought old boards and planks from destroyed homes to build this wall. After everything was ready, 13 people made their way, in turns, from the ghetto to the hiding place in the attic, including two children. Some women knitted sweaters, gloves and hats from old military sweaters and socks bought by Stefania on the market, which she washed and cleaned, then sold them to the neighbors who resold them on the market. On July 27, 1944, the Russian army drove out the Germans, and the hidden persons, after being cooped up for 20 months, were free to leave.[4]

In the Elisabeth Abegg story, she aided persons known to her before the war, to which she added some she met during the war years. Born 1882 in Strasbourg, then part of Germany, she stated that the teaching of Albert Schweitzer, of the same city, on Christian universalism and the sanctity of human life, had a life-long impact on her. Joining the Quaker movement, in Berlin, she also became a history teacher where she endeavored to impress her humanistic beliefs on her students, many of them Jewish. After Hitler's accession to power, she was dismissed and forced to retire prematurely. She would not, however, be deterred from maintaining contact with her former Jewish students and friends. For that purpose, Abegg turned the three and a half room apartment that she shared with her eighty-six-year-old mother, and invalid sister Julie, into a temporary shelter and assembly point for Jews who lived underground, or directed them to hiding places elsewhere. Of special comfort and moral edification were Elisabeth Abegg's Friday noon meals for her distraught Jewish friends, which she prepared herself. There, for a brief two hours, these hunted men and women, some of whom passed nights in dark cellars, condemned buildings and secluded places in public parks, gathered for a once-a-week session of camaraderie, companionship, and moral uplift. "It allowed us to forget that we had no more right to exist as human beings," recalled Liselotte Pereles, one of Abegg's many wards. Through her contacts, she arranged sheltering places for her former students, and some others, in Berlin or elsewhere in Germany. Gisela Heinricht, one of Abegg's wartime friends reported her saying: "Do you know Gisela, one cannot perceive how much evil Nazism brought with it. I am, after all, a convinced opponent of this regime and am not easily swayed. Nevertheless, when I previously walked the streets, I saw persons about me without making any distinctions about them. Now, when I walk the streets, I see different types of persons. I say to myself, this man looks Jewish, poor fellow." Abegg brushed off the thanks of a Jewish couple: "We are indebted to you! We have so much to amend for!"[5]

Met during the occupation period. Some rescue stories had their beginnings not in a longtime previous acquaintance, but contacts established during the war years. German-born Imgard Wieth worked in a German housing department office in Lwów, Poland (today, Lviv, Ukraine), and sheltered four Jews in her apartment, in a building that also served German army personnel. Cecilia Stern-Abaham first met Wieth in September 1942 when she was assigned to sew dresses for Wieth and other German women working in the housing department. Wieth agreed to Cecilia's request to hide her 12-year-old daughter (her only remaining child). Wieth also hid Jozef Podoshin for almost a year, a pharmacist she had met earlier when she went to get medicine at his ghetto-located pharmacy, as well as his wife and daughter.[6]

An equal wartime meeting appears in the Karolina Kmita story, when she accidentally met Sara Gewirtzman while visiting her daughter-in-law. Sara had just fled there from a mass shooting of Jews in Kovel, Poland (today in Ukraine). Karolina took Sara with her to her hometown village of Boża Dąrówka, where she hid the 21-year-old Sara in a small pit, not far from her garden. At night, Karolina secretly brought her hot food and removed and washed the pan which was used as a chamber pot. Sara remained in the pit, covered with branches and leaves, throughout the 1942–3 winter, and as late as June 6, 1943. Sara relates: "In the winter, she came wrapped up in a white sheet so that she would not be detected against the snow, and she blurred her footsteps with a twig." In June 1943, Karolina brought Sara back in her house, where she remained hidden in the attic, with three other Jewish women, with her husband's backing. All four survived the liberation on March 6, 1944.[7]

Some rescuers started with saving one or a few; then they gained confidence and determination and extended their charitable help to many more. Helena Kruk, born 1923, during the German invasion, was sent by her parents to her uncle in Warsaw. One day, in Spring 1940, she met Adam Lichtenstein, who for a while became her mathematics teacher. On the eve of her birthday (December 23, 1940), her uncle asked her what she'd like to receive, and as she recalled: "I answered nothing personal, but helping my Jewish friends. My aunt was totally shocked by my response, but my uncle said he would think about it." Helena hurried to the Lichtenstein family and immediately took with her the four-year-old Elżunia and her mother, and placed her aunt before a fait accompli. "I said these two persons are staying with me, and if no place were to be found for them, I would leave this house. After an hour-long conversation between my uncle and my aunt, it was decided that these two persons could stay." With the help of a friend in the Polish underground, she aided people fleeing from the Warsaw Ghetto. At first, she hid seven persons in the home she shared with her aunt. More persons were added, bringing up the total to thirteen persons. She later moved to a safer place with all her thirteen charges. While there, one of the hiders gave birth to a son. In summary, Helena had cared for thirteen persons, two of whom died during the war years, all of whom she first met starting 1940, in German-occupied Warsaw.[8]

Did not know each other. In such sudden encounters, the rescue could begin when the fugitive Jew, on the point of death, desperately sought a sheltering place, as in the story of Erna Härtel, who operated a roadside inn in Sorgenau, East Prussia. On January 31, 1945, her Polish maid brought to the house a Jewish woman who had miraculously escaped from a death march of Jewish women from the Stutthof concentration camp toward the Baltic coast, then had suddenly come under machine gun fire as they reached the sea shore. Frieda Kleiman was still covered with blood from freshly inflicted gunshot wounds when Härtel admitted her to her home, where she remained until the coming of the Russians on April 13, 1945. To others, Härtel concocted the story that Frieda was a fleeing Polish laborer. Erna Härtel's husband was away in the German army.[9] As for Donata Helmrich, in Berlin, she received Jewish women, unknown to her, sent to her by her husband, Eberhard, a German military major, serving in Drohobycz, Poland (today in Ukraine) under the guise of Ukrainian laborers. She arranged work for them as domestic maids, and kept tabs on them to hide their Jewish identity.[10]

In Haarlem, the Netherlands, Cornelia ("Corrie") ten Boom was part of a family watchmaking business in their home, originally created by her father, Casper ten Boom, and including her sister Betsie and other family members. Father, Casper, of the Protestant Calvinist church, believed that the Jews were still the "chosen people," and therefore one was obligated to help God's people when the need arose. Eventually, the family had a secret space laid out in Corrie's bedroom, that was located behind a false additionally constructed wall, and six people were able to hide there, via a camouflaged entrance. On February 28, 1944, the ten Boom family was arrested by the Gestapo, based on information by a Dutch informer, although despite a thorough search the hidden persons behind the fake wall were not found. Some family members were released, while the elderly Casper died while under arrest. Corrie and sister Betsie were eventually deported to the Ravensbrück women's concentration camp, where Betsie died at the age of fifty-nine. Fifteen days after her sister's death, Corrie was released. Earlier, before leaving for Ravensbrück, Corrie received a letter, stating that "all the watches in your cabinet are safe," coded words meaning that the hidden Jews in her bedroom hideout had not been discovered, but managed to escape and were safe. They were transferred by resistance associates of the Booms to other safe locations.[11]

Rescue of Children. The rescue of children presented a different set of circumstances and problems. Parents came to the difficult decision to hand over their children, even to strangers, so that if the parents did not survive, at least the children will have a better chance of survival when in other people's hands. Such as in the story of Samuel and Rachela Cygler, in the Będzin ghetto (Poland), who turned over their six-year-old daughter Tamar in the hands of Genia Pająk, a stranger to them, but known to a relative of the Cyglers. So, they began to coach Tamar to accept a new mother. In the words of Henrietta Altman, the Cygler's relative, every child in the ghetto was taught that a day may come when they will get a new name, a new "mama," and that in that event they shouldn't cry or talk about their real parents and never admit that they lived in the ghetto and are Jewish. That day had now come for little Tamar. A few days after Tamar was turned over to Genia, the girl's parents were deported to Auschwitz, and did not survive. Tamar's name was change to Bogumila, or affectionately "Bogusia." To explain the sudden appearance of an additional child in her household, she concocted a story of having given birth to a child out of wedlock, who had until recently lived elsewhere with an old aunt, and all this oblivious to her own husband. Now her aunt having died, she was forced to take the child with her, and her husband had finally agreed to adopt the child.[12] In Warsaw, Gertruda Babilińska had been engaged as a nanny by the Stolowicki family, in Warsaw, for their son Michael, born 1936. When the Germans invaded, in 1939, the boy's father was away in France. His mother, Lidia, fled to Vilna, together with Babilińska. There, Lidia suffered a stroke, and before dying in April 1941, she asked Babilińska to care for her son and take him to Palestine after war. Two months later, the Germans entered Vilna. "I was left alone, with a circumcised five-year-old child," Babilińska related. She obtained false papers and a baptismal certificate for the boy, and had him registered as her nephew. After the war, she left with Michael to Palestine, today's Israel.[13]

Still in Poland, in September 1942, in a forest near Dzieźkowice village, not far from Warsaw, a baby girl was found abandoned, after a battle between Polish farmers and Jews. The village mayor asked who was willing to care for the child, and Apolonia Oldak stepped forward and took the baby home with her, and together with her husband, Aleksander, they cared for the abandoned child. When Apolonia, who was not originally from that village, asked for fresh milk for the child, she was turned down. "Everywhere I was met with refusals," Apolonia recalled. "All claimed that a Jewish child does not deserve milk." Summoned to report to the Germans about the child, she claimed it was a foundling, a not uncommon phenomenon in those days by unwed mothers. One late night, three men burst into the house; one was wielding an axe. They looked a bit deranged and insisted on having the child turned over to them. They said they were going to behead her. One of them shouted, "Why waste a bullet, we want to kill her with the axe." Apolonia's husband, Aleksander grabbed, a gun, pointed it at them, and ordered them to leave. After the war, the former baby worked as a practicing nurse in Israel and was herself the mother of children.[14]

Moving to Italy, Kalman and Yuzzi Toth, originally from Hungary, were both dancers and musicians. In 1940, Kalman returned to Hungary and his traces were lost. Left alone with three children, in Castiglion Fiorentino (Tuscany), Yuzzi took on a helper, a 15-year-old house maid, named Ida Bruneli (later, Lenti), who at first did not know that the Toth family was Jewish. In 1943, Yuzzi became ill with a heart condition and January 1944, died of angina pectoris. On her deathbed, the mother pleaded to Ida to take care of the orphans, who she now confided were Jewish. Ida kept the secret of the children's identity to herself, and continued to care for them. When Ida visited her mother, Maddalena, in another village, near Padova, the children were presented as Hungarian refugees. Not able to further care for the children due to the difficult economic conditions, Ida arranged for them to be admitted in children's homes, with Ida often visiting them. Thus, they survived.[15]

In the following story, help started even before the child's birth. In late 1942, Ruth Abraham was on her way to her forced-labor duty at the Starke pharmaceutical plant in Berlin's Tempelhof district, wearing the obligatory Jewish star badge, and was in her ninth month of pregnancy. She suddenly noticed being followed by a woman, so Ruth quickened her pace. But the other woman caught up with her and asked if she could help in any way. Ruth Abraham curtly replied that there was nothing she needed from this other woman. That stranger woman continued to follow her in the next days. Together with her husband, Walter, Ruth concluded that this woman was either deranged or a Gestapo provocative agent. Then, on Christmas eve, of 1942, the woman appeared at the pharmaceutical plant, and presented Ruth with a basket of food. That broke the ice between the two; the woman's name was Maria Nickel and she continued to help Ruth Abraham with food until the child's birth. When a daughter, named Reha, was secretly born to Ruth, in January 1943, and the parents decided to go into hiding, Maria Nickel took care of the baby, in addition to caring for her own recently born child. She also provided Ruth's husband her own husband's ID card as a truck driver. For the next two years, Maria Nickel continued to be of help to Ruth's baby as well as her parents.[16]

In Vienna, Maria Potesil had lost her husband during the First World War in the Austrian army. In 1927, she was living with two children, when the municipal social service gave her a two-year-old boy, named Kurt, to care for as a foster child. When he reached school age, Maria Potesil learned that the child's father was Jewish. When the Nazis took over Austria, Kurt, then fourteen, was suspended from school, and Potesil stopped receiving assistance for the boy's support. She was also forced to move with Kurt to a street where Jews were required to live, as well as buy food only in stores that sold to Jews. When, in September 1944, Kurt was picked up for deportation, running from office to office, Potesil succeeded in having him released. He survived under his adopted mother's care.[17]

Moving to Hungary, we have the story of a household maid who, driven by a passionate resolve, saved her hosts' entire family; elders and children. Erzsebet (Erzsi) Fajo came to the Abonyi family, in 1931, as a thirteen-year-old nurse maid. In 1941, the Abonyis sold the pharmacy they operated in the small town of Bekescsaba, and moved to Budapest, taking Erzsi along. When deportations loomed for Budapest Jews, on July 2, 1944 (fortunately it was cancelled), Erzsi appeared at the Abonyi home (she had then lived elsewhere) determined to be deported with them. The Abonyi daughter Zsuzanna: "I still can hear her cry: 'I don't want to live without you! If I cannot share life with you, I will share death!'" On November 17, 1944, with Jews in Budapest forced to move into a ghetto, Erzsi ran from house to house, and found a deserted pharmacy whose owner allowed the Abonyi family to spend the night there. When on December 3, 1944, the Abonyi children, Zsuzanna and Ivan were taken to the ghetto—first, Erzsi managed to get a Swedish passport for the father Laszlo and took him to a Swedish "protected house" and his wife Margit to her non-Jewish cousin. Two days later she entered the ghetto, and running from house to house, she located the two children, and with Budapest under fire from Russian bombardments, Erzsi took the two children to five different places, finally reuniting them with their parents. When the Pest part of the city, where most of the events recounted here took place, was liberated on January 17, 1945, the Abonyis returned to their former home. "As we arrived," Zsuzanna wrote, "she was waiting for us outside. . . . We were crying in Erzsi's arms for months, and I still am crying there since that time." The family adopted Erzsi and looked after all her needs; sending her to school, and including her in their will when they divided their estate. Zsuzanna: "She truly is our sister, . . . a sister who gave us life then when we were sentenced to death."[18]

Moving again to the Netherlands, Marion van Binsbergen was born in 1920 to a Dutch father (a judge in Amsterdam) and an English mother. At 19 she entered the school of social work in Amsterdam. One morning in 1942, on her way to school, she passed a Jewish children's home and saw the Germans loading the children on trucks. When the children did not move fast enough the Germans picked them up, by an arm, a leg, the hair, and threw them into the trucks. "To watch grown men treat small children that way—I could not believe my eyes. I found myself literally crying with rage. I just sat there on my bicycle, and that was the moment I decided that if there was anything I could do to thwart such atrocities, I would do it." Joining a group of friends, including two

Jewish students, they helped both adults and children in many ways. One day Marion had been handed a Jewish baby, stolen from the Crèche, the day-care center opposite the Hollandsche Schouwburg (Dutch Theater), where Amsterdam Jews were momentarily held before moving them to the main transit camp of Westerbork, and from there to extermination camps in Poland. While the adults stayed in the theater, the children were momentarily held in the Crèche, across the street. Marion had been asked to take the baby to a certain village. When she arrived there, a man approached her and said that the man she was to turn over the baby had been arrested. Hungry and exhausted, "I just wanted to drop the baby and run." The man said, "Well, why don't you come to my house, you can rest, and maybe we can find some milk for the baby before you go back." Leading her to his village home, she met the man's wife and their four or five children. Totally worn out, Marion immediately fell asleep in her chair.

"When I woke up, his wife had taken the baby, changed it, fed it and was telling the children that they should pray for me because I was a sinner; I had had this baby out of wedlock, could not take care of it, and that they were going to keep it. That my punishment was that I would never see my baby again." The man walked her back to the train station and said that this story made it possible for them to keep the baby and protect themselves. When asked by neighbors where this new baby came from, the children would tell a credible, convincing story.[19]

In nearby Belgium, Andrée Geulen also became involved in saving Jewish children. Born in 1921 in Brussels, in 1941, with Belgium already under German occupation, Andreé qualified as a teacher. She then began teaching at the Gatti de Gamond boarding school in Brussels, where she discovered about a dozen Jewish pupils in hiding. In May 1943, the Gestapo raided the premises deep in the night. Andrée was asked, "What are you doing here?" "I give lessons," was the reply. Gestapo: "Aren't you ashamed to teach Jews?" Geulen: "Aren't you ashamed to make war on Jewish children?" Gestapo: "If one does not want to suffer from bugs, one must squash them when they're small." She was told to leave and not return to this place. All fourteen children were taken away including the school's heads, Odile and Remy Ovart, sent to Bergen-Belsen and Buchenwald camps. They did not survive. Geulen then joined up with the Jewish Ida Sterno, in a joint effort to save children from deportation. When the two approached parents for their children, in Andreé's words:

"We told the parents to prepare a suitcase, and we shall return in a day or two. . . . I still weep when I think of the times when I had to snatch children from their parents, especially children aged 2 or 3, without being able to tell the parents where I was taking them. . . . The number of children that I thus accompanied alone I estimate at around 300."

Reflecting on her wartime activity, Andrée humbly told: "I deserve nothing for what I did. I am not a hero. I was by nature rebellious—against the established order. Already in 1939, I worked for the Red Cross, and I went to receive children who arrived on the Kindertransport from Vienna and was assigned to find locations for them."[20]

To end this children's section, we return to Poland, and to the amazing story of Irena Sendler. Born 1910 into the Krzyżanowski family, in 1927 she studied law and Polish literature at the University of Warsaw. In 1931, she married Mieczysław Sendler, who later was captured as a soldier by the Germans in September 1939, and remained in a German prisoner of war camp until 1945. When the Warsaw Ghetto was created, Irena Sendler obtained a permit by the municipality to her and her closest collaborator, Irena Schultz, giving them the right to enter the ghetto to report on health conditions, especially for signs of typhus, a disease mostly feared by the Germans of spreading beyond the ghetto. Passing through different gates of the ghetto Sendler began to smuggle Jewish children out of the ghetto, and provide them with false identity documents and sheltering places. Depending on their age, sex, and outward appearance, and the child's knowledge of Polish (some mostly spoke Yiddish) the children were either found Polish families to live with, or were sent to convents, or, alternatively, to secular child care institutions.

Together with her colleague, Irena Schulz, the two Irenas met with the mothers of children. Sendler: "We told them we were able to save the children, to get them beyond the wall. Then they would ask the crucial question regarding what guarantees there were of success. We had to honestly answer that we could offer no guarantees. I spoke frankly; I said I couldn't even be certain I would safely leave the ghetto with a child that very day. Scenes from hell ensued. For instance, the father would agree to give us the child, but the mother would refuse. The grandmother, embracing the child most lovingly of all, tears streaming down her face, in between the sobs would declare: 'I'll never give up my granddaughter!' Sometimes I would leave such a family with their child. The next day I would return to see what happened to the family, and frequently it would turn out that the entire family was already in Umschlagplatz. [deportation point]. . . . Some Jewish mothers would spend months preparing their children for the Aryan side. They changed their identities. They would say: 'You're not Itzek, but Jacek. You're not Rachela, but Roma. And I'm not your mother, I was just the housemaid. You'll go with this lady and perhaps over there your mummy will be waiting for you.'"[21]

Sendler continues to relate how she helped Jewish children survive. "There were several ways to get infants out of the killing zone." With small children, "we would usually take them out through the court building in Leszno Street. This court had two entrances: one from the ghetto side, and the other from Ogrodowa Street on the Aryan side. Some of the doors were left open and, thanks to the courage of the ushers, and through this building one could get out of the ghetto with a child. Children were also driven out in fire engines, ambulances, or by tram, thanks to a befriended tram driver called Leon Szeszko." Some children were taken in sacks, boxes, or baskets. Babies were put to sleep and hidden in crates with holes, so that they could breathe. Other times they were driven out in the ambulance that delivered disinfectants to the ghetto, with the help of driver Antoni Dąbrowski, "who took great risks to help us." Sewage canals were also used as an escape route.[22]

As the deportations increased in intensity, in late 1942, Irena Sendler joined the newly created Council for Aid to Jews, better known as Żegota. This organization was created by the Polish underground for helping Jews survive within the general population. Working with Żegota from January 1943, she was later appointed head of Żegota's Department for the Care of Jewish children. In that capacity, she supervised a team of workers that was responsible for the, according to some estimates, up to 2,000 children in Żegota's care.

On October 20, 1943, Sendler was arrested and brutally interrogated at Gestapo headquarters, and sentenced to be executed. Luckily for her, her underground confederates were able to bribe the Gestapo for her release, and she was let go. Forced to stay out of sight for the remainder of the German occupation, Irena conducted her humanitarian activities from her new hiding place. Asked to explain the motivation of her humanitarian work, she stated: "All my life, I had Jewish friends." She added: "Every child saved with my help is the justification of my existence on this earth, and not a title to glory." Also: "As long as I live and as long as I have the strength I shall always say that the most important thing in the world and in life is Goodness."[23]

Clergy. Quite a number of the middle and lower-rank clergy were involved in the rescue of Jews, in spite, one my add, of the centuries old "teaching of contempt," in the words of French-Jewish historian Jules Isaac, by the churches towards the Jews.[24] As stated by the earlier-mentioned Andrée Geulen from Belgium, "I am not a believer, and I don't think much of priests and rabbis. However, I will admit that the lower clergy helped us greatly, and without their assistance we would not have achieved much."[25] Most of the boarding schools in Belgium where Jewish children were at placed were, in fact, under Catholic supervision.

We will mention a few of the hundreds of cases received at Yad Vashem of the role of women among the clergy, and we begin with Poland. After escaping from the Warsaw Ghetto, in August 1942, Marguerite Frydman (later, Acher) and her sister moved from one place to another for short stays, and on September 9, 1942, they were taken to Matylda Getter, Mother Superior head of the Order of the Family of Mary, who took the two sisters to the Order's home in Płudy, slightly north of Warsaw, where sister Agnela Stawowiak, was the local Mother Superior. Fourteen-year-old Wanda Rozenbaum was another resident in the Płudy home. She noted many Jewish faces among the girls there. Bianca Krance (later, Lerner), born 1929, was admitted in the Warsaw affiliate of the Family of Mary. "One morning I woke up with a rat on my bed. He was cold and hungry too." When Getter visited the Warsaw home, on Hoza street, she sent for Bianca to inquire if she was fine. "She impressed me as a good person, a really good Christian. . . . She never tried to push me to convert."[26]

Still in Poland, in 1942, sister Alfonsa (Eugenia Wasowska), of the Order of St. Joseph's Heart, was made responsible for the children in the Order's orphanage, in Przemyśl. Under her stewardship, a total of thirteen Jewish children (ten girls and three boys) were sheltered in the orphanage until the city's liberation in July 1944. Some of the Jewish children were brought accompanied by an adult person; others were left outside the gate with a note pinned to their clothing. Sister Alfonsa: "We took the children to church along with Polish children, not because we were trying to make them Catholics but just so nobody would suspect they were Jews." Miriam Klein, one of the former child residents of the orphanage, remembers some of the children screaming at night and wetting their beds. "Sister Alfonsa always knew how to calm us. Sleeping with us in the small room she was alert to every noise and often got up at night to place an additional blanket on the frightened children." Immediately upon the city's liberation, sister Alfonsa took the thirteen Jewish children to the newly constituted Jewish Committee in Przemyśl and promptly turned them over. "They were Jewish children and belonged with Jews," she emphasized in her postwar testimony.[27]

While convents and monasteries served mostly as houses of refuge for children, in some of the accounts it is rather adults who were admitted. In 1941, Anna Borkowska was Mother Superior of a small cloister of Dominican Sisters in Kolonia Wilenska, near the city of Vilna, and she agreed to allow members of a Jewish underground organization to find shelter in her convent for brief spells of time. There, behind the secure walls of the Dominican convent, and its nine nuns, the youthful Jewish men and women were plotting an eventual uprising in the Vilna ghetto. "They called me 'Ima' (mother)," Anna fondly recalled in her postwar testimony. "I felt as if I were indeed their mother. I was pleased with the arrival of each new member, and was sorry that I could not shelter more of them." In the convent cells, Abba Kovner composed his famous call of rebellion, the first of its kind for Jews in Nazi-occupied Europe, which began with the clarion words: "Let us not be led like sheep to the slaughter!" This manifesto, secretly printed in the convent was distributed in the ghetto on January 1, 1942 and served as inspiration to many ghetto and partisan fighters. Until these plans could hatch, Kovner and his sixteen colleagues worked side by side with the convent's nine nuns doing laborious work in the fields. To conceal the Jewish group's activities from the eyes of suspecting neighboring peasants, all protégés were given nun habits and thus they cultivated the nearby fields, until such time when they returned to the ghetto. Eventually, the Germans had Anna Borkowska arrested in September 1943 (coinciding with the Vilna ghetto's final liquidation), the convent shut and the sisters dispersed.[28]

Clerics were not beyond punishment when caught helping Jews, and some suffered martyrdom. Sára Salkaházi, born 1899 in Kassa (now Košice, Slovakia), worked as a journalist, then decided for a nun's life, joining in 1929 a Hungarian order, named the Sisters of Social Service. At first, she supervised the church's charities office in Košice, and published a periodical entitled *Catholic Women*. Transferred to Budapest, she opened Homes for working girls. During the German occupation of Hungary, she helped shelter hundreds of Jews in a building belonging to the Order in Budapest. Betrayed to the authorities by a woman working in the house, the Jews she had sheltered were taken prisoner by members of the Hungarian pro-Nazi Arrow Cross Party, lined up on the bank of the Danube River on December 27, 1944, and shot, together with their benefactress, Sára Salkaházi, with their bodies dumped in the river. In 2006, she was beatified in a proclamation by Pope Benedict XVI. It is told that Salkaházi's life-sustaining motto was, "Here I am; send me!"[29]

A similar bitter fate ended the life prematurely of a nun in the Russian Orthodox Church. Born 1891, Yelizaveta Pilenko at first lived in Riga (then part of the Russian Empire), where her father was the government's chief prosecutor. After his death, the family settled in St. Petersburg, where Yelizaveta wrote poetry, which was well received in literary circles. When the Bolshevik Revolution broke out in November 1917, Yelizaveta was a member of the Socialist SR Party and was sent to Anapa, on the Black Sea to further the revolutionary cause there, and was elected the town's mayor. With the capture of the town by the White forces of General Denikin, she was arrested and put on trial. Her defense swayed the president of the court, Danilo Skobtsov, to dismiss all charges. To the surprise of all, the two eventually married and fled to France via Turkey and Yugoslavia, where they arrived in 1923. In the meantime, she bore Danilo a daughter and a son.

In 1932, Yelizaveta underwent a profound religious experience, following the premature death of her four-year-old daughter of meningitis, and she decided to become a nun in the Russian Orthodox Church. Taking her vows, she chose the name Maria. She stated that she wished to dedicate herself to the cause of the needy, especially among the many Russian emigrants in France, for whom she opened a dormitory in Saxe, near Paris, and another in Paris, on Rue de Lourmel, which became the base of her charitable work.[30] With the German invasion of France, in June 1940, she decided to turn her attention to Jews in distress and help them—first by making the free kitchen available to them, then by providing temporary shelter at her center for those in need until other arrangements could be made for them, as well as issuing false baptismal certificates. Lourmel soon became known as a "Jewish Church," and the overcrowding there was great. An entire Jewish family was huddled in a private room of Father Dimitri Klepinin, her principal aide; another in Skobtsova's son Yuri.

When the Germans promulgated the wearing of the Yellow Star for all Jews, in June, 1942, Yelizabeta Skobtsova (Mother Maria) penned the following poem:

Two triangles, a star, the shield of King David, our forefather. This is election, not offense; the great path and not an evil. Once more is a term fulfilled. Once more roars the final trumpet; and the fate of a great people, once more is by the prophet proclaimed. Thou art persecuted again, O Israel. But what can human malice mean to thee; thee, who has heard the thunder from Sinai?

During the big roundup of Parisian Jews at the Winter Sports Stadium in July 1942, Mother Maria succeeded in penetrating the closely guarded stadium and snatch away two Jewish children (hidden in trash cans). Arrested on February 8, 1943, by the Gestapo, together with her son, Yuri—under interrogation, she readily admitted to helping Jews, to issuing of false baptismal certificates, and to transferring funds to Jews in hiding. Gestapo officer Hoffmann told Marie's mother: "You educated your daughter very stupidly. She helps Jews only." The old woman replied: "This is not true. She is a Christian who helps those in need. She would even help you if you were in trouble." The Nazi replied, "You will never see your daughter again." On April 24, 1943, Maria Skobtsova was deported to the Ravensbrück camp. Ravaged by hunger, disease, and torture, she finally succumbed on March 31, 1945, and was committed to the crematorium, only weeks before the collapse of the Third Reich. Skobtsova's son, Yuri, was ordered sent to the Dora camp, where he died in February 1944.

In her private notes, the following entry was found: "At the Last Judgment, I will not be asked whether I satisfactorily practiced asceticism, nor how many genuflections I have made before the divine altar. I will be asked whether I fed the hungry, clothed the naked, visited the sick, and the prisoner in his jail. That is all that will be asked." On October 12, 1945, a memorial service was held in a Parisian synagogue in her memory.[31]

We finish this section with the story of a woman who, though not a clergy, worked closely with the Catholic church in Germany in help to people in distress, including Jews. Born 1900, in Liverpool, England, Gertrud Luckner lived in Germany since early childhood. She obtained her doctoral degree, in 1938, at the Freiburg University. Since 1933, she was involved with the Catholic Caritas Association in Freiburg, that in the 1940s included helping Jews, those who had converted to Catholicism as well as regular Jews. She used monies that she received from the archbishop to smuggle Jews over the Swiss border. She stated: "I was kind of a courier. I went from one Jewish family to another, from city to city." She also dispatched money and parcels to deportees to the Łódź ghetto, and to Piaski, near Lublin, where some German Jews were deported.[32] On March 24, 1943, as she was about to transfer 5,000 Marks to some of the last remaining Jews in Berlin, she was arrested, as she was leaving the train station in Berlin. In her interrogation, when the Gestapo asked who her bosses were, she replied: "My Christian conscience." She asked to be taken to Theresienstadt (to be where Rabbi Leo Baeck was). Response of the Gestapo interrogator: "For you, Jew-lover, we have something better—Ravensbrück." She spent nineteen harrowing months until the camp's liberation on May 3, 1945. After the war, she published the *Freiburger Rundbriefe*, which sponsored more positive dialogues between Jews and Christians, and to the building bridges of understanding between both religions.[33]

Romance. In Nazi Germany, non-married lovers, where one side was Jewish, was forbidden by the 1935 Nuremberg Laws, but such relationships nevertheless existed, as in the following story. From February 1943 to May 1944, Konrad Latte, an aspiring musician, originally from Breslau, lived illegally in Berlin, under the name of Konrad Bauer. When most organists in Berlin were conscripted in the army, "I replaced them, playing in churches for services, at funerals, as well as regularly in the prayer services for Martin Niemöller in the Annenkirche, in Berlin-Dahlem." With the help of a trustworthy colleague, he was able to get membership in the Music Chamber. In early 1944 Konrad learned that the director of the *Hessische Volkstheater* was looking for a conductor of an orchestra to accompany his tours in army bases throughout Germany.

I presented myself to Bodo Bronski [the director], was hired, but I declared to have no other documents than of the Music Chamber, since I was bombed out in an air raid. He told me that this fact was not decisive at the moment, as he, Bronski, was working for the Propaganda Ministry, and was considered trustworthy. I promised to continue my efforts to retrieve my lost documents.[34] Konrad then joined up with the ensemble in Goslar, south of Hannover, in May 1944. There, he also met Ellen Brockmann, one of the singers of the Hessian People's Theater, and the two fell in love. "Very soon, she found out everything about my real origin, and from that time on, she helped me whenever possible, until May 1945."

When in September 1944, all theaters in Germany were closed, and Konrad was at loss where to go, Harald Poelchau, his pastor friend in Berlin sent him a fake cable, informing that the State Opera needed Konrad urgently. He left by train to Homburg, Ellen's hometown, where she waited for him, in a flat that she kept, and presented him as her fiancé. "As an aspiring pianist, I soon took part in concerts. . . . and I conducted the Protestant church choir. . . . Ellen Brockmann's reputation being spotless, my connection with her proved positive for me." The two were married on April 28, 1945, in the already liberated Homburg.[35]

In yet another romance story, it was of a different kind, and ended tragically for one of the parties, and severe hardship for the other. On August 21, 1944, the Gestapo arrested two women—not for the lesbian relationship between both, but because Elisabeth Wust, a non-Jewish German, was sheltering in her home her lover—the Jewish Felice Schragenheim. "She was my life's love," Elisabeth Wust, known better as Lilly, stated after the war. "I shall not forget the beautiful moment fifty years ago." Born in 1913, Lilly was married to Gunther Wust and gave birth to four sons, for which she was decorated by the Nazi state. Her marriage with Gunther was on the rocks, as he carried on love affairs on the side. So did Lilly. Then Elisabeth met Felice, and her life underwent a dramatic emotional change.

Felice Rachel Schragenheim, born 1922 in Berlin, lived underground, and was aided by friends in the lesbian community of Berlin. In November 1942, she met Lilly Wust in the posh "Berlin" café, near the city's zoo—a known hangout of homosexuals and lesbians. "I was attracted to her from the first. It was the meeting that changed my life," Elisabeth wrote, not knowing at the time the truth of Felice's Jewish origin. Elisabeth-Lilly wrote that "with Felice I understood who I am and what I want. With Felice I felt like walking on the clouds." Felice gave her lover a new name, "Aimée" (beloved), based on the heroine of a 1930s popular Berlin theater play. Felice chose for herself the name "Jaguar." One day, Felice decided to lay her cards open on the table. "Will you love me even if I disclosed to you a secret," she asked Elisabeth? Lilly responded by swearing that Felice was the only love of her life. At that, Felice continued, "Lilly, I am Jewish and my name is Schragenheim, not Schrader." For a moment, Lilly did not move. "Then, suddenly," Elisabeth wrote, "I realized the danger Felice was in. . . . From the moment that she disclosed to me her identity, it was as though she had placed her fate in my hands. All that night, we wept together, and swore to be faithful to one to another." Lilly's husband was then away in the German army.

The secret love affair lasted from March 1943 to August 1944, when both women were arrested. In consideration of her four sons, her decoration for this by the Nazi state, and her husband's service in the army, Elisabeth was released, and sent home. On September 8, 1944, Felice was deported to Theresienstadt camp across the Czech border. As long as Felice was in Theresienstadt, she was able to correspond with Lilly, as was the policy in that camp for other prisoners. In the meantime, Lilly decided to secretly shelter in her home several more Jewish women of the lesbian community, but as she noted in her diary, she continued to yearn for Felice, as she wrote on a February 24, 1945 entry: "Felice, I love you so much. I am so lonely, although I am surrounded by people who deserve my love and care. Through them, I love you even more . . . I miss you so ardently. . . . You—my only beloved person." After the war, Lilly was informed that Felice was no longer among the living. The date of her death was set for December 31, 1944, probably coinciding with the day she arrived either in Auschwitz or Gross-Rosen camps.[36]

Protest. Some women, too few unfortunately, made no secret of their opposition to the Nazi anti-Jewish persecutions. Ilse Sonja Totzke made her opinion clearly on this point. This led to a summon, on September 5, 1941, for a Gestapo interrogation. She stated that born in 1913, in Strasbourg to Protestant parents (her father, Ernst Totzke, an orchestra director), the family moved to Mannheim (after Strasbourg reverted back to France). She, then, studied music in Würzburg. She stated that Schwabacher, to whom the Gestapo charged she was befriended, was actually not Jewish, but married to a Jewish man who left for America. While not taking any interest in politics, at the same time she did not agree with the treatment of Jews. "I cannot agree with the measures in this regard." She was not a communist; simply, every decent person was acceptable to her, without regard to one's nationality.[37]

On October 28, 1941, Totzke was summoned for another session with the Gestapo, and made to sign a statement, including: "To the charge that I have many contacts with Jews, that is true. . . . As for my attitude toward National Socialism, I don't mix in politics. At the same time, I find it not right the measures against the Jews. I wish to emphasize I am not a communist. I find that every decent person is acceptable, irrespective of whatever nationality one belongs. I am not preoccupied with the Jewish question, and have not yet formed an opinion on this. Therefore, I did not think much about my contacts with Jews . . . I hereby declare that henceforth to cease all contacts with Jews, including Schwabacher. . . . I am aware that in the event I shall again be reprimanded, I will face the possibility of immediate arrest and admittance in a concentration camp."

Then, suddenly, on March 4, 1943, the Mülhausen (today, Mulhouse, France) Gestapo informed of the arrest of Totzke on February 28, 1943, together with the Jewess Sara Basinsky (a kindergarten teacher), from Berlin, and that the two were turned over by the Swiss to the German border police. Totzke then admitted that she had decided to flee the country—not alone, but in the company of the Jewess, Basinsky. She added: "I have been thinking about fleeing Germany for a long time, because I do not feel comfortable under the government of Adolf Hitler. Above all, I found the Nuremberg Law incomprehensible, which is why I have maintained relations with the Jews I know. ("*Ich trage mich schon seit längerer Zeit mit dem Gedanken aus Deutschland zu flüchten, da ich mich unter der Regierung Adolf Hitlers nichtwohl fühle. Vor allem habe ich das Nürnbergergesetz unbegreiflich gefunden, aus diesem Grunde habe ich auch die Beziehungen zu den mir bekannte Juden aufrecht erhalten*"). In the face of the renewed Gestapo summons, I decided to flee to Switzerland."

As for her fleeing Jewish partner: "I was not asked by anyone to take the Jewess along. I only felt compassionate toward her and wished to free her from deportation. It is I who persuaded her to join me. For this, I did not receive from Basinsky or anyone else any payment. . . . I would like to repeat that I wanted to flee Germany because I reject National

Socialism. Above all, I cannot support the Nuremberg laws. I had the intention to let myself be interned in Switzerland. I don't want to continue living under any circumstances in Germany." ("*Ich möchte nochmals erwähnen, dass ich aus Deutschland flüchten wollte, weil ich den Naltonalsozialismus ablehne. Vor allem kann ich die Nürnbergergesetze nicht gutheissen. Ich hatte die Absicht, mich in der Schweiz internieren zu lassen. In Deutschland möchte (wollte) ich unter keinen Umständen weiterleben*").

On March 13, 1943, the Würzburg Gestapo ordered Totzke's internment in a concentration camp. In a lengthy report on the case, the Gestapo wrote that her motivation for helping Basinsky was compassion ("*mitleid*"), to help her avoid deportation. That furthermore, Totzke makes no secret of her opposition to Nazism. She is a "Jew-woman" ("*Judenweib*"), and in light of her behavior, she is beyond "corrective action." ("*besserungsfähig*"). On May 23, 1943, she was ordered sent to Ravensbrück camp. It is not known whether she survived, nor the fate of Sara Basinsky. Her open declaration before her Nazi interrogators of her opposition to Nazism due to its persecution of Jews, and she therefore wished to leave Germany—that took enormous courage.[38]

We finish with a different form of protest; against a German head doctor in Auschwitz, in charge of pseudo-medical experiments on the bodies of Jewish prisoners. Adelaïde Hautval, born 1906, in Hohwald (Alsace, France), was qualified as a medical doctor and psychiatrist. During the German invasion of France, in May 1940, she fled the Alsace region (annexed to Germany) to the interior of the country. She related what then happened to her.

"In April 1942, I was arrested for trying to pass the demarcation line into Alsace without a permit, after having learned of my mother's death. I was imprisoned in Bourges, where at this moment large numbers of Jews arrived. I protested to the Gestapo the treatment of the Jews. The Gestapo told me: 'Since you defend them, you will share their fate.' I was to be freed on July 5th, but the previous evening the Gestapo brought me a Jewish Star and a large banner, on which was written 'Friend of the Jews,' and ordered me to have them sown on my coat. In January 1943 I was placed on a convoy for Auschwitz, where we arrived after a journey of three days. Our group of women alighted from the train and entered the camp singing the Marseillaise [French national anthem]."

After a three-month stay in Birkenau, in April 1943, Hautval was transferred to Block 10, in Auschwitz, which was reserved for medical experiments, including various forms of sterilization. Dr. Eduard Wirths, the SS camp head physician asked Hautval to participate in these experiments. She was assigned to help out Dr. Carl Clauberg, who practiced sterilization by inserting a caustic liquid in the uterus of women. After witnessing one such experiment, she refused to participate, and was told to report to Dr. Wirths. "He asked me whether it was true that I was refusing, and asked for the reason. I answered that it was absolutely against my conception of a doctor. Wirths responded: 'But can't you see that these people, that is to say the Jews, are completely different from you?' I replied that there were in this camp many people different from me, starting with himself." Many SS-men were present at this exchange, but no one intervened. She was dismissed, wondering what her fate would be.

> I told my colleague, Dr. [Dorota] Lorska, "The Germans will not allow people who know what is happening here to get in touch with the outside world, so the only thing that is left to us is to behave, for the rest of the short time that remains to us, as human beings." I was then sent to Birkenau, where I was told to hide. A little while later, I was asked to work in the Revier, the name of the camp's medical dispensary, which was a far cry from a regular and fully equipped dispensary.

In August 1944, all French prisoner women were transferred to Ravensbrück camp. "By then, of our convoy, which consisted of 230 women, in August 1944 we were only 50 left. Selections to the gas chamber still took place there, as late as March 1945. We were liberated on April 28, by the Russians, and in July, we returned to France, and to my practice as a medical doctor." The story, however, does not end there.

Nineteen years later, on April 29, 1964, Adelaïde Hautval appeared as the star witness for the defense, during a highly charged atmosphere in a London court, in the case of Wladyslaw Dering versus Leon Uris. In his best-selling novel, *Exodus*, Uris had inserted a paragraph in which he charged Dering, a Polish prisoner-doctor at Auschwitz, with performing surgery, without proper anesthetics, on ovaries and testicles of Jewish women and men, after they had been sterilized with X-ray by SS doctors. After the war, Dering fled arrest to England, where he set up a private practice. He was now suing the American author for defamation of name. In his testimony, Dering admitted to having performed numerous ovaries and testicle removing operations in Auschwitz, at the request of Dr. Horst Schumann, but claimed innocence since in Auschwitz, "all law, normal, human and God's law were finished. They were Germans' law." If he refused to perform them, he claimed, he would certainly be killed. "To refuse would be sabotage. That meant only one thing in the camp."

Then Dr. Dorota Lorska was summoned to appear and she stated that one could bypass the orders of the SS in such a way as to avoid punishment. "I know of many who did not carry out their orders, . . . in the first place, Dr. Hautval," who then testified. To the court's question: "Were you ever punished?" Hautval replied: "No, I was never punished. I refused afterwards to carry out experiments for Dr. Mengele and they said, 'We cannot force her to do what she does not want to do.'" A gynecologist was brought in to remind the court of the Hippocratic Oath: "I will abstain from abusing the bodies of men and women, either free or slave."

The jury handed a verdict in favor of the plaintiff, Dr. Dering, but awarded him the sum of only one-half penny, the smallest denomination in currency—in effect, a vindication of the defendant author Leon Uris. In a 1972 article, Hautval wrote that this case demonstrates what can happen to a man, an ordinary doctor, when he participates in a process leading to the degradation of man. She also spoke out against the "arrogance" of present-day doctors, many of whom regard themselves as "superior beings," who know everything, and treat their patients, especially the elderly, as if they were "complete morons." Primitive tribes treat their old people better. "They would never let them rot away in institutions." As for her own life philosophy—one should try and remember the good things. Even inside Auschwitz, with all the horror and the degradation, there was an enormous amount of heroism, of daily acts of courage and devotion. "I think we ought to love life too much to remember only the hatred and bitterness of the past." She later commented that she had no right to hold the Righteous title, for such a title is reserved to God alone, and not to mortal beings.[39]

In conclusion, the women appearing in this article are a fitting reminder that during the Nazi era, in a world gone mad, these persons by their commitment to the welfare of others, at great risks to themselves, kept alive the ultimate meaning of civilized life—the individual human person, his/her welfare and his/her right to a life for as long as it may last. Women were in the forefront of that quest, and thanks to them, there is hope.

Notes

1. Statement in the Mishna, Tractate Sanhedrin 4, 5.

2. Files at the Yad Vashem Righteous Among the Nations Department are listed as: YVA M31.2/ followed immediately with the file's number. Thus, for the Richter story, YVA M31.2/53.

3. Also, Peter Kunze, *Dorothea Neff: Mut zum Leben*. Vienna: Orac Pietsch, 1983. After the war, Lili Wolff continued her costume designing, in Dallas, Texas, especially for contestants for the Miss Texas pageant. *YVA M31.2/1652.*

4. YVA M31.2/1524.

5. In a booklet dedicated to her seventy-fifth birthday in 1957, and entitled "And a Light Shines in the Darkness" (*Und ein Licht Leuchtet in der Finsternis*), her former charges offered profuse praises to her dedication, care, and humanity from which some of the above quotes are taken. The collection ends with a quote by the French novelist Romain Rolland: "A single great man who remains human always saves faith in humanity for all!" YVA M31.2/403.

6. An SS officer took a liking to Wieth and was in the habit of dropping in with only a short early notification. Imgard Wieth had to scurry to hide her Jewish charges in another room, until she could politely see the enraptured SS officer off at the door. YVA M31.2/403.

7. YVA M31.2/301.

8. The file lists the names of the 13 persons helped by Helena Kruk. She later was married to Jacob Korzeniewski, with whom she moved to Israel. YVA M31.2/77.

9. YVA M31.2/243.

10. Donata's husband, army major Eberhard Helmrich, was also honored by Yad Vashem as a Righteous for saving Jews in his military station. YVA M31.2/154 and 154a.

11. It is also told that during her interrogation, ten Boom mentioned her work with the mentally disabled, and the interrogator scoffed at her; probably, since in Germany such people were being killed in accordance with Nazi racial policies. Ten Boom told the interrogating officer that in the eyes of God, a mentally disabled person might be more valuable "than a watchmaker; or a military lieutenant." After the war, Corrie ten Boom told her story in, *The Hiding Place*. Toronto and New York: Bantam, 1974. YVA M31.2/330.

12. After the war, Tamar was sent to Israel to be raised by a relative. YVA M31.2/2349.

13. A circumcision sign on one's male genitals was ineluctable proof of one's Jewishness; hence, a death warrant to that person, for in Poland only Jews were circumcised at birth. YVA M31.2/11.

14. YVA M31.2/272.

15. In 1998, I arranged for Ida Lenti to be one of the visiting group of Righteous to participate in the celebrations of Israel's fiftieth anniversary. YVA M31.2/5641.

16. YVA M31.2/474.

17. YVA M31.2/1400.

18. YVA M31.2/3449.

19. After the war, she married the American Anton Pritchard and moved with him to the USA, where as a psychoanalyst she treated school children with difficult behavioral tendencies. YVA M31.2/1993.2.

20. After the war, she made efforts to locate the children she and Ida Sterno had dispersed in various family homes, based on secret wartime lists that both kept, and return them to their surviving families, relatives, or to Jewish children organizations. YVA M31.2/4323.

21. Anna Mieszkowska, *Irena Sendler: Mother of the Children of the Holocaust* (Santa Barbara, CA: Praeger, 2011), 73–5.

22. Sendler added: "That is how four-year-old Piotr Zysman (today 70-year-old Piotr Zettinger, an engineer living in Sweden) got out of the ghetto." Mieszkowska, *Irena Sendler*, 75–6.

23. In 1969, Irena Sendler was added to the Righteous roster, and in 1991, she was made an honorary citizen of Israel. Several schools in Poland are named after her. On a personal note, I helped her with needy medicine, when she wrote to me when I headed the Righteous Department at Yad Vashem. I also visited her in 1988, during a trip to Poland. She died in 2008, aged 98. YVA M31.2/153.

24. Jules Isaac, *The Teaching of Contempt* (New York: McGraw Hill, 1965).

25. YVA 31.2/4323.

26. YVA 31.2/3097.

27. After the war, Sister Alfonsa renounced her nun's vows and left for Australia, where she married, and became Eugenia Renot-Wasowska. YVA 31.2/1929.

28. After the war, Anna Borkowska asked to be released from her nun's vows, and she moved to Warsaw. In Israel, Abba Kovner dedicated a poem to her, "Anna of the Angels." YVA 31.2/2862.

29. YVA 31.2/495.1.

30. Klepinin was already married to Tamara, and two children were born to them: Helen and Peter. The Russian Orthodox Church does not require priests, already married, to divorce when taking their clerical vows.

31. YVA 31.2/3078.

32. Gertrud Luckner, *Lebenszeichen aus Piaski* (Münchenz: Biederstein Verlag, 1968), 101–2.

33. YVA 31.2/2080.

34. Konrad Latte explained the method he used to avoid perilous encounters with security agents for lacking a bona fide ID card under his false name. "I did it the following way: every fortnight, I wrote a letter to the military district office in Berlin-Schoeneberg. I threw away the original and sent, by registered mail, an empty envelope. I attached the receipt to a copy

of the letter. With these papers every control by either the Wehrmacht, police or Gestapo, accompanied with long explanations, was O.K." YVA 31.2/1404.

35. After the war, Konrad Latte (he resumed his family name) was chief conductor of the Berlin Baroque Orchestra, and director of the Wilmersdorf music school. See also: Peter Schneider, "Saving Konrad Latte." *The New York Times Magazine*, February 13, 2000. YVA 31.2/1404.

36. Elisabeth Wust was recognized by Yad Vashem as a Righteous for sheltering Felice Schragenheim in her home, and later three additional Jewish women (names are in the file). Also, see Erica Fischer, *Aimée and Jaguar: A Love Story, Berlin 1943* (New York: Perennial, 2015). A film also appeared in 1999 under the same title, in Germany. Check Wikipedia, *Aimée and Jaguar,* for more on this story. YVA 31.2/6097.

37. During her interrogation, the Gestapo raided her home and reported finding the following "suspicious" literature: "The Mother," by Schalom Asch; "Der Gezeichnete," by Jakob Picard; "Eine Zeit stirbt," by Georg Hermann; "Jewish History," by S. Miller; "Theodor Herzl - a Biography," by Alex Bein; "Palestine Diary," by Manfred Sturmann; "The New Crusade," by Benjamin Disraeli, and brochures of the magazine "Um die Frau."

38. YVA 31.2/6335. Among men, we have the stories of Armin Wegner (YVA 31.2/306) and Catholic Reverend Bernhard Lichtenberg (YVA 31.2/10292), who openly declared their opposition to the Nazi antisemitism. Both spent time in Nazi jails.

39. YVA 31.2/100. Also, Adelaïde Hautval and Hallam Tennyson, "Who Shall Live, Who Shall Die?," *Intellectual Digest* 2, no. 7 (1972): 52–4. "Auschwitz in an English Court: the Dossier on Dr. Dering," *World Jewry: Review of the World Jewish Congress* 7, no. 3 (May/June 1964). Mavis Hill and Norman Williams, *Auschwitz in England* (London: Macgibbon & Kee, 1965).

CHAPTER 3
RESISTING OBLITERATION
LEARNING ABOUT THE LIVES AND DEATHS OF JEWISH WOMEN DURING THE HOLOCAUST
Judy Baumel-Schwartz

I would like to begin with a story, because, as Prof. Yehuda Bauer, one of the world's most prominent Holocaust historians always says, to be a good historian one has to be a storyteller. Many years ago, while I was in the process of interviewing women survivors about their wartime experiences, I asked one of them, a former Auschwitz prisoner, about the differences between the lives of Jewish men and women during the Holocaust.[1] Her answer was succinct. "They were the same. The Nazis wanted to kill us all." But when I pressed the subject she relented and admitted that maybe one of the differences was in the ghetto where in most cases, women were responsible for maintaining the household and obtaining food while often still being forced to work in a ghetto factory, or perform slave labor for the Nazis. In other words, there were domestic differences between the lives of men and women during the Holocaust.

When pressed further she added another point. There was a difference in how men and women reacted to what happened when they arrived at Auschwitz. While both groups were forced to undress in front of the Nazi guards, the experience, at least for the women in her transport, appeared to be a lot more traumatic with regard to personal modesty, than it was for the men. Yet another difference that she remembered was the men's and women's reaction to having their heads shaved upon arrival. While men could still recognize each other without their hair, women often became anonymous, and thus were unable to locate mothers, sisters, and friends in the crowd of newly shorn prisoners. She remembered not being able to recognize her sister who had been with her on the transport from Hungary, after their heads had been shaved. Their female identity, and indeed as many felt, their entire identity, had been completely wiped out by this act.

Ultimately she remembered three additional gendered differences between men's and women's Holocaust experiences as she had experienced them, gender, in this case, referring to the cultural expectations of men and women determined by their sex, during the historical period in question. One was in the sphere of physical strength. As many women were often not used to hard physical endeavors, they found the forced labor in Auschwitz to be more difficult than did the men who worked nearby doing similar tasks. A second had to do with gendered education. Traditionally, women in her generation were responsible for teaching the younger female generation domestic skills. She recalled how women in her block in Auschwitz often tried to continue teaching young girls how to run a household, at least in theory, even by teaching them recipes by heart at night.

A third had to do with what I term women's "double jeopardy" during the Holocaust.[2] Being targeted simultaneously as Jews and as women, she recalled how women often made great efforts to remain gender-anonymous in order avoid molestation and worse by the Nazi guards, regardless of the racial laws. "Don't be attractive, don't stand out, don't draw any of the men's attention," she recited to me. "Those were our unofficial rules. Sure, there were always women prisoners who used their looks to obtain favors from the local male guards. There was even one woman who became a paramour of a German there. But the rest of us? We didn't want them to know that we existed, not as women, and not at all."

What we can learn from the discrepancy between this former prisoner's initial response and her later elucidations after I pressed her about gender differences in camp? And what can we learn from her examples about the differences between men and women's lives, behaviors, and experiences during the Holocaust? The answer to the first question is that many still tend to examine the Holocaust through the prism of "Auschwitz," in other words, of extermination. If the Holocaust is examined by looking at how people died and not how they lived, one may initially be oblivious to the uniqueness of women's Holocaust experiences. Until that perspective is changed, there is no need to answer the second question as one never gets past the first one. The first stage is therefore to avoid the pitfall of looking at the Holocaust through the "Auschwitz prism." To do so, it is necessary to change one's focus, one's perspective. And as changing one's perspective is often a long, drawn-out process, that can explain why our understanding of women's lives and deaths during the Holocaust has changed over a period of time and along with that, how our perspective of the legitimacy of studying women's Holocaust experiences has changed as well.

Throughout the course of studying history, which is almost since "history" began, new topics have been identified, new disciplines have emerged, and new perspectives on previously existing issues have developed that changed people's viewpoints. This pattern holds true for Holocaust studies as well. Since the end of the Second World War the study of the Holocaust has changed, as have the topics upon which Holocaust research focused. Holocaust study was rarely calm and benign. Many topics aroused deep emotion and grief, such as the Jewish fate during the Final Solution. Others touched off painful and vehement discussion, such as the behavior of the Judenrätes, the role of different Jewish political movements during the Warsaw Ghetto uprising, or the activities of the Jewish police. But the legitimacy of exploring these topics never came under question.

Until now, that has happened with one Holocaust-related topic: women and the Holocaust. The first studies of women during the Holocaust began during the Second World War,[3] but it only became a serious topic of Holocaust scholarship during the late 1970s and early 1980s. It was, however, a topic whose legitimacy came under attack by scholars, writers, public figures, and even survivors. The dynamics of how and why that occurred has been written about elsewhere but ultimately, the study of women during the Holocaust developed, albeit slowly, until it is today considered by most to be a mainstream Holocaust theme.[4] How did that happen? How could a historical topic whose very existence was threatened by scholars and public figures nevertheless grow and develop to become a well-accepted subject of study?

This question belongs to a larger body of research: that which examines how subjects that were initially not considered legitimate research quests, crossed the barrier to become accepted and even mainstream topics of study. In their article on the state of scholarship about graffiti and street art Jeffrey Ian Ross, Peter Bengsten, John F. Lennon, Susan Phillips, and Jacqueline Z. Wilson describe the metamorphosis of how the academic study of street art and graffiti moved from being considered an unaccepted fringe topic to one that has become more legitimized in recent years.[5] The six stages they mention are as follows: focusing on promoting publication, overcoming scientific rejection, ensuring a growing availability of sources, giving a topic an "area studies" focus, developing undergraduate and graduate courses on the subject, and creating researcher networks.

Ross et al. posit that the initial difficulty begins with finding a publisher or journal willing to publish serious scholarly research on what is then considered a "fringe topic." Once that literature is published, the next step to overcome its rejection by parts of the scientific community who see such research as violating social taboos or being related to sexuality and its derivatives, topics which may produce discomfort, even among academics. Then there are various scholars' personal opinions and prejudices which can also influence whether they will consider a topic as being legitimate.

The next step in making a topic mainstream is ensuring a growing availability of sources upon which one can base academic studies. The dissemination of those studies is the key to making larger numbers of researchers aware of the topic's existence. Once the topic is "on the academic map," so to speak, it must be moved out of existing disciplines and given an "area studies" focus of its own. A common method of doing that is to hold interdisciplinary conferences on the subject instead of sporadically including it through individual papers at various disciplinary conferences. An important stage in mainstreaming a topic is to develop undergraduate and graduate courses focusing on it, which are predicated on a solid and robust corpus of academic studies to serve as a reading list along with primary textual materials. A final stage is to create informal and formal networks of researchers writing about that topic, to help them identify and negotiate the challenges they encountered as individual scholars.

Does this template hold true regarding the development of women in the Holocaust as a legitimate discipline? To answer this question we must first examine how themes related to the Holocaust, and later, those related to women during the Holocaust, developed over the years. After that, I will give a few examples of the unique experiences of Jewish women during the Holocaust, referring to the second question asked earlier, pertaining to the observations of the Auschwitz survivor quoted at the beginning of this chapter regarding the differences between men and women during the Holocaust. Finally, I will return to the aforementioned template to examine whether the topic of women during the Holocaust went through the same stages of acceptance for it to become a legitimate topic of study.

The Development of Holocaust Study

During the two decades following the war's end, only "mainstream topics" relating to Holocaust experiences were granted legitimacy by Holocaust historians, many of whom were themselves survivors. These included topics which they considered central to understanding the framework of the Holocaust experience such as "Jewish leadership," "Jewish resistance," "rescue," and the "Final Solution." Only later did Holocaust historians begin to study social and cultural topics, starting with those pertaining to what they termed "daily life in the ghettos and camps." The manifold reasons for this tendency have been discussed elsewhere[6], but their result was identical. During the first three decades after the war, there was virtually no Holocaust research that focused on women's lives during the Holocaust.

There were, however, a growing number of studies focusing on *Jewish leadership* during the Holocaust, both in ghettos and in occupied but not-ghettoized areas. Initially only male groups such as Judenräte were studied by researchers.[7] There is anecdotal evidence of a women's Judenräte formed after all the men of that town were deported, but we have no documents referring to it. It was also the exception that proved the rule, mentioned in passing but never examined in depth. At a later stage researchers began to deal with alternative leadership frameworks such as those of youth movements and alternative educational frameworks, where one could find large numbers of women active in leadership positions. These included Zionist-pioneering movements such as Hashomer Hatzair, Dror, and Gordonia, communist-Jewish groups such as the Bund, and ultra-orthodox girls' educational frameworks such as the Bais Ya'akov (Beth Jacob) school network. However, the women involved were almost never examined as women, but rather as part of a more general "alternative leadership framework."

Jewish resistance was another topic whose study began soon after the Holocaust and the first diaries and memoirs of Holocaust survivors published in Israel were written by former resistance fighters and partisans. The direction that such research took was usually guided by a narrow definition of terms. During the first postwar years "resistance" usually meant one thing—armed resistance. Other forms of defiance, also termed "passive resistance," "spiritual resistance," or "day-to-day stand," only became topics worthy of note almost a generation after the war's end. This had to do with the development of what the public, along with most historians at that time, considered "resistance." The Hebrew terminology is clear and dichotomous. It uses the terms *hitnagdut* to describe physical resistance, and *amida,* literally translated at the first Yad Vashem conference devoted to the topic of resistance (1968) as the "day-to-day stand," to describe the other forms. Since that time, the almost binary view of "resistance" has softened to include numerous shades and nuances of that term. Today we speak of variations of resistance; rescue, underground schools, and even going about your daily life as much as possible under impossible circumstances, as "resistance" during the Holocaust. As soon as there was a broader definition of "resistance," it also began to include actions which were often intrinsically connected with daily life of Jewish women during the Holocaust. Thus, the defiance of women during the Holocaust was a major factor in broadening the scope of behaviors identified as resistance and rescue, reshaping our models for that behavior.

The Final Solution was yet another topic upon which early Holocaust research had focused. In most cases the emphasis was on Nazi anti-Jewish policy, but there were also studies of Jewish response to this policy. Concentrating primarily on the extermination process was, in some ways, detrimental to the development of gender studies. Why? Begin here, too, scholars emphasized that the destiny of all Jews during the Holocaust was supposed to be the same, regardless of gender.

Sometime during the 1970s and 1980s, Holocaust research began to change course, focusing on social and cultural topics that had initially not been considered mainstream. These included *daily life in ghettos, camps, and other areas under Nazi domination*. This change of focus encouraged studies about the lives of different groups of Jews under the Nazis, including those living in various countries, the lives of children under the Nazi regime, those of Jewish communists, the Orthodox and ultra-Orthodox Jews, and eventually, the lives of Jewish women under the Nazis. Thus, the developmental shift in Holocaust studies from the 1950s to the 1980s opened new fields of interest in which it would be possible to focus separately on the female Jewish experience during the Holocaust. All that was missing was the awareness that it was a topic of merit, separate (and parallel) to the male experience, and worthy of independent examination.

The Development of Women's Studies and Its Impact on Holocaust Studies

I now move our focus to Women's Studies, a rapidly growing topic from the 1970s onward. Initially an outgrowth of the burgeoning women's movement of the late 1960s, its impact was felt first on the social sciences and later on the humanities. In history, women's studies attempted to contrast the previous male perspective that had permeated most studies ("his-story") with that of the female perspective of those incidents ("her-story"). Although the process was deemed necessary in order to fill in the missing parts of the story, there were those who argued against it. They claimed that by separating the study of women from that of men, feminist scholars were creating a bifurcated history which lacked cohesion. Only after seamlessly integrating women's studies with the existing historical narrative would it be possible to present a complete historical study from the point of view of all humanity, and not only that of a particular gender. This could only be achieved at a later stage, after a narrative equilibrium had been achieved between two different, and at times opposing gendered narratives of historical events.

The focus on women during the Holocaust was built on the crossroads where Holocaust studies, already a well-accepted discipline, met Women's Studies, a new and not always revered academic invention. This already meant that from its inception, a disciplinary "burden of proof" was put on studies of women during the Holocaust. Unlike examinations of leadership, resistance or the Final Solution, mainstream topics whose research was carried out by acclaimed scholars who were often survivors, from the outset, studies of women during the Holocaust were usually conducted by younger women, some children of refugees and survivors, and others with no personal connection to the cataclysm. This, too, set the stage for such studies being critically viewed as minor, trivial, and in some cases, even threatening examples of what some termed "quasi-research."[8]

The first group of academics focusing on women during the Holocaust included not only historians, but scholars from various disciplines, some from the humanities, others from the social sciences, many with a radical feminist agenda. Scholars who had written these early studies were often accused of having this agenda compromise the accuracy of a number of their conclusions. These included evaluations of the power of women's relationships during the war as opposed to men's, the depth of such relationships as opposed to those of another gender, statements about women being persecuted under the Nazis as part of the persecution of women and not the persecution of Jews, etc.[9] As time passed a number of scholars who wrote these early studies reworked many of their conclusions, and it became rarer to find blanket statements such as those appearing in such early studies, that lacked empirical or historical basis. But it took time.

Consequently, during its first years as an academic discipline, scholars involved in women's Holocaust studies were often accused of not having utilized rigorous academic methodology, and were even considered by some as being a dangerous aberration. I found this out early in my academic career when I began thinking about a topic for my doctoral dissertation. Turning to one of the world's prominent Holocaust historians of the time, Prof. Yisrael Gutman of the Hebrew University and Yad Vashem, I proposed that I write about women during the Holocaust. "Don't do it," replied Gutman; "you want to be taken seriously, don't you?" So what should I study, I asked him? Big topics, he replied such as leadership, resistance, and rescue. It is interesting to note that when we discussed the possibility of studying resistance he brought up examples of women such as Ruzka Korchak or Zivia Lubetkin, central figures in the Zionist underground movements during the war, but he never suggested examining them as women.

The same thing happened when I discussed rescue with another major Holocaust scholar of the time, Prof. Yehuda Bauer, who suggested writing about women such as Gizi Fleischmann or Recha Freier, considered major figures in the field of rescue, but not as women. Both scholars ultimately recanted and became extremely supportive of my work and those of others who have dealt with aspects of women's lives during the Holocaust. However, their response at that time was telling, as it was a picture of what the historical establishment of the early 1980s thought about the topic at that time. For them, women may indeed have played an important role during the Holocaust, but they did not yet view gender issues as being worthy of mention. In their minds, Jewish women during the Holocaust functioned as Jews, and the category of "women," at least to most Holocaust scholars of that era, was superfluous.

In the early and mid-1980s when the first studies about women during the Holocaust appeared, it was still difficult to convince people that it was a serious research topic. That only happened later, when a group of historians, mostly women but also some men, began to study various aspects of women's Holocaust experiences. I was privileged to be one of them.

And this brings us back to the title of this chapter, Resisting Obliteration: The Lives and Deaths of Jewish Women During the Holocaust. Much of the research about Jewish women during the Holocaust deals with various aspects of women's daily life, *amida bashoa*—the "day-to-day stand" during the Holocaust, as it is referred to in Hebrew, or what I have chosen to call "resisting obliteration—variations of women's resistance during the Holocaust." What comes to mind when using that term?

Symbols of the Holocaust: Many symbols of the Holocaust have feminine overtones. There has been much discussion about the Jew as a victim during the Holocaust, with "victim" traditionally being a feminine symbol. Hence it is not surprising that one of most universal symbols of the Holocaust is a girl, Anne Frank, author of the most widely written and translated Holocaust-authored book in the world. In addition, quite a number of the earliest Holocaust memoirs published in the western world were written by women. One example is "The Diary of Mary Berg," published in 1945, which focused on the story of a young girl in Warsaw whose father lived in America, enabling her and her mother to be removed from the Warsaw Ghetto and transferred to the United States late in the war.[10]

Resistance: Survivor memoirs written by women lead us to "women's resistance." In pre-State Israel, one of the major centers that absorb Holocaust survivors, the first Holocaust books published there were written by women, particularly women partisans such as Rozka Korchak who had survived the Holocaust. Urged by her political movement to write her story, the account naturally stressed the topic of resistance but not necessarily "women's resistance."[11] As the term "resistance" broadened, scholars, along with survivors, began to realize that women's day-to-day lives was actually a form of "resistance" against the Nazi dehumanization of Jews, in this case of Jewish women, that preceded their annihilation.

Day-to-Day Lives: To understand these "day-to-day lives," we have to first explore a number of unique aspects of Jewish women's lives during the Holocaust. This examination begins with the stories of Jewish living in Germany during the 1930s. From there one moves into the 1940s and Jewish women's experiences in occupied areas, ghettos, the Nazi camps, the underground movements, in hiding and finally, during the Final Solution, the death marches, and ultimately liberation.

Germany Under the Nazis: Historian Marion Kaplan, who had studied this topic in depth, has focused upon a number of interesting aspects of Jewish women's lives in Germany under the Nazis.[12] One is awareness. During the early years of the Nazi regime, Jewish women were often the first to realize the depth of anti-Semitic sentiment that had become prevalent in Nazi Germany. While shopping, taking their children to play in public parks, swim in public pools, and socialize with their neighbors, they could sense the changes going on around them. Neighbor women would no longer greet them, they were forbidden to enter parks with their children or take them to swim in public pools, certain stores informed them they were not welcome anymore as they were no longer willing to sell to Jews, etc. Busy with work and other public frameworks, Jewish men, often exempt from Nazi anti-Jewish employment legislation due to their military service in the Great War, were often more protected from social encounters and daily dealings with the general German population where such things were felt.

Jewish women were therefore often the first in the family to press for immigration, and scores of files in the Central Jewish organizations in Germany's emigration departments (*Auswanderungs Abteilung*) show how mothers begged to have their children join children's transports to get them out of the country.[13] Women in Nazi Germany were therefore the barometer of political and social anti-Jewish sentiment, and were often instrumental in saving their families, leaving no stone unturned in their quest to leave Germany, or at least save their children, before the outbreak of the Second World War.

In Ghettos: With the outbreak of the Second World War in September 1939, following Poland's surrender on September 21, Nazi policy decreed that the majority of the Jews of the newly formed General Government would be incarcerated in ghettos. This policy would later be enforced throughout occupied Eastern Europe. In some areas Jews were sent to forced labor outside the ghettos while in others, they worked in factories and workshops which had been established inside the ghettos in order to prove to the Nazis that they were productive, and thus to postpone their "resettlement" (in other words, annihilation) for as long as possible.

Under such circumstances, women were faced with a two-pronged task. Not only were they required to work to stay alive, but in many if not most cases, they also had full responsibility for maintaining a household under impossible conditions: standing on line for hours for the little food that was available in the ghetto; finding additional food on the black market, cooking and serving the food to try and make inedible remnants edible and give everyone enough sustenance when there was not enough food; making provisions for children to be cared for and fed while they themselves were at work.

We have numerous stories from ghetto diaries of how Jewish women went hungry, would faint at work, and how it turned out that they were giving their food to their children and husband, who they thought needed it more. This was a continuous struggle in which women not only multitasked to stay alive, but actively sacrificed their own sustenance to give it to their families. Contemporary gender studies have pointed out that although this appears to have been the normative behavior of wives mothers under such circumstances, it was not the only pattern. There were also stories of mothers who were overcome by hunger and ate food meant for their families. Were the mothers who gave their own food to their husband and children acting automatically out of an existing gendered norm of women sacrificing for their families more than their making a thought-out choice? How were they seen at that time? Were those who ate their families' food acting against an accepted gendered norm? Were they considered "worse" at the time, than starving ghetto fathers who may have eaten their family's entire rations? These are all questions that contemporary gender and Holocaust studies must address.

Underground Movements: Jewish women played a major role in the underground movements, for example as couriers. Why? The automatic answer, in fact one that I taught for years, was anatomical. Because Jewish men were circumcised, it was easy for the Nazis and their accomplices to discover whether a young man they might find traveling from place to place in Eastern Europe was Jewish. Women, on the other hand, had no bodily signs of their Jewishness and could therefore travel much more safely from place to place during the war.

It was only in a discussion with Prof. Yisrael Gutman, a Warsaw Ghetto and Nazi camp survivor, that I discovered a very different answer. Just the fact that a young man would be walking around freely in certain areas in Eastern Europe in the middle of the day was in itself a cause for suspicion. He didn't have to be told to lower his pants in order to realize that he was not a local Pole, so Gutman told me. Young Polish men during the war did not have free time: they worked, were laborers on a farm, were serving as forced German labor, etc. On the other hand, peasant girls traveled freely, primarily to sell farm goods in the cities, and were therefore less suspect of espionage. This teaches us that to understand gendered wartime issues regarding Jewish during the Holocaust, it is necessary to understand not only prewar gendered Jewish behavior but also that of their non-Jewish environment and surroundings.

Bronkla Klibanska, a Jewish courier in Eastern Europe during the Holocaust, told the following story. At some point she was using a false identity, hiding as a kitchen farm girl on a Polish farm. One day she was standing in the kitchen cutting carrots with a few of the other Polish girls when one of them turned to the others and pointed to Bronka. "Look at her, she is cutting carrots just like a Jew!" the girl exclaimed. It seemed that without thinking, Bronka was cutting the carrots into thin slices as if for carrot *tzimmis*, a common Jewish sweet carrot dish, instead of into coarse large pieces as Polish girls were wont to do. Even something like cutting a carrot correctly was part of "Polish women's society" and a Jewish woman, trying to appear as if she were Polish, needed to know all the nuances necessary in order to maintain her cover. Here, too, we see how women's behavior changed our understanding of the models of rescue and resistance, broadening definitions and categories.

Mutual Assistance: One of the means by which Jewish women in ghettos, and even more so, in camps, attempted to resist and survive the Holocaust was through helping each other as individuals or in groups, a phenomenon better known as "mutual assistance." This meant forming groups of two, three, and more girls or women who stayed together, supporting each other throughout their incarceration. Not all forms of assistance were physical; others could be emotional, educational, or spiritual. A similar phenomenon existed among men and it is therefore not the phenomenon of "mutual assistance" that comes into question but rather its contents.

One form of women's mutual assistance included teaching young women how to keep house, cook, or various domestic forms of education. This is connected to a gendered difference between men and women when coping with hunger. Hunger, or the fear of hunger, dominates Holocaust narratives and was the silent accompaniment to many if not most wartime experiences. While survivor testimonies of men in concentration camps speak about their coping with hunger by talking talk about the food that they would want to eat after liberation, women's survivor testimonies speak of how women would discuss what they would cook, owing to the domestic gendered differences in the world from which many, if not most of them they had come.[14] One aspect of the discussions about cooking was educational: women were used to imparting domestic skills and such discussions enabled them to teach the younger generation of girls in the camp who had no chance to learn domestic skills before their incarceration, how to act in a "normal world." Such acts should be seen as part of these women's resistance: to carry out their domestic-educational tasks, even in the framework of a Nazi camp.

One such documented case took place among women in Teresienstadt, where a group of older women would teach younger ones how to cook by reciting recipes to them by heart. Even though there was no food available they wanted to pass on their culinary knowledge to the younger generation, as part of a gendered educational form of mutual assistance and resistance. Some of these recipes have been published in a book edited by Cara De Silva, "In Memory's Kitchen."[15]

Another form of mutual assistance was the formation of groups of girls and women who stayed together throughout the war and acted as each other's "camp sisters." Sometimes the groups had a family basis, sometimes they were prewar friends or neighbors. At times the groups just got together "ad hoc" during the war and remained as such. There were also similar men's groups of "camp brothers" in which the ties appear to have been equally strong, and the difference between the groups was not the intensity of commitment but the group size.

In my study of the "Zehnnerschaft," a group of ten young women who banded together in the Nazi camp of Plaszow and remained together for two and a half years in Auschwitz and Bergen-Belsen, I show that it was more common for women's groups to be larger than it was for men's. Anything that would draw attention to prisoners was dangerous, but for women, the larger the group, the more protection it gave its members from Nazi guards who wished to harm them physically or intimately. Thus, it was a balance for these women. The larger the group, the greater the chance that they would be noticed, but on the other hand, the larger the group, the greater protection it afforded to its members.

Research Framework and Discussion

Here we have seen only a few illustrations of the types of topics that have been studied within the framework "Jewish women during the Holocaust." All of it was ostensibly serious research, well grounded in primary sources, and heavily relying on oral documentation. And yet, for years it was labeled by historians and public figures as "unscientific," "agenda driven," and "not serious." The matter came to a head in 1998 when *Commentary* editor Gabriel Schoenfeld published an article entitled "Auschwitz and the Professors" in which he attacked Holocaust scholarship in general and contemporary studies of women in the Holocaust in particular. Moving from the academic to the educated reader, he then published a short article against gendered Holocaust scholarship in *The Wall Street Journal* that touched off an ongoing debate on the subject.[16] The articles elicited a reaction which touched off a counter-response, starting a dialectic with far ranging repercussions for some of the women involved in women's Holocaust scholarship. It took several years until the matter began to die down and even when contacted at the end of the second decade of the twenty-first century, Schoenfeld claimed to still be of the same mind in this matter as he was two decades ago.

How, then, did "Women in the Holocaust" move from being a fringe or unaccepted topic of study to a fully legitimate research subject? It appears that the process involved all of the stages that Ross et al. listed with regard to studies of graffiti and street art. Initial studies were often met with criticism, whether focused on the sources, or on the perceived agenda behind these studies. But scholars persevered, more sources (testimonies, diaries, oral documentation) were discovered or created, and additional research was published. As in the case of street art, there was often academic opposition to the topic of women in the Holocaust, even leading to public debate on the matter, but it nevertheless began to gain broader acceptance, leading it to become a discipline within Holocaust studies.

Apart from being a research theme, it also became a topic of academic courses. The first such course was organized by Konnilyn Feig in California in 1984,[17] but it was only in the 1990s that additional courses on the subject were offered first in the United States and later in Israel. As more studies and several anthologies on the topic were published during the 1990s, some of it published by those of us teaching such courses, it became easier for us provide our students with lists of required reading.[18] Then there were the conferences. The first conference on the topic of women in the Holocaust was organized by Joan Ringelheim and Esther Katz in New York in 1983.[19] Only a decade and a half later was it followed by a workshop that Dalia Ofer and Lenore Weitzman convened on the topic in Jerusalem during the summer of 1995. Since then, a number of workshops, symposia, and conferences devoted to women and the Holocaust have been held in various locations, each strengthening the topic's perception as an accepted academic discipline.

Finally we come to the issue of a scholar's network. The last stage that Ross et al. list in the stages of granting academic legitimacy to a topic that was initially considered "fringe" or "unworthy" is the creation of a network for scholars involved in its research or teaching. During the summer of 2019, almost four decades after the publication of the first contemporary studies about women and the Holocaust, such a network was finally created. When I became Director of the Finkler Institute of Holocaust Research at Bar-Ilan University in Israel, I founded an international forum entitled "Women Recall the Holocaust" in which close to thirty women scholars from different disciplines formed an international network in which they could discuss their work and experiences. Ultimately, with the assistance of the Fanya Gottesfeld Heller Center for the Study of Judaism at the university, the network acted as the core body for a book of ego-documents (memoirs) written by each of its members. Studying women in the Holocaust now became the basis for a new form of "sisterhood," uniting more than two dozen women into a single framework with international meet-ups in New York, London, Munich, and Ramat Gan, Israel.

This brings me to my conclusion regarding Resisting Obliteration. While Jewish women resisted the obliteration of their lives during the Holocaust, women studying women during the Holocaust resisted attempts to obliterate the developing discipline whose disappearance would wipe out those Jewish women a second time. Arousing the ire of scholarly traditionalists, they posited probing questions and critically examined women's Holocaust-related valorization, asking, for example, whether women sacrificing their health, food, and lives for their families had done so out of choice or gendered conditioning. Daring to discuss those testimonies that mentioned women who acted otherwise, they emphasized that understanding the lives, actions, and deaths of Jewish women during the Holocaust is a matter of perspective that must be liberated from traditional gendered approaches. It is that ever changing perspective that gives this relatively new discipline its uniqueness, fueled by scholars worldwide who have devoted much of their research to exploring its depths. By braving new research frontiers, they have ultimately bonded in the knowledge that in unity there is strength, and that when it comes to creating a new scholarly discipline and giving it legitimacy, the whole is indeed much more than the sum.

Notes

1. Author's interview with Zipporah Goldstein, Petach Tikva, August 31, 1988.

2. See my book *Double Jeopardy: Gender and the Holocaust* (London: Vallentine Mitchell, 1998).

3. Such as that being conducted within the framework of Emmanuel Ringelblum's clandestine archive in the Warsaw Ghetto, "Oneg Shabbat." See: Dalia Ofer, "Her View through My Lens: Cecilia Slepak Studies Women in Warsaw," in *Gender, Place and Memory in the Modern Jewish Experience: Re-placing Ourselves*, eds. Judith Tydor Baumel and Tova Cohen (London and Portland, OR: Vallentine Mitchell, 2003), 29–50.

4. For the debates over the topic's legitimacy see: Judith Tydor Baumel-Schwartz, "Why Deal With Women During the Holocaust as a Separate Topic?" (Hebrew), *Yalkut Moreshet* (forthcoming 2021).

5. Jeffrey Ian Ross, Peter Bengsten, John F. Lennon, Susan Phillips, and Jacqueline Z. Wilson, "In Search of Academic Legitimacy: The Current State of Scholarship on Graffiti and Street Art," *The Social Science Journal* 54, no. 4 (December 2017): 411–19.

6. See, for example, Judith Tydor Baumel, "Gender and Family Studies of the Holocaust," in *Lessons and Legacies II: Teaching the Holocaust in a Changing World*, ed. Donald G. Schilling (Evanston: Northwestern University Press, 1998), 105–17.

7. Dan Michman, "Jewish Leadership in Extremis," in *The Historiography of the Holocaust*, ed. Dan Stone (London: Palgrave Macmillan, 2004), 319–40.

8. See, for example, Gabriel Schoenfeld, "Auschwitz and the Professors," *Commentary* 105 (June 6, 1998): 42–6.

9. For example the early studies by Joan Ringelheim, "Women and the Holocaust: A Reconsideration of Research," *Signs* 10 (1985): 741–61; Joan Ringelheim, "The Unethical and the Unspeakable: Women and the Holocaust," *Simon Wiesenthal Center Annual* 1 (1984): 69–87.

10. Mary Berg, *Warsaw Ghetto: A Diary*, ed. S. L. Shneiderman (New York: L.B. Fischer, 1945).

11. Ruzka Korchak, *Lehavot Ba'efer* (Flames in the Ashes) (Merhavia: Hakibbutz Ha'artzi Hashomer Hatzair, 1946).

12. Marion Kaplan, *Between Dignity and Despair: Jewish Life in Nazi Germany* (New York: Oxford University Press, 1998).

13. Judith Tydor Baumel, *Unfulfilled Promise: The Jewish Refugee Children in the United States, 1934-1945* (JuneAQ: Denali, 1990).

14. Myrna Goldenberg, "Food Talk: Gendered Responses to Hunger in the Concentration Camps," in *Experience and Expression: Women, the Nazis and the Holocaust*, eds. Elizabeth R. Baer and Myrna Goldenberg (Detroit: Wayne State University Press, 2003), 161–79.

15. Cara De Silva, *In Memory's Kitchen: A Legacy of the Women of Terezin* (Lanham: Roman and Littlefield, 1996.)

16. Schoenfeld, "Auschwitz and the Professors"; Gabriel Schoenfeld, "The Cutting Edge of Holocaust Studies," *The Wall Street Journal,* May 21, 1998: 16.

17. R. Ruth Linden, "Troubling Categories I Can't Think Without: Reflections on Women in the Holocaust," *Contemporary Jewry* 17, no. 1 (January 1996): 18–33.

18. I taught the first such course in Israel at the University of Haifa and at Touro College in Jerusalem during the early 1990s.

19. Joan Ringelheim and Esther Katz, Women Surviving the Holocaust, Stern College, March 20–21, 1983.

CHAPTER 4
DEFIANCE AND RESISTANCE TO NAZISM FROM THE PERSPECTIVE OF GENDER, CLASS, AND GENERATION
Volker Berghahn

This contribution attempts to examine if, when it comes to defiance and resistance inside Nazi Germany after 1933 and in occupied Europe during the Second World War, it is possible to gain additional insights into anti-Nazi activities and motives by looking at the question in terms on gender in relation to socioeconomic class and generational difference.

It has long been accepted among scholars of this period that the use of physical violence and murder was endemic to the Nazi movement well before 1933. The Nazi seizure of power on January 30, 1933, then saw an escalation of this violence inside the country during the 1930s. It then spread throughout Europe by means of German military aggression. From the autumn of 1939, there were waves of ethnic cleansing directed by the SS from Berlin's Reich Security Main Office against Europe's Jewish populations and other minorities, such as the Sinti and Roma as well as the Slav majorities in the East and in the Balkans.

After Hitler had seized power on January 30, 1933, it was in the first instance his paramilitary Stormtroopers (SA) who in early February unleashed a truly vicious wave of violence against their supposedly most dangerous enemies, that is, Communists, Social Democrats, and trade unionists.[1]

Leftist anti-Nazis were arrested without warrants, beaten up, and, together with other alleged "enemies of the state," put into makeshift concentration camps, where the guards murdered some of them with impunity. This was not a temporary phenomenon and by the end of the year, Hitler had turned Germany into a terroristic one-party dictatorship.

Knowing from the bitter experience of the previous years of virtual civil war in the urban centers of Weimar Germany, it was both Communist and Social Democrat working-class men and women who tried to organize an active resistance against Nazi violence and criminality as quickly as possible. They formed small underground cells of no more than three people whose members went out at night to paint anti-Nazi slogans on factory walls or produced flyers on Roneo machines that were then left in factory lavatories and public places. There are a number of studies on these grassroots movements, and only one that was active in Mannheim—the city where Hitler never came to make a speech because he knew there would be no welcoming cheers—shall be mentioned here.[2] This book shows, how improvised these activities were. Leaflets had to be smuggled from France across the border in bicycle tubes. While it was young male and female activists who went out in the middle of the night, their parents not only knew about their work but often also supported it, as all of them saw themselves as belonging to a specific working-class milieu in which friendship and solidarity held them together. Relatively few of them left the fold and became National Socialists.

The trouble is that few working-class activists had some experience doing underground work, with the exception of a group of older communists from earlier periods when the Communist Party and its affiliates had been banned from time to time before 1933. Given these handicaps, the Gestapo took about two years to identify and arrest working-class resisters. With brutal torture the men in those long black leather coats soon also got hold of these groups and the leaders of various resistance networks that had been built up in 1933. While women took an active part, the Gestapo targeted mainly the men who were tried, imprisoned, or executed.

For these reasons, the left-wing resistance largely fell silent by 1936 when Heinrich Himmler was not only Reichsführer SS, but also became Chief of the German Police and the head of a ubiquitous machinery of surveillance and brutal repression. There existed but very small pockets, such as the *Onkel Emil* cell founded in 1938 by Ruth Andreas-Friedrich and other Social Democrats to help German Jews to escape.[3] Andreas-Friedrich was later also involved in saving active resisters on the left, such as whom the Gestapo was looking for after the failed July 1944 Plot.[4] Liselotte Herrmann must also be mentioned here who, born on June 23, 1909, had begun her studies of chemistry at the Universities of Stuttgart and Berlin in the early 1930s, but had been relegated in July 1933 because of her communist activism.[5] Returning to her parent's home in Stuttgart and married to a leader of the party's illegal CP in Württemberg, she acted as a liaison across the nearby Swiss border until she was arrested in December 1935, tried, imprisoned, and finally executed on June 20, 1938.

If men and women like Herrmann were not sent to a concentration camp where many of them perished without trial, they were hauled through the still existing traditional court system whose judges imposed draconian sentences, and many of the defendants were guillotined without the chance of an appeal. The Mannheim study interviewed a few men, but otherwise relied quite heavily on interviews with the widows who had participated in underground work, but had survived. By the beginning of the war, there were, at the grassroots level, only individuals left, such as Georg Elser who, without being able to rely on a support network, tried to kill Hitler, and almost succeeded when he planted a bomb in a pillar of the assembly hall where Hitler was scheduled to appear.[6] The only larger resistance group was the one that the Gestapo began to trace, calling it "Red Orchestra." But as will be seen in a moment this was in many ways a misnomer.

With the once significant Communist and Social Democrat resistance and its quest to overthrow the Hitler dictatorship for all practical purposes obliterated, the conservative and military resistance in which the German nobility had assumed a dominant position moved into the center of the resistance against the "Third Reich." With the regime now firmly established and protected by a pervasive and ubiquitous police state, the officer corps were the only ones who disposed of the weapons and the organizational capacity to confront Hitler with superior military power. However, this resistance had been moving on a different time-scale from that of the working-class resistance. Many men and women who became active opponents of the Nazi regime either openly supported it in the early years or they had tolerated it, while it fought the Left and implemented a public expenditure program officially propagandized to revive the economy devastated by the Great Slump in the early 1930s with its six million unemployed.[7]

What the regime camouflaged, however, was that, in preparation of Hitler's plans to acquire by violent means "living space" in the East, it had adopted what has been called a "military Keynesianism."[8] While Hitler's public investments provided the desired stimulus for the revival of the economy and job creation, it produced armaments to be used in Hitler's projected wars of conquest. When unemployment had disappeared by 1936–7, the economy should have reverted back to civilian production, but did not. With the specter of war on the horizon, it was now the military leadership in alliance with prominent civil servants and retired conservative politicians that became so concerned about a conflict that Germany could not win that they thought of removing Hitler. Accordingly, plans were made by the Army leadership in 1938 and in the early 1940s, but for various reasons were never implemented.[9] This being very much a man's world, it was only later at the height of the war that women began to play an important role in the resistance movements.

When the tide of the global war was turning against Hitler and a German defeat looked very likely a conspiracy of officers and civilians around Claus von Stauffenberg reached the point of action, culminating in the attempt on the "Führer's" life at his Rastenburg headquarters on July 20, 1944.[10] It failed. While this event and the men involved in it, most of whom here tried and executed, has been the subject of many studies, the question is what was the role that women played in this drama. Here the main point is that some of the plotters had kept their conspiratorial activities secret from their wives in order to protect their families. As Dorothee von Meding has written, the participation of the women of July 20 was more "private" and shaped by "prevalent gender roles."[11] Thus, the wives of Wessel Freytag von Loringhoven, Elisabeth, and of Fritz-Dietlof von der Schulenburg were largely ignorant.[12] Others such as Nina Schenck von Stauffenberg, the wife of Claus, the key figure in the attempt on Hitler's life, had some knowledge, while Marion York von Wartenburg, who was married to Peter attended meetings of the Kreisau Circle of Nazi opponents and had more detailed information, but also stressed that her own and her friends' marriages were strong and absolutely trusting.[13] Clarita von Trott zu Solz, the wife of Adam, on the other hand, later claimed that she knew everything through her husband.[14] This also seems to have been true of the Dohnanyi family, where Hans was married to Christel Bonhoeffer.[15]

Emmi Bonhoeffer, the wife of Klaus and sister-in-law of the famous theologian Dietrich, was tasked with encoding telephone messages and walked around the block at night as a guard while the plotters held their meetings in an apartment upstairs.[16] Marion Countess Dönhoff, who was single, took a step further and acted as a messenger and was asked by von der Schulenburg to approach Heinrich Count zu Dohna to join the Plot.[17] After its failure, she was hauled into the Gestapo office in Königsberg.[18] But, as she quickly discovered, her interrogators did not have any incriminating evidence against her. She had merely been denounced by a relative, Bogislav von Dönhoff, who had persuaded a post office clerk to record the senders of letters that she had been receiving and had then handed them over to his friend Erich Koch, the Gauleiter of East Prussia. After a very uncomfortable night in a Gestapo cellar, not knowing what would happen in the morning, she was let go. There is also the drama that took place on July 20, 1944, on the estate of Heinrich von Lehndorff.[19] When the coup failed he knew that the Gestapo would be looking for him. At first he tried to hide in the adjacent woods, but then gave himself up for fear that his wife and his four children would be taken hostage (Sippenhaft, as the Nazis called it).

The Lehndorff children were given new names and made to disappear in an orphanage at Bad Sachsa.[20] This was also the fate of the children of several other plotters, among them the Freytag von Loringhoven offspring who were renamed "Braun," and the children of Caesar von Hofacker.[21] Fortunately, all of them were found and reunited with their surviving mothers. The widow's ordeal was likewise horrific. Nina Stauffenberg was imprisoned and her daughter Konstanze was born in her solitary confinement.[22] Marion York was locked up from August till October 1944 and Clarita Trott zu Solz for six weeks from the middle of August.[23] Inevitably, the levels of constant anxiety and worry were high, the more so since there was little or no information about the fate of their husbands and children.

Another steadfast woman was Elisabeth von Thadden who did not belong to the Stauffenberg and Moltke groups.[24] Born in 1890, she came from an ancient Pomeranian clan rooted at Trieglaff, now Trzyglow in Poland, and, having trained as a teacher, had been working as the director of a private school near Tutzing south of Munich and later during the war for the presidium of the German Red Cross. She had appeared in the crosshairs of the Gestapo as an opponent of Nazism, partly because of an informer who had been trailing her. She was finally arrested on a trip to northern France in Meaux, near Amiens. Brought back to Germany, she was tried in July 1944 just before the Stauffenberg coup and executed on September 8. Her fate is relevant for two reasons that reflect the terrible dilemmas in which quite a few conservative Germans found themselves. In October 1933, she published an article in which she praised the role of private boarding schools like hers. Its aims coincided with those of the "new Germany."[25] These schools supposedly offered "more opportunities to educate German youth to become German *Volksgenossen*." They would thus be able to become "fully conscious members of the National Socialist state" and "help construct the new Germany." There is also a brochure advertising the school, stating that "since the National Socialist assumption of power the decisive cooperation of women for the new construction of Germany has been determined."[26] This did not prevent the regime from forcing the dismissal of several Jewish teachers. If Elisabeth von Thadden ever pondered joining the party, she was now so devastated by the government's anti-Semitic policies that she distanced herself from the regime that now followed her work ever more closely until the Gestapo decided to pounce in 1944 and to execute her.

In 1994 her school held a small commemoration on the fiftieth anniversary of her execution at which Elisabeth's nephew Rudolph by then a professor of history at Göttingen

University and director of studies at the Ecole des Hautes Etudes en Sciences Sociales in Paris spoke very movingly of her life and international connections.[27] There followed another speaker at the memorial who remarked on what was required to rise against an all-powerful apparatus of domination. After all, "acting in resistance constituted a liminal situation of human existence, doubt, and powerlessness, but [was nonetheless always] driven by a courageous wager."

Having examined the role of anti-Nazi women among both the working-class and the nobility, the experience of middle-class women is even more complex. Just as many German bourgeois men, millions of women who came from these families gave their enthusiastic support to Hitler and his regime before and after 1933.[28] Many of them did so initially because they believed, all too naively, in the political and economic promises that the new Reich chancellor had been making. But some of them, especially if they were faithful Catholics or Protestants, did so increasingly reluctantly. They kept their distance and also encouraged their children not to join any of the Nazi youth organizations. Nor did many of them welcome Hitler's waging of war in Poland and Western Europe. Many of them may have been swayed again by Hitler's military victories in 1940, but they were positively alarmed when he invaded the Soviet Union in June 1941. Still, overall it is fair to say that during the 1930s millions of German women remained largely passive, even as they witnessed the anti-Semitic outrages, culminating in the Pogrom of November 1938.

During the war, it was only a small minority of women who openly resisted. Among the best researched subversive activities are those by Hans and Sophie Scholl siblings in 1942.[29] Once members of the Hitler Youth and the League of German Girls, the two of them had become strong opponents of Nazism. In late 1937 Hans had spent five weeks in prison. He was then drafted into the Army to fight in the East, where he learned about the mass murder of Jews and other minorities in the occupied Soviet Union. Hans and Sophie, mentored by Professor Kurt Huber at Munich University, began to rally a larger group of fellow students and to distribute a series of anti-Nazi leaflets in the university, and mailed many more. They took enormous risks and eventually got caught by one of the lecture hall custodians. There was a brief trial, and Sophie and Hans died under the guillotine in Munich's Stadelheim prison. Of the 1,381 victims murdered there, 121 were women.[30] As the end of the war was approaching, there were also other stirrings of working-class adolescents in the Rhineland or at the Christianeum high school in the middle-class western suburbs of Hamburg whose members were arrested and sent to the Neuengamme concentration camp near Hamburg.[31] As late as April 23, 1945, thirteen women were hanged there.[32] This is how merciless the Hitler regime was virtually up to the last minute. Nor should it be forgotten that during that time the last trains with Jewish deportees left the railway station in Berlin-Grunewald.

Thanks to the research of Anne Nelson and Stefan Roloff we now also know much about the "Red Orchestra" resistance group of the Luftwaffe lieutenant Harro Schulze-Boysen and Arvid and Mildred Harnack.[33] Arvid was the son of a famous theologian; Mildred was an American who thought that her being a woman and foreign citizen protected her from execution in 1942. She was wrong and they all died, being deemed part of a communist cell, when more recent research has shown that they were in touch with British intelligence in Switzerland and that their main goal was to get rid of the Nazi dictatorship. In short, as this volume shows, complemented by the additional cases presented in this section based on class and generational differences, there is by now a good deal of research on the role of women who defied and resisted the Nazis and who gave their lives for this cause. No less important, others risked severe punishment because they hid and rescued the victims of Nazi anti-Semitic persecution.

While recent research has shown that women rescuers also existed inside Germany and helped Jews to survive, their numbers were even greater in Nazi-occupied Europe. Yad Vashem has identified larger number of male and female "righteous gentiles" and the *American Jewish Foundation for the Righteous* has also honored and financially supported many of them in Eastern Europe after the collapse of the Soviet Bloc in 1989–90.[34] Especially in Eastern Europe hiding Jews meant deportation and death for those families but also execution for the rescuers. Inside Germany, the penalty was imprisonment, while those in hiding were deported and murdered. It is a field that still requires a lot more research, including the extent of self-rescue without clandestine support, often in the most incredible circumstances of rescue and also self-rescue.[35]

However, women in Nazi-occupied Europe were not only rescuers of Jews and other persecuted minorities, but also actively joined underground resistance groups as well as partisans.[36] The latter grew enormously in the East once the Nazis had begun to round up young men and women to work as forced laborers on farms and in the armaments industries of the Reich. German atrocities began straightaway in the autumn of 1939 in Poland, when not only Jews but also intellectuals and priests were summarily executed. After the occupation of Western and Northern Europe, resistance groups formed in France, Belgium, The Netherlands, as well as Denmark and Norway, increasingly supported by Britain's Special Operations Executive (SOE) and the American Office of Strategic Services (OSS). Women were invariably among the resistance cells. As Anne Nelson has shown in her contribution, Suzanne Spaak was both associated with "Red Orchestra" and built up a network of women friends in Paris to save Jewish children from deportation. There probably was an unspoken more patriarchal assumption among the leaders of these resistance movements that the work of sabotage was too dangerous to involve women in partisan operations and the dynamiting of railway lines. But there is the example of a Jewish resistance unit in Lithuania whose members, understandably did not know how to build a bomb. But there was a librarian who was prepared to look up the relevant information which she passed on to this unit.

One difference should be pointed out, though, with regard to women who resisted the Nazi regime. For patriotic West and East Europeans, the Germans were the invaders, occupiers, and murderers of their families and neighbors. So, they had a moral right to help defeat them.

For Germans, including women, the situation was different in so far as they worked for the defeat of their own native country. If, on top of this, they had even welcomed the establishment of the Hitler government in 1933, they found themselves in a more conflicted position.[37] Nor, unless they were Communists or Social Democrats who had combated the Nazis in the streets of the big cities, could they have imagined how ruthless this Nazi regime would become. So, it was clearly more difficult for middle-class Germans to reverse course. They did eventually, but often not until Hitler's total war revealed his regime's ultimate aims. Yet ultimately all Europeans, women and men, were confronted with the existential question of whether they were prepared to face death in their quest to remove a criminal regime.

Given how brutal and indeed lethal this regime was practically from 1933 onwards, it is important for the retrospective historian to come to grips with the terrible dilemmas that anti-Nazis faced and to realize how much courage it took to become an active opponent, whether as a lonely individual or as a member of a group that could only survive in the underground. So, it is not surprising that some of these avowed anti-Nazis took time before they made a decision. That decision was further complicated by the fact that they did not know the future and that this may have led them at first to take a wait-and-see attitude before they committed themselves to a dangerous life on the margins of society, whether inside Germany or in the occupied territories. This is why it is also important to ponder how far these anti-Nazis chose, at least temporarily, to life in the "gray zone" that Nathan Stoltzfus discusses in his Introduction to this volume. If we ignore these aspects of life under the Nazi regime, we are likely to miss a point without which defiance and resistance by women and men in this period cannot be understood, just as their class background and generational differences—basic themes of this chapter—provide fruitful insights.

Notes

1. See, e.g., Ian Kershaw, *Hitler, 1889-1936: Hubris* (New York: W. W. Norton & Company, 1999), 377ff.
2. Erich Matthias and Hermann Weber, eds., *Widerstand gegen den Nationalsozialismus in Mannheim* (Mannheim: Edition Quadrat, 1984), 139ff., 256ff.
3. See Martha Schad, *Frauen gegen Hitler. Schicksale im Nationalsozialismus* (Munich: Heyne Verlag, 2001), 282, 321.
4. Ruth Andreas-Friedrich's first husband was Otto Andreas Friedrich. She was a "modern woman" and Social Democrat, he rose to a high position in the rubber industry in the 1930s, but while he collaborated with the regime, they stayed in touch. It seems that she sent Dr. Gleissner to his apartment in Berlin and to his credit, he took him in and hid him for a while. If the Gestapo had found them, not only Gleissner's life would have been in jeopardy, but also Otto Friedrich's. The story is a good example of how precarious life had become. See Volker R. Berghahn and Paul Joachim Friedrich, *Otto A. Friedrich. Ein politischer Unternehmer. Sein Leben und seine Zeit, 1902-1975* (Frankfurt: Campus, 1983), 17. See also Ruth Andreas-Friedrich, *Berlin Underground, 1938-1945* (New York: Henry Holt and Co., 1947).
5. See Schad, *Frauen gegen Hitler*, 203ff., also for the following.
6. Peter Steinbach, *Georg Elser* (Berlin: Be.bra Wissenschaft, 2008); Ulrich Renz, *Georg Elser* (Stuttgart: Kohlhammer, 2014).

7. See, e.g., Hermann Beck, *The Fateful Alliance: German Conservatives and the Nazis in 1933* (New York: Berghahn Books, 2008). Examples of this can also be found in the early careers of Fritz-Dietlof von der Schulenburg, Henning von Treskow, Claus Schenck von Stauffenberg. Others, such as Helmuth von Moltke and Peter York von Wartenburg were anti-Nazis of the first hour. Some who joined the Wehrmacht officer corps, turned against the regime when they learned about the atrocities that the SS committed in Poland and later in the Soviet Union. See also the remark by Barbara von Haeften in Dorothee von Meding, *Courageous Hearts: Women and the Anti-Hitler Plot of 1944* (Oxford: Berghahn Books, 1997), 153: When she took a walk with her husband Hans-Berndt one evening, they passed a hospital in Berlin-Lichterfelde where SS-men were treated whose involvement in mass killings in Poland had led to their mental breakdown. Hans-Berndt had learned this from Helmuth von Moltke. The latter had got this from a Catholic priest to whom the nurses in that hospital had been complaining.

8. See Volker R. Berghahn, *Modern Germany: Society, Economy and Politics in the Twentieth Century* (Cambridge: Cambridge University Press, 1987), 138ff.

9. See, e.g., Harold C. Deutsch, *The Conspiracy against Hitler in the Twilight War* (London: University of Minnesota Press, 1968).

10. See, e.g., David C. Large, ed., *Contending with Hitler. Varieties of German Resistance in the Third Reich* (Cambridge: Cambridge University Press, 1991); Peter Hoffmann, *German Resistance to Hitler* (Cambridge, MA: Harvard University Press, 1988); Jörgen Schmädecke and Peter Steinbach, eds., *Widerstand gegen den Nationalsozialismus* (Munich: R. Piper, 1986).

11. von Meding, *Courageous Hearts*, xii.

12. Ibid., 36, 118.

13. Ibid., 186f., 110.

14. Ibid., 173.

15. Ibid., 16.

16. Ibid., 15.

17. Schad, *Frauen gegen Hitler*, 268f.

18. See Volker R. Berghahn, *Journalists between Hitler und Adenauer: From Inner Emigration to the Moral Reconstruction of West Germany* (Princeton: Princeton University Press, 2019), 91ff.

19. See, e.g., Antje Vollmer, *Doppelleben. Heinrich und Gottliebe von Lehndorff im Widerstand gegen Hitler* (Gütersloh: Eichborn Verlag, 2012).

20. See Petra Behrens and Johannes Tuchel, "Unsere wahre Identität sollte vernichtet werden," Die nach dem 20. Juli 1944 nach Bad Sachsa verschleppten Kinder, Berlin 2017.

21. See Dorothee von Meding, *Courageous Hearts* (Providence: Berghahn Books, 1997).

22. Ibid., 184ff.

23. Ibid., 167, 105. See also Marion York, *Die Stärke der Stille. Erinnerungen aus einem Leben im Widerstand* (Moers: Brendow-Verlag, 1998).

24. See Schad, *Frauen gegen Hitler*, 145ff., also for the following.

25. Quoted ibid., 148.

26. Ibid.

27. Quoted ibid., 166f.

28. See, e.g., Claudia Koonz, *Mothers in the Fatherland. Women, Family and Nazi Politics* (London: St. Martin's Press, 1987). This book unleashed a debate spearheaded by Gisela Bock that Koonz gave too one-sided a picture of the situation of women in the Third Reich.

29. See Schad, *Frauen gegen Hitler*, 298ff. See also Barbara Beuys, *Sophie Scholl: Biografie* (Munich: Hanser, 2010); Fred Breinersdorfer, ed., *Sophie Scholl – Die letzten Tage* (Frankfurt: Fischer Taschenbuch Verlag Gmb, 2005).

30. Schad, *Frauen gegen Hitler*, 310.

31. Detlev Peukert, *Edelweisspiraten* (Cologne: Bund Verlag, 1980).

32. Schad, *Frauen gegen Hitler*, 317.

33. Anne Nelson, *Die Rote Kapelle* (Munich: Verlag, 2010); Stefan Roloff, *Die Rote Kapelle* (Ullstein Hc: Munich, 2002). See also Hans Coppi and Geertje Andresen, eds., *Dieser Tod passt zu mir. Harro Schulze-Boysen. Grenzgänger im Widerstand. Briefe, 1915-1942* (Berlin: C. Bertelsmann, 1999).

34. See Chapter 2 in this book, by Mordecai Paldiel, *Whoever Saves One Life Saves an Entire World*. See also, Gay Black and Malka Drucker, *Rescuers. Portraits of Moral Courage in the Holocaust* (Santa Fe: Radius Books, 2020).

35. See Michael Skakun, *On Burning Ground. A. Son's Memoir* (New York: St. Martin's Press, 1999).

36. See, e.g., Jan T. Gross, *Polish Society under German Occupation* (Princeton: Princeton University Press 1979); Alexander Dallin, *German Rule in Russia, 1941-1945* (London: Palgrave Macmillan, 1957); Rolf-Dieter Müller and Gerd R. Ueberschär, *Hitler's War in the East, 1941-1945* (Oxford: Berghahn Books, 1997); Henri Michel, *The Shadow War. Resistance in Europe, 1939-1945* (London: Harper & Row, 1972).

37. See, e.g., Hermann Beck and Larry E. Jones, eds., *From Weimar to Hitler* (New York: Berghahn Books, 2019).

CHAPTER 5
THE WOMEN'S PROTEST ON ROSENSTRASSE BETWEEN COMMEMORATION, IDEALIZATION, AND DEBATE
Susanne Heim

Helga Löwenthal was not yet eleven years old when in late February 1943 she accompanied her mother to Rosenstrasse in the center of Berlin where her father was imprisoned. When she wrote her memoirs many years later for her children and grandchildren, she couldn't recall how they had received the information about the place of internment. But she remembered quite clearly that they met several hundred people there: wives and mothers of the incarcerated Jews as well as other relatives and passers-by. The protest meeting lasted from February 28 to March 11, and Helga and her mother went there several times. They saw Helga's father, Kurt Löwenthal, at the window of the building on Rosenstrasse that served as a provisional prison for the Jews living in "mixed marriages" who had been arrested during the so-called Fabrik-Aktion. During this roundup in Berlin and some other places of the remaining Jews who had not yet been deported because of their employment as forced laborers in armament factories, Jews living in mixed marriages had been separated from their Jewish colleagues without non-Jewish spouses. Helga remembered the protest as a spontaneous and nonviolent action: "While the detainees defiled at the windows of the house [Rosenstr. 2] we shouted on the street: 'Give us our husbands, our fathers back!'" In the beginning there were only policemen, but according to Helga Löwenthal on March 4 troops with machine guns appeared and threatened to dissolve the gathering by force. "This finally didn't happen, and the fact that Berlin's Gauleiter and Minister of Propaganda, Joseph Goebbels, ordered the release of the prisoners in the first instance seemed to us like a miracle."[1]

The interpretation of this "miracle" doesn't cease until today. For years now there has been a controversy among historians about whether the intermarried Jews imprisoned at Rosenstrasse were released due to the protest of their non-Jewish spouses or if the Nazis had in fact never intended to deport them.[2] Those who participated in the protest, and those incarcerated at and finally released from Rosenstrasse, too could only venture a guess whether the release was a result of the protest or not. They were given no official information, much less a reason for their release. Their eyewitness accounts about how many people gathered on Rosenstrasse differ considerably, as do the descriptions of the protest. The lack of unambiguous documents on decisions concerning the prisoners at Rosenstrasse in late February and early March 1943 leaves room for all kinds of interpretation and conjecture. Over time the controversy became more and more heated and it now tends to distract from the most important fact which nobody doubts: the amazing courage of the non-Jewish spouses who could not know what reactions their protest might provoke and which consequences it might have for them. Over the past thirty years the public commemoration of the Rosenstrasse event has become more and more important. Once a year, on February 27, there is a celebration on Rosenstrasse to honor the protest. In the relevant museums in Berlin, however, there is hardly a trace to be found about this unique event.

In my contribution to this volume, I want first to reflect on the way in which the Rosenstrasse protest is commemorated—and at the same time ignored—in Germany today. Second, I'll summarize the main arguments of the dispute and discuss them in a broader context of reactions of "ordinary Germans" to the persecution of the Jews, and third I will point out questions which have up to now remained unanswered and might stimulate further research.

The Commemoration of the Rosenstrasse Protest Today

Commemoration of the protest in Rosenstrasse did not start until the 1980s, more than forty years after the event, during the final phase of the German Democratic Republic.[3] In 1985 Heinz Knobloch was the first author in the German Democratic Republic (GDR) to mention the women's protest in his book about Mathilde Jakob, the secretary of Rosa Luxemburg. He asked why there was no memorial plaque, or better yet a memorial, on Rosenstrasse which was then located in the capital of the GDR.[4] At about the same time the artist Ingeborg Hunzinger, a communist and daughter of a Jewish mother, learned about the women's protest in February 1943 and started to campaign for a memorial on Rosenstrasse. Three years later, in 1988, she succeeded in getting an assignment to create a sculpture in commemoration of the women's civil disobedience. By the end of the 1980s the government of the GDR abandoned its hostile attitude toward the state of Israel and by this the Jewish community felt encouraged to act more publicly. In March 1992 students of the University for Applied Sciences temporarily installed a 1940s-style advertising column on Rosenstrasse on which they provided some information about the historical event of 1943. After one week, however, the column was removed. About a year later, on the fiftieth anniversary of the women's protest, the first large public commemoration took place. At that time very few people knew about the Rosenstrasse protest, as was pointed out in one of the speeches delivered at the commemoration: "Hardly any history book writes about it. Not even a commemoration plaque reminds us of this important act of civil disobedience."[5] A few months after recently unified Germany had been shaken by a racist pogrom in the city of Rostock and an arson attack committed by Neo-Nazis in Solingen which killed three members of a Turkish family and left several others seriously wounded, the commemoration of the women's protest as an example of courageous defense of a discriminated minority appeared more urgent than ever.

In October 1995 the sculpture by Hunzinger was finally inaugurated. Its inscription reads: "The power of civil disobedience and the power of love subjugate the dictatorship."[6]

Another three years later a commemoration plaque was installed at a hotel which had been erected in the place where once the administrative building of the Jewish community of Berlin stood which at the time of the protest had been utilized as a prison for the intermarried Jews. In her speech at the unveiling of the plaque, Rita Süßmuth, then president of the German Bundestag, warned of exclusion, anti-Semitism, and the violence of neo Nazi groups at present, and expressed her hope that the commemorative plaque would provide a stimulus for further remembrance. She not only praised the resistance of the women of Rosenstrasse, according to her still "hardly known in the larger public," but also claimed that their protest resulted in the release of their Jewish husbands. Furthermore, she pointed out that especially in the center district of Berlin many so-called ordinary people had resisted National Socialism and had protected the persecuted Jews. Süßmuth went on: "Despite all propaganda Hitler never achieved the same mass-following in Berlin that he had in other cities."[7] This seems more wishful thinking than a statement based on proven facts. But it points at the need to keep a positive image of the so-called ordinary people as being opposed to the evil high-ranking Nazis.

There are very few examples of heroic and collective action taken by non-Jews to defend the persecuted Jews. Thus, the history of German Jews during the Nazi era provides hardly any relief for German feelings of guilt. Out of the desire to emphasize (and perhaps overestimate) the few examples of protests, the ambiguous documentary evidence regarding the success of the women's protest is ignored in the public commemoration although it has been set forth several times. Of course, there is nothing wrong with praising the courage of the women who gathered on Rosenstrasse. But their protest was courageous regardless of whether it caused the release of their relatives or not. In recent years more and more people have participated in the annual commemorative meetings on February 27 organized by an association of the memorial sites in the Berlin area and several nongovernmental organizations in the field. Even the right-wing "Alternative for Germany" (Alternative für Deutschland—AfD) has joined other political parties in the celebration and has publicly demonstrated its support. This attempt to highlight one of the positive moments in German history can be seen as a part of the party's general effort to minimize the historical importance of the Nazi dictatorship and reduce it to, as one prominent AfD politician put it, a bit of "bird dropping" in German history—a history which on the whole is seen as magnificent and a matter of national pride. It also suggests that the ceremony has become subject to a competing commemoration policy. While the AfD is eager to be present in all public events that other parties take part, in, they didn't play a major role in this celebration. The main speech was held in 2018 as well as 2019 by Petra Pau, vice president of the German parliament and one of the leading politicians of the Left-wing party "Die Linke." She spoke out against anti-Semitism, the increasingly violent attacks on Jews and called for an active alliance of all democratic forces (which obviously did not include the AfD) against anti-Semitism and hostility toward other minorities.

In contrast to the eagerness to commemorate, there is extremely little information, if any, to be found in the relevant museums in Berlin. The Topography of Terror, a museum about the rule of the SS and Gestapo in Nazi Germany, once provided such information but doesn't do so today. This is also true for at the Memorial to the German Resistance. The latter presents several examples of individual acts of support for Jews in the permanent exhibition but doesn't even mention the Rosenstrasse. Visitors might come across some information if they read a book about resistance in the center of Berlin which is offered for free and provides eye-witness accounts and photos on eight of its more than 400 pages.[8] Hopefully, a soon to be launched new research project on women's resistance against National Socialism will fill this gap.

The increasing interest in public commemorations of the protest has left some visible results on Rosenstrasse itself but overall there is only limited documentation to be found in the public space and since Rosenstrasse is a tiny street it is unlikely that people who don't know about the history of the protest will chance upon it when walking through Berlin. In 1999 two advertising columns were installed which featured eye-witness accounts of men who had been imprisoned there in spring 1943, diary entries, deportation lists, and other documents of the perpetrators, as well as photos of Jewish life in Berlin in the 1920s and 1930s taken by the photographer Abraham Pisarek who in February 1943 was also held at the Rosenstrasse prison. Since 2016 an information board next to the sculpture of Ingeborg Hunzinger gives some details about the round-ups during the so-called Fabrik-Aktion and the protest on Rosenstrasse. For several years a small exhibition in the hotel where Süßmuth unveiled the plaque in 1998 provided some information about the history of the building once owned by the Jewish community and the protest of February 1943. But in 2019 with the renovation of the hotel the exhibition disappeared. This is just one example for a more general trend: while public commemoration increases and historic events like the Rosenstrasse are gaining importance in the context of politics of the past, the documentation of such events is decreasing. Actually, commemoration and documentation appear to be diverging more and more.

In 2002 the author Gernot Jochheim wrote about a "growing public recognition" of the women's protest which could be seen from the fact that there were theater plays as well as schoolbooks documenting the events of Rosenstrasse. Indeed, an analysis of schoolbooks published by the most important publishing houses in this field shows that the Rosenstrasse was first mentioned briefly in 1981[9] while high school students of the 1990s apparently didn't learn about the protest. From 2002 onwards at least some of the books deal with the Rosenstrasse either by quoting eye witness accounts or by giving at least brief information.[10] In the years 2010–11 there were three textbooks which not only provided information about the women's protest but also about the controversy among historians and asked the students to discuss the different positions.[11] One of these books, however, does no longer mention Rosenstrasse in its most recent edition.[12] The granddaughter of Helga Christoph, née Löwenthal, too, indicates that although the subject of Nazi rule in Germany played an important role in history lessons at her school, Rosenstrasse was never mentioned. She knew about the event only from her grandmother's memoirs and decided to interview her and write a paper to present in her history class.

For a long time, only a direct and militant confrontation with dictatorship aimed to fight the regime as such was regarded as resistance. For years, the Memorial to the German Resistance predominantly honored the German army officers who tried to assassinate Hitler on July 20, 1944. In the cold war years, the integration of communist resistance fighters such as the Rote Kapelle into the permanent exhibition was accepted only reluctantly. In the public perception of resistance very few individual women, if any, were recognized as playing an important role. The general image of the typical resistance fighter was an armed man. Decorative postcards showing young female Italian partisans proudly presenting their weapons were the proverbial exception which confirms the rule. Only very slowly the importance of women's role in organizing the infrastructure of resistance was recognized. The women of the Rosenstrasse still did not fit this picture. A public collective protest aimed not to alter Nazi policy in general, not to speak about ending the dictatorship, but to achieve a very concrete aim which was decisive for their personal fate and that of their families, was unique at least in Germany. Not least due to the fact that it were mostly women who shaped this protest, it took more than fifty years until such action was publicly recognized. Until today the protest obviously doesn't have a solid position in public commemoration.

A Dispute Among Historians

The information which is lacking in the public space is, however, available in several scholarly books on Rosenstrasse. The disagreements among historians briefly mentioned earlier about the interpretation of the "miracle" were openly discussed only from the early 2000s on and more vehemently after the motion picture "Rosenstrasse," directed by Margarethe von Trotta, reached a larger public and provoked some criticism. The debate has been conducted for several years and in a wide range of publications, in scholarly meetings, and online platforms which cannot be discussed here in detail. A comprehensive overview of the controversy with extensive information on literature is provided by Antonia Leugers who herself has weighed in on the debate.[13] In this chapter I can only summarize the main arguments.

In 1996 Nathan Stoltzfus was the first to dedicate an in-depth study to the "resistance of the heart" as the protest is referred to in the title of his book.[14] From the mid-1980s on he conducted sixty interviews, many of them with women who took part in the protest to release their Jewish husbands, with so-called Mischlinge, who protested on behalf of Jewish family members and with former prisoners from Rosenstrasse, including three who in a group of twenty-five had been deported to Auschwitz during the Fabrik-Aktion and returned after about twelve days. Furthermore, Stoltzfus interviewed some former Nazi officials. In his book Stoltzfus describes the general situation of the "intermarried," the pressures imposed on them, and tells about the lives of the protesters. In the vast majority of the approximately 35,000 intermarriages the wives were not Jewish. Due to their Jewish husbands the household was regarded as Jewish by the Nazi authorities. Compared to these couples, Jewish women married to an "Aryan" husband and thus regarded as living in "non-Jewish households," were sometimes better off: the Jewish wives were not obliged to wear the yellow star or to have their apartments registered as Jewish. A non-Jewish husband regarded as head of the household could protect his Jewish wife against persecution, while a non-Jewish woman married to a Jew became subject of discrimination because of the intermarriage.[15] Several of Stoltzfus' non-Jewish interviewees had experienced social exclusion, job loss, humiliation, and legal discrimination due to their intermarriages. One of them was even barred from seeing her daughter who grew up with the grandmother.[16] The fact that most of them refused divorce despite considerable social and administrative pressure to do so leads Stoltzfus to the conclusion that they saved the lives of their husbands who would have been immediately deported after a divorce or the death of the non-Jewish wife. Most of the Jews who survived Nazi Germany without going into hiding did so thanks to their non-Jewish spouses.

Stoltzfus raises a number of questions about how "ordinary Germans" reacted to the persecution of the Jews. According to him the protest was spontaneous and unorganized but fueled by years of discrimination that turned at least some formerly apolitical Germans into opponents of the Nazi regime while "Germans collectively were a powerful force, working mostly in favor of Nazism."[17] Leading Nazis were well aware of the fact that the power of the regime was based not only on terror but on a consent, a silent one at least, among German society. Thus, they were particularly sensitive to disagreement and protest. The delicate political situation in the beginning of 1943 also helped the protesters of Rosenstrasse. A few weeks after the German defeat in Stalingrad the Nazi regime didn't dare to brutally oppress the protest. Another factor which according to Stoltzfus contributed to the women's success was the fact that their protest was unarmed and only aimed at defending their families, not defeating the regime.[18]

Apart from such considerations and testimonies Stoltzfus bases his argument on several written documents among which the report of Gerhard Lehfeldt plays a prominent role. Lehfeldt, a lawyer who according to the Nazi laws was categorized as "half-Jew" had good connections among high-ranking Nazis. In March 1943 he wrote a report about the situation of the "Mischlinge" in Germany which reached leading circles of the Catholic Church. Lehfeldt writes that during the roundup which was later called Fabrik-Aktion, the Jews and "Mischlinge" imprisoned at Rosenstrasse had been released against the original intention, due to public protests. In order to disguise this defeat, leading Nazis such as Joseph Goebbels the Reichsminister for propaganda, later claimed that no deportation had been planned anyway—at least not at this point in time.[19] This view was confirmed by Goebbles deputy Leo Gutterer in an interview with Stoltzfus.[20]

A year after Stoltzfus, Nina Schröder published a book on the Rosenstrasse protest.[21] She too interviewed Jews who had been arrested in February 1943 and their relatives. Like Stoltzfus she didn't ask them only about the women's protest but also about their entire life stories and their experience as Jews or spouses of Jews living in "mixed marriages." Their accounts about what happened on Rosenstrasse in late February and early March 1943 differed in some aspects: some of them confirmed Stoltzfus' evaluation that in the difficult situation after Stalingrad the regime was afraid that the protest might spread due to the general dissatisfaction among the non-Jewish population, others assumed that the separation of the intermarried Jews from the others arrested during the Fabrik-Aktion indicates that the Nazi leaders were planning to treat them differently from the very beginning.[22] Sometimes the accounts even seemed to be contradictory: while Gad Beck, who had been imprisoned at Rosenstrasse, stressed that it was not the SS, but policemen who guarded the building during the protest,[23] Hans Oskar-Löwenstein de Witt, also a prisoner, whose mother was among the protesters, said that during the first days SS-men had mounted a machine gun in front of the building. After one of the women screamed at them that they should be ashamed of themselves and would do better to defend Germany's women and children on the Russian front, they allegedly dismantled the weapon.[24] In his more general assessment of the protest Löwenstein argues that the women would have run away if the police had threatened to otherwise shoot or deport their relatives.[25] The interviewees had no idea why the prisoners were released from Rosenstrasse.[26] Even though Schröder admits that "there is no definite proof that the release was a reaction to the demonstrations," in the preface of her book she nevertheless claims that the protesters liberated their relatives.[27]

The antithesis is put forth by Wolf Gruner, a historian who in 2005 published a book about the Rosenstrasse protest. In it he sets out to give a comprehensive reconstruction of the events of February 1943.[28] Based on a number of documents he also draws the conclusion that the protest was not the reason why the Jews were released from the Rosenstrasse prison but that their deportation had not been intended at that particular time.

There are several indications, Gruner argues, that from November 1942 on Nazi authorities intended to deport the remaining Jews from Germany to the death camps in the occupied Eastern territories, including even those working in the German armament industry. Nevertheless, according to the deportation guidelines issued on February 20, 1943, only the Jews who were still living in "mixed marriages" with non-Jewish spouses were to be excluded from deportation.[29] The centerpiece of Gruner's argument is a decree of the Gestapo of the city of Frankfurt (Oder) from February 24, 1943, stating that all Jews still working in the industry are to be arrested in order to be registered. This affected especially those Jews living in "mixed marriages." Their detention was not to attract any attention, and assaults were to be avoided, especially in public or at the workplace. But any impertinent behavior by Jews living in "mixed marriages" was to be punished by "taking them into custody and by making an application for their accommodation in a concentration camp." This decree could be interpreted quite freely, however, "the impression that this campaign aims to comprehensively solve the problem of mixed marriages must be avoided." If there was no reason for their detention, Jews living in "mixed marriages" were to be released to their homes; but on no account were they to return to the company where they had been working or to any other business. Further instructions regarding their treatment were pending.[30] Gruner reads the document as proof that the Jews with non-Jewish spouses were only to be registered but not deported—at least not for the time being, while Stoltzfus dismisses this interpretation hinting at the fact that the decree is a document of only regional importance. The dates of the two documents quoted by Gruner seem to contradict the assumption that the Gestapo claimed only in retrospect that their intention had always been to release the prisoners.

According to another interpretation, the Jews married to non-Jewish spouses might have been imprisoned for several days or even weeks because the Gestapo expected an imminent decree to deport them. According to the deportation guidelines of February 20, 1943, they were explicitly only temporarily exempted from deportation while the general aim to make Germany "free of Jews" had been pointed out several times. Thus, the detention of the intermarried Jews at Rosenstrasse, separate from the other Jewish forced laborers, might also have been intended to gauge the reactions of the non-Jews, relatives or not. In this case the women's protest would indeed have been decisive.[31]

If the Jews living in "mixed marriages" were only to be registered but not deported why were they kept in the Rosenstrasse prison for several days or even weeks instead of being released at once? The historian Beate Meyer, author of a seminal study on Jewish "Mischlinge," has examined the process of registration in an article published in 2002.[32] She analyzed the testimonies of 235 German Jews who in 1963 were living in East Berlin or in Eastern Germany and had been asked by the authorities of the GDR about the persecution during the Nazi era. Of those witnesses who explicitly talked about the reason for the release, sixteen assumed that this happened because they had non-Jewish relatives while six saw the protest as a cause.[33] According to Meyer, the Jews living in "mixed marriages" were separated from the other detainees immediately after their arrest and brought to Rosenstrasse where their marital status was checked. Those who could easily prove that they were living with their non-Jewish wives (or husbands) were released at once. Some were not even arrested at all but only registered. Others were kept up to five weeks in detention in order to check if their spouses had died or divorced them. Some of the non-Jewish spouses were located by the Gestapo and urged to divorce their Jewish husbands. Only after their marital status had been confirmed and attempts of pressuring the wives into divorce had failed were the Jewish husbands released. Meyer concludes that the release of the Jews living in "mixed marriage" was not a result of the women's protest in Rosenstrasse but had been intended anyway.[34]

Gruner gives another explanation why the Jews were only released from their imprisonment gradually. According to him the 2,000 Jews incarcerated at Rosenstrasse were not to return to the armament factories because they were regarded as a security risk there. Instead they were envisaged to replace several hundred employees of the Jewish community who were not protected by a non-Jewish spouse and thus were to be deported. The discrepancy of numbers he explains as follows: "The internment of 2000 men in Rosenstrasse was the most effective way to recruit several hundred persons suitable for working in Jewish institutions, many experts among them."[35] But if in the critical situation after Stalingrad the Gestapo was so eager not to create the impression that their campaign "aims to solve the problem of mixed marriages comprehensively" why did they register and check the marital status of the intermarried Jews at this very moment?

Historians on both sides of the controversy at least agree on the fact that the deportation of the "Mischlinge" and intermarried Jews was intended for the near future. Goebbels had already been insisting on making Berlin "free of Jews" for quite a while. On March 2, 1943, a few days after the Fabrik-Aktion, he stressed: "We will now get the Jews out of Berlin definitely and expel them to the East in the shortest possible time." News of the roundup had leaked into the general public and many Jews had managed to escape. Nevertheless Goebbels went on in his diary he would not rest until the capital was completely "free of Jews."[36] Only a few days later, on March 6, 1943, he insinuated that it was the Security Service's lack of political instinct that led them to arrest the Jews in such a delicate political situation. It would have been better to have waited for a few weeks. "Then we can do it even more rigorously." On 11 March Goebbels claimed that the arrest of intermarried Jews had led to some disagreement "which caused anxiety and confusion."[37]

While the intentions of the regime are not clear there is, however, a consensus that a considerable amount of courage was needed to publicly request the release of incarcerated Jews and that the relatives who gathered on Rosenstrasse could not have known how the Nazi regime would react. Beside this remarkable fact, one must take into consideration that most of the relatives had been urged to divorce their Jewish spouses, many of them had lost their job and/or social standing, or had to do forced labor, they were excluded from large parts of the non-Jewish society and had to endure the disdain of "Aryan" neighbors or even family members. Nevertheless, they had resisted this pressure for many years, despite the strain it undoubtedly put on their relationship to their partners. As Mary Fulbrook has pointed out, people living in "mixed marriages," who had closer connections to non-Jewish Germans than Jews without "Aryan" relatives, observed what is called the "suicide of a nation": the loss of any kind of empathy for the victims of persecution.[38] At the beginning of the Nazi era some non-Jewish Germans might have disagreed with the persecution of the Jews, but they soon learned not to intervene and gradually became used to remaining silent. This, however, caused a feeling of humiliation in the bystander, who subsequently defended his or her conversion as allegedly voluntary, in order not to have to question it. Thus, the environment in which intermarried couples had to live became more and more hostile. The resistance to this hostility might have been no less courageous than taking part in the protest on Rosenstrasse.

Remaining Questions in the Historiography of the Rosenstrasse Protest

Even those historians who share the view that the protest was not the reason for the release from Rosenstrasse disagree about some crucial aspects. There are various other controversial topics such as the number of protesters. Was it just a handful of non-Jews or several hundred or even 6,000 as Ruth Andreas-Friedrich wrote in her diary?[39] Did the women shout to demand the release of their husbands or not? Were there soldiers in uniform who took part in the protest and who might have protected the women?

Were there police or SS-men who threatened the women in front of the building? Was the protest organized and if so by whom? If it was spontaneous, as Helga Christoph, née Löwenthal, remembered it, how did the relatives know about the imprisonment on Rosenstrasse?

Definite proof to answer these questions is lacking. Some of the differences in accounts of eye-witnesses might be caused by the fact that people gathered in front of the building of the Jewish community on Rosenstrasse over several days. Throughout this time span the situation might have changed with regards to the vigor of the protest, the number of protesters and the presence of soldiers, SS, or policemen.

The Nazi policy regarding "mixed marriages" was contradictory. There appear to have been different factions, such as Gestapo, Goebbels, the Reichs Security Main Office, and the Wirtschaftsverwaltungshauptamt, who differed in their ideas about how to deal and what to do with couples in "mixed marriages." There is a possibility that even when the Fabrik-Aktion started, none of these factions could be sure that they would be able to enforce their plans. Why did the Gestapo order that Jews living in "mixed marriages" should at least temporarily be arrested and not return to their former workplace? If they were regarded as a security risk while working in the armament factories, why did this aspect come up only in February 1943? If the intermarried Jews and "Mischlinge" were detained in order to replace the so-called full Jews still working in the Jewish institutions, why did the Gestapo arrest so many of them while only a few hundred were to be replaced? An investigation into how the Jews released from Rosenstrasse were finally employed might give an indication of the reasons why they were arrested and reveal if their subsequent employment followed a pre-arranged plan. Focusing on such questions which are still not definitively answered—and at least some of them probably never will be—and pointing out what still has to be researched in more detail will help to move the discussion away from the unproductive dispute about the effectiveness of the protest and open up more interesting lines of enquiry. This makes all the more sense in times when commemoration is increasingly aligned with the Politics of the Past and tends to ignore historical facts.

Notes

1. Lebenserinnerungen notiert von Helga Christoph, geborene Helga Löwenthal, über eine ereignisreiche und schwere Lebenszeit [memoirs of Helga Christoph, née Löwenthal, about an eventful and difficult life time]; typoscript in private property, copy in possession of the author of this article. In her memoirs Helga Christoph wrote that soldiers had appeared with machine guns. When interviewed by her granddaughter in autumn 2018, she corrected herself by speaking about SS-men. She wasn't present at Rosenstrasse on this day but remembered that the women had been threatened with the violent dissolution of the protest already during the first days when she and her mother attended; Leah Hermsdorf, Vergleich einer Zeitzeugenbefragung mit entsprechender Literatur am Beispiel des Protests in der Berliner Rosenstrasse im Jahr 1943, 2.11.2018.

2. Beate Meyer, "Die Inhaftierung der, jüdisch Versippten' in der Berliner Rosenstrasse im Spiegel staatsanwaltlicher Zeugenvernehmungen in der DDR," *Jahrbuch für*

Antisemitismusforschung 11 (2002): 178–97. Jana Leichsenring, *Frauen im Widerstand* (Münster: Lit Verlag, 2003). Antonia Leugers, *Berlin, Rosenstrasse 2–4. Protest in der NS-Diktatur. Neue Forschungen zum Frauenprotest in der Rosenstrasse 1943* (Annweiler: Plöger, 2005). Wolf Gruner, *Widerstand in der Rosenstrasse. Die Fabrik-Aktion und die Verfolgung der "Mischehen" 1943* (Frankfurt a. M.: Fischer Taschenbuch Verlag, 2005).

3. The following paragraph is based on the book of Gernot Jochheim, *Frauenprotest in der Rosenstrasse Berlin 1943. Berichte, Dokumente, Hintergründe* (Berlin: Hentrich & Hentrich 2002), 84–6.

4. Heinz Knobloch, *Meine liebste Mathilde: Geschichte—zum Berühren* (Berlin: Buchverlag Der Morgen, 2002), 274.

5. Jochheim, *Frauenprotest*, 89.

6. Ibid., 93.

7. Quoted in ibid., 97 f.

8. Hans-Peter Sandvoß, *Widerstand in Mitte und Tiergarten* (Berlin: Gedenkstätte deutscher Widerstand, 1999), 320–8.

9. Etienne Schinkel Holocaust and Vernichtungskrieg, *Die Darstellung der deutschen Gesellschaft und Wehrmacht in Geschichtsschulbüchern für die Sekundarstufe I und II* (Göttingen: V&R unipress, 2017), 206.

10. Ibid., 287–9.

11. Ibid., 358–60.

12. Björn Onken, ed., *Das waren Zeiten—Berlin/Brandenburg. Unterrichtswerk für Geschichte, Band 2 für die Jahrgangsstufen 9 und 10* (Bamberg: C.C. Buchner, 2017).

13. Antonia Leugers, "Widerstand gegen die Rosenstrasse. Kritische Anmerkungen zu einer Neuerscheinung von Wolf Gruner," *theologie.geschichte* 1 (2006): 131–205.

14. Nathan Stoltzfus, *Resistance of the Heart: Intermarriage and the Rosenstrasse Protest in Nazi Germany* (New York, London: W.W. Norton & Company, 1996).

15. Nathan Stoltzfus, "Der ,Versuch in Wahrheit zu leben' und die Rettung von jüdischen Angehörigen durch deutsche Frauen im 'Dritten Reich,'" in *Frauen im Widerstand*, ed. Jana Leichsenring (Münster: Lit Verlag, 2003), 74–88, here p. 80.

16. Stoltzfus, *Resistance*, 55 f.

17. Ibid., 279.

18. Stoltzfus, "Versuch," 84.

19. The report is printed—as are the most important documents the discussion relies on—in Leugers, *Berlin, Rosenstrasse 2–4*, 233–8. See also Stoltzfus, *Resistance*, 203–5.

20. Stoltzfus, *Resistance*, 244.

21. Nina Schröder, *Hitlers unbeugsame Gegnerinnen. Der Frauenaufstand in der Rosenstrasse* (München: Wilhelm Heyne Verlag, 1997).

22. Ibid., 84, 151–3.

23. Ibid., 151.

24. Ibid., 213.

25. Ibid., 219 f.

26. Ibid., 84, 219.

27. Ibid., 9, 38.

28. Gruner, *Widerstand*.

29. Ibid., 51.

30. Ibid., 53 f.

31. Joachim Neander, Die Rosenstrasse von außen gesehen—Wechsel der Perspektiven, in *Berlin, Rosenstrasse 2–4,* 163–202, here: 179–88.

32. Meyer, "Inhaftierung der 'jüdisch Versippten.'"

33. Ibid., 194.

34. Ibid., 189.

35. Gruner, *Widerstand*, 121.

36. Elke Fröhlich, ed., *Die Tagebücher von Joseph Goebbels,* part 2: *Diktate 1941-1945,* vol. 7 *Januar—März 1943,* (Munich: Saur, 1993), 449 (entry March 2, 1943).

37. Ibid., 487 (entry March 6, 1943), 528 (entry March 11, 1943).

38. Mary Fulbrook, *Bystanders to Nazi Violence? The Transformation of German Society in the 1930s.* (Jerusalem: Yad Vashem publications, 2018), 36. Froukje Demant, "The Many Shades of Bystanding: On Social Dilemmas and Passive Participation," in *Probing the Limits of Categorization. The Bystander in Holocaust History*, ed. Christina Morina and Krijn Thijs (New York and Oxford: Berghahn, 2019), 90–106.

39. Ruth Andreas-Friedrich, *Der Schattenmann. Tagebuchaufzeichnungen 1938-1945* (Berlin: Suhrkamp, 1947), 109 (entry: March 7, 1942).

CHAPTER 6
RESCUE THROUGH INTERVENTION IN THE NAZI DECISION-MAKING PROCESS
PROTEST IN GOEBBELS'S BERLIN
Chris Osmar and Nathan Stoltzfus

In February and March 1943 "Aryan" spouses of Jews rounded up in Berlin demonstrated on Rosenstrasse before the Jewish welfare office where their family members had been collected. Despite efforts to disperse them, the protests continued, day after day, until the Rosenstrasse detainees were released. To date, consideration of the significance of the Rosenstrasse protests has centered on the question of whether the protesters effected the release of their partners or, alternately, if the Nazi regime had never intended to deport Berlin's intermarried Jews in the first place and had not told this to the week-long gathering of hundreds of women protesting on behalf of Jews in order to disperse them. This dispute cannot be adjudicated without an investigation of how the regime made decisions about intermarried Jews. Though the delicate political problem of deporting intermarried Jews had previously been deferred, in the critical moment of early 1943 a variety of the Reich's power centers aligned in an effort to move ahead with removal. The dynamics of this process reveal how the regime managed difficult cases that could damage the cult of Hitler as it worked toward its historic mission to clear the Reich of Jews.

The regime's approach to mixed marriages underwent an iterative process, evolving through formal and informal negotiations between parties with a stake in the issue. This process continued up to and through the February 1943 deportation operation in Berlin, which would see the apprehension of 2,000 intermarried Jews in Berlin, with interested state agencies still working out the precise scale, scope, and destination of the action just days before. Nazi ideology required every trace of Jewish blood to disappear from the Reich, and Himmler's aims for the Elimination of Jews from the Reich territory coincided with Goebbels's intentions to declare Berlin *Judenfrei*, removing as many intermarried Jews as possible who wore the star by March 1943. A telegram of March 2, 1943, on the fourth day of the arrests and protests, from the SS Main Economic and Administrative Office (WVHA) shows that the concentration camp apparatus, too, was counting on the inclusion of intermarried Jews in the contingent of Jewish workers they were receiving from Berlin at that time.

In late winter 1943, with the crucible of the encirclement and destruction of the German 6th Army at Stalingrad, the Third Reich experienced a liminal moment. The crisis at the front shattered the notion of the inevitability of German victory, opening the way for significant change in the Nazi regime's war effort and way of rule. The exact contours of this impending transformation had not yet been worked out, but all the same it was fertile ground for radicalization. Hitler had previously determined that the final removal of Jews from Germany would have to wait until the war in the East had concluded, and although Germany had lost that battle for the moment, the intention thereafter was to proceed with clearing Berlin of Jews in early 1943, within the fluid environment that followed the Stalingrad defeat.

Joseph Goebbels, Reich Propaganda Minister, Gauleiter of Berlin and chairman of the national Air Raid Damage Committee as of January 15, 1943, was one of the central personalities vying to impose his vision of National Socialism on the German nation during this period of uncertainty. In the wake of the Stalingrad debacle, and drawing on ideas of leadership developed during the period prior to Hitler's seizure of power, he sought to mobilize Germany for total war on a wave of enthusiastic public support. He further imagined that he might win de facto control of domestic policy for himself by demonstrating that the people were behind him and his plan, outmaneuvering his more bureaucratic-minded rivals. Berlin, as Goebbels's personal satrapy, was to serve as the centerpiece for this effort—evidence of the effectiveness of his approach and a model to be emulated in the rest of the Reich. The removal of Jews from Berlin, in turn, was an integral part of Goebbels's project to transform the capital into an example of a National Socialist Volk in action. In his mind, ridding Berlin of Jews would eliminate a potential "fifth column" of sedition, which both endangered racial purity and, he feared, might attempt an insurrection in league with foreign workers. He had secured Hitler's blessing that Berlin should be the first German city to be entirely free of Jews in September 1942 as well and his authorization on December 6, 1942 to remove Berlin's "nonprivileged" full Jews.

The political boost that Goebbels hoped to gain from freeing Berlin of its Jews was predicated on the successful and seamless conduct of the deportation action. The operation went afoul from the outset, however, when protests began to develop the first day of the arrests and, according to a well-cited portion of Goebbels diary, some 4,000 Berlin Jews, tipped off by their employers, went underground prior to the roundup.[1] On the third day of the massive arrests, Berlin experienced its heaviest bombing to date, which by itself jeopardized Goebbels's position by threatening to undermine support for total war. When the Rosenstrasse protests continued despite efforts to disperse them, visibly contradicting Goebbels's pretention that the people of Berlin were prepared to follow him in lockstep to total war, he finally intervened and ordered a cessation to the operation.

Negotiating the Fate of Jews in Mixed Marriages

Just prior to the National Socialist seizure of power, nearly half of all newly married Germans of Jewish heritage were taking non-Jewish spouses. Though the Nazi Party had been demanding an end to the rapidly growing number of unions between Jews and

"Aryans" since the 1920s, there were some 35,000 intermarried couples in Germany when Hitler came to power in early 1933. Thereafter Nazi propaganda and social pressures quickly reduced the proportion of Jews who married out to non-Jews by two-thirds.[2] Further, the Law for the Restoration of the Civil Service of April 7, 1933, identified Jews as anyone with one or more Jewish grandparent and ousted Jews working at all levels of the German government.[3] Still, intermarriage remained legal up until the institution of the Law for the Protection of German Blood and German Honor in September 1935. These Nuremberg Laws, however, did not dissolve existing mixed marriages despite the efforts of party ideologues, who also wanted the law to count intermarried gentiles as Jews themselves.[4] Instead, sexual intercourse between German gentiles and Jews, not excluding those in intermarriage, was prohibited by law under pain of death.[5] Reich leaders surmised that existing intermarriages would dissolve under such a mounting burden of adversities, whether stemming from propaganda and the Gestapo or from neighbors and colleagues. Nonetheless, the vast majority of these couples defied the regime from the beginning, where its fundamental ideology of race threatened their personal lives.

The regime took numerous legal measures to discourage mixed marriages. A June 30, 1933, law barred anyone married to a Jew from taking a position in the civil service. Intermarried gentiles hired before 1933 were not discharged from government employment until 1937, but they were denied eligibility for promotions in June 1934.[6] In December 1935 intermarried gentiles were prohibited to display or salute the national flag.[7] Gentiles who divorced their Jewish partners were promised an immediate return to Hitler's heroic "racial" community without further disadvantages, in accordance with regulations Hermann Göring had proposed to Hitler for his signature in December 1938. Göring, who had recently fallen into disfavor with Hitler for pushing peace rather than military aggression at the Munich Conference of October 1938, saw to it that both partners in an intermarriage would be "treated as Jews as soon as the heightened emigration is put into effect."[8]

Only a small fraction of the intermarried couples succumbed to the pressure to divorce, leaving the leadership of the Third Reich to wrestle over how to handle this politically and ideologically troublesome population. In an effort to simplify the problem, two categories of intermarriages were established in April 1939. Those marriages which had produced children not considered to be Jews, or in which the Jewish partner was a woman, enjoyed "privileged" status while the remainder were relegated to the "unprivileged" category.[9] The severe consequences of this differentiation became apparent when the law of April 30, 1939, concerning Jewish tenants, required only "nonprivileged" intermarried couples to move into "Jewish Houses." Non-Jewish partners in intermarriages who were not privileged were required to divorce or move with their partner. Jews in privileged intermarriages were also exempted from the September 1, 1941, "Star" decree. Joseph Goebbels, ever conscious of maintaining the image of his fiefdom as a model for the rest of the country, had introduced an initiative to mark Jews in Berlin with badges the previous spring, but the "Star" decree made this a national policy. The "Star" decree also refined the categories of privilege, exempting Jews in already privileged marriages from wearing the star and extending privilege to Jewish parents of a Mischling child even if death or divorce brought the marriage to an end.[10]

The introduction of the star badge in the Reich was a necessary prerequisite for the deportation and murder of German Jews, a process that began in the fall of 1941. While neither Jews in privileged nor unprivileged marriages were initially included in the deportations, authorities within the Reich Security Main Office (RSHA) certainly wanted to remove intermarried Jews from Germany as well and began exploring approaches that might achieve this goal. The main sticking point, which persisted throughout subsequent maneuvering on the intermarriage question, was how to deal with the "Aryan" spouse. Participants at an RSHA conference convened by Reinhard Heydrich on October 10, 1941, determined that the proper course would be to pressure the "Aryan" half of mixed marriages to divorce and simply deport both partners if they refused.[11] Nonetheless, Heydrich recognized that pursuit of his genocidal project required assent from other interest groups within the Reich in order to be successful. To secure this support, Heydrich on January 20, 1942, brought together fifteen representatives from an array of agencies at a villa on the Wannsee in Berlin. According to meeting minutes, discussion of intermarried Jews consumed nearly half of the Wannsee Conference, and produced general agreement that such Jews should be deported regardless of privilege. At this point Wilhelm Stuckart of the Interior Ministry interjected that existing mixed marriages would have to be dissolved before proceeding, as efforts by "Aryans" to legally end their marriage after the deportation and the murder of their spouses would prompt uncomfortable questions which might jeopardize the secrecy of the entire endeavor.[12]

When the Wannsee Conference participants convened once again on March 6, 1942, to revisit these issues they were joined by a representative from the Propaganda Ministry, which had not previously been involved. The Propaganda Ministry opposed Stuckart's blanket forced dissolution of mixed marriages, arguing that such a measure would incite opposition from the Vatican, and in any case the Germans who had their marriages invalidated against their will would not separate but go to the courts. In order to placate the Propaganda Ministry, the proposal was modified so that "Aryan" spouses could apply for a divorce that would automatically be approved by the courts. If the "Aryan" declined to take this step, a public prosecutor could initiate a divorce petition unilaterally with the guarantee that the courts would grant it. While this adjustment may have placated the Propaganda Ministry, its encroachment into the autonomy of the Justice Ministry produced a backlash. In an April 8 letter to this latest conference's cohort, Justice Ministry State Secretary Franz Schlegelberger expressed his approval for easing the divorce process but opposed any measure that would end a marriage against the will of the "Aryan" spouse "since the couples will be separated anyway by the deportation of the Jewish partner." He was skeptical that this would work, however, since persons married a long time would be expected to stay together regardless of whether the state declared their marriages annulled.[13]

True to the Nazi decision-making style of allowing regional leaders to solve the challenging problems without directives from Berlin, some districts forcibly annulled local intermarriages. Still, the question of how to separate intermarried couples without compromising secrecy languished through the spring and summer of 1942, only to resurface once again in the fall as preparation to clear all Jews from Germany moved from the theoretical to the operational. On September 9, 1942, Goebbels reported a briefing from Gerhard Schach of the Berlin Gau offices that there were still 46,000 Jews in Berlin, which included Jews in intermarriages.[14] In early October 1942, as his mind turned to how he would deal with Berlin's intermarried Jews, Goebbels called the exemptions the regime had made for partners of intermarriages a "social evil" (*übelstand*). Persons married to Jews did not serve in the war itself, a concession in the fourth year of the war that they would "welcome as a ticket to a more comfortable life."[15]

On September 22, Goebbels received a letter from Bormann stating that the Jews in privileged intermarriages—those with children baptized as Christians or in which the Jewish partner was the wife—must also be made to wear the star and be included in the deportations. Goebbels agreed, but Hitler did not. On November 5, 1942, Reichsführer SS and Chief of Police Heinrich Himmler issued a decree for the "Elimination of Jews from Reich Territory" by which "half-Jews" (Mischlinge) were to be removed from Reich territory, which meant that all "full" Jews including those in intermarriages would go too. On February 27, 1943, Himmler's RSHA unleashed arrests it called the Elimination of Jews from Reich Territories Actions, which in Berlin led to the arrest of intermarried Jews and the Rosenstrasse Protest.[16]

Goebbels, who had been agitating to remove Jews from Berlin for years, made no effort to conceal his conviction that he would soon be able to realize this goal. He took the issue of the remaining Berlin Jews to Hitler on October 4, 1942. Hitler approved of a mass deportation action in Berlin so long as Goebbels cooperated with Speer to ensure there were no production disruptions. On the issue of mixed marriages, Hitler would not hear of Goebbels's interest in ordering Jews in nonprivileged intermarriages to wear the star just like those in nonprivileged marriages, saying they would be dealt with later. He expressed his desire that "first . . . we should get the pure Jews who have nothing more to do with Aryan Volksgenossen out of Berlin." Goebbels, however, floated a suggestion on how to severe these ties between Germans and Jews so that deportations of intermarried Jews could go forward: "Aryan" spouses could be drafted into Organization Todt and sent to work on the eastern front. Hitler agreed, and instructed Goebbels to draw up a proposal.[17]

Nevertheless, plans remained fluid. A third major "Final Solution" conference, staged by the RSHA on October 27, 1942, instead opted to go forward with the plan to compel divorce. According to Otto Hünsche, Eichmann's deputy and a participant at the conference, the meeting also produced an agreement that intermarriages would be legally annulled, and that all intermarried Jews, as well as intermarried half-Jews who wore the star, should be deported regardless of privilege status.[18] This two-part plan is reflected in Goebbels diary for December 6, 1942, when he discussed it with Hitler. He rejected the proposal for annulling mixed marriages, and then reported that Hitler had commissioned him to "push out the unprivileged full Jews from Germany."[19]

A new proposal for the liquidation of Jewish marriages was presented to me. . . . It would bring about so much unrest and confusion in public opinion that at least at the moment the affair is not worth it. In addition the Führer commissioned me to first ensure that the unprivileged full Jews are removed from Germany. Once they are all gone we can approach the remnants of the Jewish problem that still remain.

Goebbels's use of the word "privileged" at this point indicates that he wanted to deport all Jews wearing the star—including those full Jews in intermarriage who lived in "nonprivileged intermarriages." [20]

Two weeks later the Catholic Church caught wind of the plan for compulsory divorce and, as Goebbels had predicted, registered their disapproval. In an November 11 letter to Wilhelm Frick of the Ministry of the Interior and the new Minister of Justice Otto Thierack, Cardinal Adolf Bertram expressed the Church's opposition to such an assault on the sacrament of marriage.[21] This complaint was not by itself sufficient to alter the trajectory of the unfolding movements against intermarried Jews. The Ministry of Justice, already hesitant to abrogate its authority on the issue of divorce, dithered on its position for over a month before Thierack finally wrote to Eichmann's office to inform him

I have no reservations on the prospective measures to be taken. As soon as the fundamental decision of the Führer is procured, I intend to propose the adoption of a regulation to the Council of Ministers for the Defense of the Reich through which the question of the separation of racially mixed marriages will be settled in accordance with the outcome of the conferences.[22]

Though he certainly did not disagree with the effort to remove Jews from Germany, Goebbels favored gradual escalation and caution, moving against Jews in unprivileged marriages first, so as to maintain the support of the people. As the reality of the impending deportation action seeped into his own sphere of authority he would become even more concerned and involved.

Goebbels's Leadership of a Model Berlin

By late winter of 1943 Hitler, consumed by the operational aspects of the war in the East, had largely withdrawn from domestic politics. A so-called Committee of Three made up of Martin Bormann, Wilhelm Keitel, and Hans Lammers would attempt to capitalize on this vacuum to exert their own influence. Bormann maintained control of Hitler's appointments as well as access to the Leader, while Lammers oversaw the Cabinet, which began meeting in Hitler's absence in January 1943. For the faction of party leadership straining to intensify Germany's wartime economy, the Committee of Three represented a significant obstacle.[23] Goebbels, in particular, chaffed at the leadership style of Bormann and Lammers. He felt that their rule through party and state administration was not radical enough to meet the moment, that they had lost touch with the German people. The leadership model that Goebbels favored in early

1943 was one rooted in the *Kampfzeit*, the period before the Nazi Party seized all of the instruments of the state, when the Party drew its strength from its ability to mobilize throngs of supporters. The drive for total war, precipitated by the military collapse in the East, offered Goebbels an arena to prove the effectiveness of his leadership approach while also significantly expanding his influence over the German economy and the day-to-day lives of the German people. He aimed to achieve this goal by forging new alliances and, above all, by demonstrating that the Volk enthusiastically supported his position. He would lead Berlin into total war and, he hoped, the rest of Germany would follow, but as a consequence Goebbels was particularly vulnerable to any appearance of dissent or unrest in Berlin.

Goebbels's first opportunity to demonstrate the strength of his leadership during crisis came in late January, as the Party glitterati gathered in Berlin for a three-day celebration of the tenth anniversary of Hitler's ascension to power. Though Hitler would not himself attend the event, he did issue a proclamation for the occasion and charged Goebbels with reading it out to a crowd of Berliners at the grandiose Sportpalast arena. Goebbels regarded the whole affair as a plebiscite of sorts. "We want to gauge the reaction of the broader Volk for the first time in a long time,"[24] he reflected. "I am now undertaking a psychological propagandistic maneuver that, under the circumstances, will set Germany on a determined struggle of unprecedented strength."[25] Goebbels, aware of the morale effects of the air war, had been rightly concerned that the Royal Air Force might try to disrupt the tenth anniversary celebration.[26] Embarrassingly, the appearance of three British Mosquito aircraft in the skies over Berlin prompted Hermann Göring to delay his speech for an hour. More conscious of appearances, Goebbels went ahead with his reading of Hitler's proclamation despite a second British nuisance raid. "From outside the din of flak penetrates into the Sportpalast," he remembered, "The air alarm is naturally heard from all sides; but no man rises from his seat or gives even the slightest sign of unrest or nervousness. Of course, this makes an enormous impression especially on the foreign journalists."[27] Once he began to speak, the crowd rallied to him enthusiastically. Overjoyed, Goebbels praised their behavior, writing "the Berliners behaved quite politically in the Sportpalast and made a great contribution to the interests of the Reich in the current situation."[28] Goebbels emerged from the celebration, with the people behind him, poised to advance his total war agenda and his personal influence.

Following the conclusion of the festivities, Goebbels set to work cajoling Reich authorities into implementing his radical total war measures, in particular raising a levy of women for armaments work and dramatically reducing nonessential sectors of the economy and state administration. Towards this end, he determined to offer Berlin, the Reich capital and seat of his own authority, as a model for emulation ahead of a greater propagandistic push for total war in mid-February. "I am going to proceed rather radically here," he wrote, "because I have a mind to create an example in Berlin for the other Gaue. I will then announce the measures that I have taken in a Sportpalast speech to the public."[29] He had already met with Ludwig Steeg, the City President of Berlin, on January 29 to secure his commitment to streamline city administration and support the total war effort over the course of three months, promising in exchange to furnish him with an allotment of women newly drafted for work.[30] On February 2 he sat down with a contingent of the city's elite in order to feel them out on the question of compelling women to work. While they did not come to any conclusion on the labor question, they resolved to move forward with the shuttering of bars and luxury shops.[31] This initiative, however, put him at odds with Göring, who sought to bring Berlin's gourmet Horcher restaurant under his personal protection.

Goebbels had anticipated that he might face opposition to his efforts to transform Berlin, but he clung to the conviction that such resistance could only be overcome by fostering the image that the people themselves demanded radical action. Still, this was not the only course available to him. During a February 1 phone conversation with Sepp Dietrich, the commander of the elite *Leibstandarte SS Adolf Hitler*, Dietrich had offered to detach a company from his now sizable *Leibstandarte*, which maintained its headquarters in Berlin, so that Goebbels could use them to cut through resistance with "brute force." Goebbels declined, opining that "in view of the current situation, [force] is not exactly the appropriate means of asserting oneself."[32] All the same, Dietrich's personal support remained a potent arrow in Goebbels's quiver, and one that he would draw during the Final Roundup in Berlin. Goebbels certainly did not dismiss the potential of forceful action, but in early February 1943 he was staking his total war project on the people moving the instruments of the state rather than the other way around. The way in which he endeavored to resolve the conflict with Göring over the Horcher restaurant is a better indicator of his modus operandi. At his instigation, a crowd descended on the restaurant, demonstrating and breaking windows and precipitating its closure to the public—though it would continue to operate within the context of total war as a private Luftwaffe club.[33]

At a two-day Gauleiter conference on February 5–6, and at a subsequent reception at Hitler's eastern headquarters in Rastenburg the following day, Goebbels succeeded in extending his support beyond Berlin. In a conversation with Speer, Hitler expressed his admiration for Goebbels's initiative, which the Berlin Gauleiter interpreted as encouragement to redouble his efforts. Hitler further endorsed Goebbels's position in an address to the assembled Gauleiters, even weighing in on the spat between Goebbels and Göring by referencing Horcher by name.[34] In his speech, Hitler also broached the topic of the Final Solution, indicating that the elimination of Jews from Europe was critical for the war effort and, reiterating a decision from the previous September, declaring that Berlin should the first German city to become free of Jews. Goebbels, encouraged by Hitler's embrace of Berlin as a model Gau, boasted in his diary afterwards that "the ruthlessness that he recommends to all Gauleitern in the face of Jewry is already a political imperative in Berlin."[35] At the conclusion of the evening Hitler sealed the impression of his wholehearted support for Goebbels by receiving him alone.

Though Goebbels emerged from the Wolf's Lair on February 7 with Hitler behind him, after Hitler once again retreated into seclusion the Committee of Three reasserted its power of obstruction, prompting Goebbels to opine that "today there is no doubt that the Volk are much more radical than their current leadership." He determined, in a February 12 meeting with Speer and Robert Ley, that he could counteract this by staging a mass rally in the Sportpalast, where he might demonstrate to the Party leadership how wholeheartedly the people stood behind the total war effort. He was confident that Hitler would approve the initiative, given his embrace of the "optics of the war in Berlin," though the effort depended on Ley and Speer penetrating the shell that Bormann and Lammers had built around the Leader.[36] Goebbels's Speech in the Sportpalast was intended as a coup de grace to the Committee of Three, an opportunity for the people of Berlin to catapult him to the very top of the Reich's power structure. "More and more," he wrote, "I am recognized as the spiritual rector of this whole movement," asserting further along that "the Reich capital city is well on its way to making up for what it did wrong in the last war."[37]

In stage-managing the total war rollout in Berlin, Goebbels also took into account the optics of the continued presence of Jews in his domain. He was well aware that a major deportation action would soon take place in Berlin. In fact, he already had operational knowledge of the date, timetable, scope, and procedure of the impending action before delivering his total war speech. Goebbels hoped that purging Berlin of its Jews would bring "a great relief in the psychological situation" and thereby advance his goal of mobilizing fanatical support for total war among the people of Berlin.[38]

When it finally came, Goebbels's Sportpalast speech was a resounding success. Radio broadcast of the event projected the roar of the masses, speaking in one voice in response to Goebbels's ten questions. Riding this wave of support, Goebbels and Speer would set a plan in motion to restructure domestic political decision-making and decisively circumvent the Committee of Three. Goebbels hoped that Hitler would endorse his bid for domestic leadership because, to all appearances, the people were already following him. The final roundup of Berlin's Jews, coming as it did at this critical juncture, represented both an opportunity and a liability for Goebbels. The Final Roundup might serve as a chance for Berlin to once again provide a shining example to the rest of the Reich, but if it did not come off smoothly it could instead threaten the façade that Berlin stood behind Goebbels.

Final Negotiations on the Contours of the Berlin Deportation Action

While Goebbels's enthusiasm to complete the removal of all Jews from his model Gau of Berlin exerted an important "push" to force them out, as Joachim Neander has framed it, intermarried Jews in Berlin were also subject to a "pull" force produced by the voracious appetite for labor in the concentration camps. The deportation of German Jews was to make up one leg of a triangle trade of sorts. In an effort to Germanize occupied Poland, a program was underway to settle ethnic Germans in the Lublin District of the *Generalgouvernement*. In order to make way for these new inhabitants, Poles still living in Lublin were to be deported into the Reich for forced labor. This influx of Polish labor, in turn, would serve to offset the loss of Jewish armaments workers deported to Auschwitz, while providing the concentration camps with a fresh workforce to advance the economic projects that the SS Main Economic and Administrative Office (WVHA) had been pursuing in earnest since September 1942.[39]

The Jews slated for deportation from Berlin in February 1943 were to fortify one of these economic projects: the synthetic fuel and rubber plant operated by the chemical giant IG Farben at the Auschwitz-Monowitz camp. IG Farben began building its factory in April 1941, and the construction of a dedicated fifty-seven barracks sub-camp to house prisoners on site commenced the following March.[40] The camp began to fill up in late 1942, reaching 3,700 inmates that December, but by early February 1943 severe attrition had ground the population down to just 1,450 capable of work. On February 10 the head of WVHA Office D-II responsible for prisoner labor, Gerhard Maurer, visited the camp and pledged to increase the captive workforce to 4,500. Shortly thereafter,[41] the camp Gestapo within Auschwitz, responding to disquiet among Poles both within the camp and in the community surrounding Auschwitz, initiated the transfer of 6,000 Polish prisoners from Auschwitz to concentration camps within the Reich. As a consequence, in mid-February 1943 Auschwitz faced a looming labor deficit of 9,000 workers, the resolution of which was an imperative for both the WVHA, with its interest in protecting the camp's productive capacity, and the camp Gestapo, which was concerned with forestalling a Polish uprising.[42]

The impending roundup of Berlin Jews offered an opportunity to bridge the gap in the labor supply at Auschwitz. On March 2, with the deportations already underway, a teletype message arrived in Auschwitz from the Chief of the Concentration Camp Central Office in the WVHA, Arthur Liebehenschel. It stated, "As is known there, the Jewish transports from Berlin begin on 1.3.43. It is once again pointed out that these transports involve around 15,000 healthy Jews perfectly fit for work, who have to date worked in the Berlin armaments industry." A few minutes later a second message arrived, this time from Maurer, in which he wrote "I would like to point out once again" that the Jews inbound from Berlin would be fit for work and should be treated accordingly, further expressing his expectation that the Monowitz population would be brought up to the desired levels.[43] The language used in this correspondence indicates that Auschwitz administration was already aware of the scope and purpose of the deportations from Berlin. More importantly, however, the total deportation number of 15,000 offered by Liebehenschel indicates that the WVHA believed that intermarried Jews would be among those transported to Auschwitz. Though roughly 9,000 Jews were actually sent to Auschwitz and some 4,000 who would have otherwise been arrested went underground before the roundup began, a total of 15,000 could only have been arrived at by including the 2,000 intermarried Jews imprisoned at Rosenstrasse. Because those 9,000 deportees were sufficient to meet Auschwitz's immediate labor requirements, the WVHA may have been willing to accept a curtailment in the deportations to exclude the intermarried Jews if problems arose. Nonetheless, they had expected more and reducing the total number of Berlin Jews who arrived at Auschwitz would have restricted their leeway to perform selections on the newcomers while still meeting their labor needs.

The negotiations between the WVHA, Auschwitz camp administration, and the Gestapo over labor questions point towards an improvised deportation process that, while still fluid in mid-February 1943, was beginning to coalesce around a consensus that the intermarried Jews of Berlin should be deported. By February 17, at the latest, the Gestapo had begun the process of removing the 6,000 putatively dangerous Poles from Auschwitz, and they would presumably have already secured replacements in order to placate the WVHA. On February 18 Goebbels recorded details of the coming roundup in his diary, rejoicing that "The Jews in Berlin will now finally be deported."[44] At about the same time, preparations within Berlin for a deportation action that would include intermarried Jews were underway. On February 15, the Jewish community received instructions from the Berlin Gestapo to assemble a contingent of Jews, including those in mixed marriages, to assist in the roundup. The Gestapo in Berlin also initiated a concurrent effort to identify and locate intermarried Jews in the city, compelling the Relief Help Office of the Catholic bishop of Berlin to query its parishes, on February 17, for the names, addresses, and privilege status of intermarried couples in their congregation.[45]

While the political leadership of the likes of Goebbels and Himmler pointed towards a clean sweep of Berlin's Jews, and though such an all-inclusive approach aligned with the economic and security interests of the WVHA and the Gestapo, respectively, the question remained of how to realize the project so that no "psychological problems" with popular perceptions arose. There was some recent precedent for how deportation of intermarried Jews might be achieved. In January 1943 the Gestapo in Frankfurt am Main, acting on instructions from the RSHA, had experimented with removing intermarried Jews individually by falsely accusing them of crimes, taking them into "Protective Custody," and interning them in a work education camp, thereby lending their incarceration a veneer of legality. The Darmstadt Gestapo pursued a parallel course, but in both instances the process was ponderously slow and required direct application to the RSHA to transfer each prisoner to a concentration camp when their three-month term at the work education camp expired.[46] Dozens of intermarried Jews would be dispatched from Berlin as Protective Custody cases as well in early March. As long as appearances were kept up, procedures might be curtailed: several Berlin intermarried Jews who the regime had identified as intellectuals were taken into protective custody and sent to Auschwitz, and twenty-five men sent from Rosenstrasse to Auschwitz were sent as "Protective Custody cases." They were charged with treason but without evidence, speeding the process. In a telegram of March 8, 1943, the WVHA in Auschwitz referred to the twenty-five men from Rosenstrasse as Protective Custody cases.[47]

On February 25, 1943, the Gestapo in Frankfurt/Oder issued guidelines for the coming roundup in its locale which mirrored the practice developed in Frankfurt am Main and in Darmstadt. It instructed that

all Jews still employed in factories are to be removed from the factories for the purpose of *Erfassung*. Insolent behavior of Jews who live in intact mixed marriages is to be punished by taking them into protective custody and application for placement in a concentration camp. One can proceed quite generously here, however the impression that the mixed marriage problem should be fundamentally resolved at this time should be avoided. Insofar as no rationale is available to justify the imprisonment of the Jewish partner living in a mixed marriage, they are to be released to their homes.[48]

While this document has been offered as evidence that the RSHA had no intention to deport intermarried Jews from Berlin, it can more productively serve as an indication of how the RSHA pursued its goals: through open-ended instructions that allowed lower levels of leadership to improvise, drawing on their intimate knowledge of their sphere of responsibility to develop innovative and inconspicuous solutions to difficult problems. The Frankfurt/Oder decree made appeals to RSHA authority, but was drafted locally and is shot through with references to specific work-camps that are to be exempted from deportations. Where the decree does invoke the RSHA, it is to identify the "*Erfassung*" of all Jews as the objective of the action. *Erfassung* could, and has, been understood to mean "registration," implying that the purpose of the roundup was to collect information on intermarried Jews before releasing them. Alternatively, *Erfassung* could be understood in the sense of "assembly," indicating that arrested Jews were to be concentrated together.

Given that, within the decree, the purpose of *Erfassung* applied to all Jews and not just to those in intermarriages, the RSHA likely intended its subordinates to come away with the latter interpretation, although intentional ambiguity of this kind had long been part of the process of genocide. The array of euphemisms employed even in internal correspondence (special treatment, evacuation, shot while trying to escape, enhanced interrogation) created conceptual tools whose real meanings evolved through usage, concealing criminal activity while opening space for innovation. The operational program the RSHA put in place with the Frankfurt/Oder decree certainly aimed at proceeding "generously" in order to remove as many intermarried Jews as possible while taking care not to draw inquiries from the local population.

The RSHA included similarly slippery language in its Reich-wide *Guidelines for the Technical Implementation of the Evacuation of Jews to the East (KL Auschwitz)*, issued on February 20, 1943. Beyond employing both "Evacuation" and "the East" in their euphemistic sense, the Guidelines also excluded *Mischlinge* and intermarried Jews from deportation "for the time being" (vorerst) with no further clarification.[49] The noncommittal nature of this exemption indicates that the RSHA recognized the political sensitivity of the intermarriage issue, but wanted to preserve some flexibility. Indeed, by February 20 the RSHA was certainly well aware that other potent interests, from the WVHA to the Gauleiter of Berlin, were driving for the broadest possible deportation operation. If the RSHA was, in fact, still opposed to including intermarried Jews in the roundup, Goebbels had one last chance to intervene. On February 26, the eve of *Entjudung des Reichsgebietes* action, Goebbels received Ernst Kaltenbrunner, the newly installed head of the RSHA, for the first time. While Goebbels does not record any discussion of the impending roundup in his diary, it is highly unlikely that the two would have overlooked the following day's massive roundup altogether.[50]

The Council of Ministers Plot

His conversation with Kaltenbrunner notwithstanding, Goebbels does not appear to have been terribly concerned that the roundup would cause him any troubles, and in any case he was preoccupied with other matters. On the evening before what the RSHA called the "Elimination of Jews from the Reich" arrests, Goebbels received Speer, along with Funk and Ley, at his residence in Berlin. Speer recalled that Goebbels's home gave a "gloomy" impression that night, as optics-conscious Goebbels had removed many of the light bulbs in his home in order to model the austerity measures of total war. Goebbels himself was no less gloomy. He confessed to his three guests that he was losing confidence in the highest echelons of party leadership. "We are not having a 'leadership crisis,'" he quipped, "but strictly speaking a 'Leader crisis.'" The issue, Goebbels asserted, was that Bormann's sway over Hitler had advanced to the point that he had effectively usurped Hitler's power in the domestic sphere. "Hitler does not hear what we have to say about the situation," he said, invoking a potent component of the Hitler myth that problems could be resolved if only the Führer knew.[51]

In reply to Goebbels's concern, Speer floated a plot to unseat Bormann and the Committee of Three while securing control of domestic politics for Goebbels himself. Two days before the invasion of Poland in 1939, Hitler had created the Council of Ministers for the Defense of the Reich, a war cabinet entrusted to Göring and empowered to issue decrees on its own authority. In theory, this council was "the highest legislative and executive organ in wartime next to the Führer," as Frick had described it in the spring of 1940,[52] yet an indolent Göring had declined to exercise this power in a meaningful way. Speer proposed reconvening the Council of Ministers for the Defense of the Reich and deputizing Goebbels to act on Göring's behalf. Goebbels, who was quite taken with the plan, imagined "I would assemble a group of around ten men, who are all excellent people, and I would then rule with them, i.e. establish a domestic political leadership." The entire endeavor, however, hinged on the consent of Göring, who was still upset with Goebbels following their show down over Horcher's Restaurant. Consequently, when the group of conspirators retired from Goebbels's darkened home at two in the morning they agreed that Speer would fly to Berchtesgaden and appeal to Göring for his support. If Göring proved amenable Goebbels would follow.[53]

The sun came up the next morning on what the Berlin Gestapo called the "final roundup" (Schlussaktion) of Berlin's Jews. Across the city the Gestapo and uniformed police, along with the detachment from *Leibstandarte SS Adolf Hitler* which Sepp Dietrich had promised to place at Goebbels's disposal,[54] raided Jewish workplaces and snatched Jews wearing the star off the street. Martha Mosse, then a leader of the Berlin Jewish community, remembered that *Leibstandarte* proceeded brutally during the course of chaotic arrests, hustling their quarry to waiting trucks without giving them any opportunity to collect important belongings. Elderly Jews who could not board the truck quickly enough were simply hurled into the back, and forty-five children were unintentionally separated from their families.[55] The roughly 2,000 intermarried Jews taken during the arrests were concentrated in the Jewish community building in the heart of Berlin at Rosenstrasse 2–4, one of the six assembly points designated for the deportation. Before the end of the day that February 27, a crowd began to develop on the Rosenstrasse, a sizable contingent of "Aryan" women come to find their Jewish husbands that would develop into a protest of hundreds in the coming days.

Goebbels was not initially aware of the protest developing on the Rosenstrasse. On the second day of the roundup, Speer phoned him, informing him that he had succeeded in persuading Göring to cooperate in their scheme. Goebbels immediately set to making arrangements to travel to Berchtesgaden, and the next afternoon he found himself seated in a car next to Speer ascending the Obersalzberg to seal his pact with Göring.[56] The subsequent meeting went swimmingly for all parties: Goebbels was encouraged when Göring "received me with the greatest kindness and approached me with an open heart," entirely overlooking their recent feud. Göring shared his visitors' concern regarding the Committee of Three, whom he referred to as the "three holy kings," and expressed his belief that Bormann was maneuvering to succeed Hitler. Goebbels assured him "depend on it, Herr Göring, we are going to open the Führer's eyes about Bormann and Lammers." As he departed from the meeting, Goebbels confided in Speer his belief that "this is going to work."[57]

It was only after he had arrived in Bavaria that Goebbels began to recognize that back in Berlin his efforts to make the city free of Jews were running into difficulty. The implications of the entire project appear to have already been weighing on him during his conversation with Goering. He reflected that Göring certainly had "no illusions" about what would happen if they lost the war. "Particularly in the Jewish question we are so implicated that there is no longer any escape for us," he wrote, "and that is just as well. Experience shows that a movement and a people who have burned their bridges behind them fight much more wholeheartedly than those who still have the possibility of retreat."

According to this view, the deportation of Jews underway in Berlin might bind Berliners together and harden them for total war. But Goebbels lamented that,

the better circles, particularly the intellectuals, do not understand our Jewish policy and in part take the side of the Jews. As a result, our action was betrayed prematurely, so that a whole host of Jews slipped through our fingers. But we will still get hold of them. In any case I will not rest until the Reich capital city at the least has become entirely free of Jews.[58]

Here Goebbels appears to have been referencing heroic efforts by individual Germans to help Jews go underground prior to the roundup rather than the protests on the Rosenstrasse, which he remained ignorant of. Nonetheless, this first setback did not dissuade Goebbels. He had demonstrated that the people of Berlin were enthusiastically behind him in his speeches at the Sportpalast on January 30 and February 18, and now with Göring's assistance he was poised to formalize his domestic leadership role.

A second and more consequential setback came shortly after Goebbels and Speer parted ways with Göring. While Goebbels and Speer were enjoying a late supper along with Speer's wife in the couple's home three-quarters of a mile down the mountain from Göring's residence, 251 aircraft from the Royal Air Force descended on Berlin in the largest attack on the German capital city to date, killing over 700 people. As had been the case with the air raids on the tenth anniversary of Hitler's seizure of power, the RAF chose to strike Berlin on March 1, Germany's "Day of the *Luftwaffe*," due to its symbolic significance. While the British were certainly not aware of the rendezvous between Goebbels and Göring earlier that day, they could not have orchestrated a more effective countermeasure to duo's fledgling alliance. Göring's prestige was inexorably intertwined with the unfolding air war, Berlin was Goebbels's city, and Hitler on January 15 had appointed Goebbels chairman of the national Air Raid Damage Committee, charged with managing the increasingly mounting challenges of civil air defense and bombing relief efforts across the Reich.[59] Goebbels first learned of the bombing raid the next day when his train stopped off in Halle while en route back to Berlin, and he observed some of the damage firsthand as he rolled into the capital. There he noted that Göring was already garnering what he considered "unjustifiable" blame for the attack and, projecting some latent concern that the people might turn against him as well, postulated that some of the ill will towards Göring might stem from the fact that he was in Berchtesgaden rather than Berlin during the attack. Making his own presence felt, Goebbels toured damaged areas of the city, and was encouraged that he was "greeted with the greatest kindness, even with joy and enthusiasm."[60]

Compromise in a Climate of Crisis

Goebbels first stopped at St. Hedwigs Cathedral, the seat of the Berlin Diocese under Bishop Konrad von Preysing, which had been completely gutted by bombs and fire. Soliciting favor from his Berliner constituents with compromises deviating from the demands of ideology, he recalled: "The priests of the Hedwig Cathedral insistently urge me to at least have a small chapel repaired and to place the hall at the Singakademie at their disposal for their worship. I willingly commit to this. Small gifts sustain friendship."[61] Margarete Sommer, the director of Preysing's Welfare Office of the Berlin Diocesan Authority, may have recognized that Goebbels had found himself in a position requiring compromise. On the day of Goebbels's visit, she penned a letter to Cardinal Bertram outlining the Jewish deportation action underway in the city, stressing that intermarried Jews had been apprehended as well despite promises that they would not be affected. She appears to have been aware of and moved by the ongoing protest on Rosenstrasse, writing "all efforts by the Aryan spouses and the half-Aryan children to free the non-Aryan spouse or parent are in vain. They were repulsed and literally expelled in the hardest form. The streets in which the men and women from mixed marriages are housed has been cordoned off by the police." She concluded by asking Bertram to solicit an attempt at intervention by Bishop Heinrich Wienken. Bertram complied, personally relating his impression of the situation to Frick, Thierack, Lammers, and the RSHA while instructing Wienken to deliver an oral protest against the "separation of racially mixed marriages" to relevant ministries.[62] The following day Nuncio Cesare Orsenigo lodged a similar complaint with the Ministry of Foreign Affairs.[63] Entrepreneurs and military officials also lodged protests privately and singly: "from military industrial factories, private firms, and also from the military itself came protests . . . work letters showing military authorizations . . . all with the aim of getting their Jewish workers released. . . . They didn't do a bit of good."[64]

But given the protests, men of the RSHA advocated separate courses of action, even issuing conflicting orders according to a Gestapo driver's postwar court testimony.[65] The bombing, the unrest on Rosenstrasse, and the voices of opposition from the Catholic Church to forced separation, expressed to Goebbels's political rivals Lammers and Frick no less, threatened to undermine Goebbels's claim to be leading a model city at a critical moment. An investigation into the protest on Rosenstrasse, seeking out leadership or organization so that it might be decapitated, yielded no results,[66] and after each effort to break up the demonstration it simply came together once again. The RSHA, stymied by the resilience of the protesters and facing questions from the Church, began to soften its position. On March 4, Adolf Eichmann granted Wienken an audience, promising that non-Aryan Catholics in mixed marriages would be released, even if the marriage was childless and thus not privileged.[67] Still, this did not mark an abandonment of the effort to deport intermarried Jews.

The Gestapo had manufactured criminal charges to support the removal Jews in mixed marriages under protective custody in some cases, deporting eighteen intermarried Jews from Berlin on the day of Eichmann's discussion with Wienken. They were taken from a Jewish home for the elderly on Berlin's Grosse Hamburger Strasse, a site used as an assembly point for arrested Jews now taking in intermarried Jews, because Rosenstrasse was filled to capacity, along with the fraction of "half-Jews" who wore the star (*Geltungsjuden*), whom Eichmann had expressly stated would be deported. The following day, however, relatives of captive Jews began to gather at Grosse Hamburger Strasse in vigilant protest as well.[68]

On March 5 Goebbels chose to intervene. In his diary he positioned this decision within the context of the chaos produced by the March 1 bombing, writing,

> at this very moment the SD considers it opportune to proceed with the Jewish evacuation. Unfortunately some rather unpleasant scenes played out in front of a Jewish retirement home, where the population assembled in great numbers and in part even took the side of the Jews. I give the SD the order not to continue the Jewish evacuation in such a critical time at least. We would rather save that for a few weeks; then we can carry it out all the more thoroughly.

He further criticized the entire endeavor in the same vein that he had been criticizing the bureaucracy that was obstructing his total war effort, forfeiting the goodwill of the people in the name of following procedure. "The fundamental evil of our leadership," he reflected, "and above all our administration is that everything is done by the book [nach Schema F]."[69] Most of the Rosenstrasse Jews living in privileged marriages were released that day,[70] and nearly all of the rest followed a few days later.

Goebbels's submission to the will of the street, as he called the regime's reaction following its conciliation of a second mass demonstration by women seven months later, was a component of his effort to consolidate his delicate political position. Still, without support from Hitler he would not be secure in any of his endeavors, whether that be outmaneuvering the Committee of Three through the Council of Ministers for the Defense of the Reich, overcoming the devastation of the March 1 air raid, or proceeding "thoroughly" with the removal of all Jews from Berlin, and he had not been able to speak to Hitler face to face for a month. Consequently, as releases from Rosenstrasse began on March 5 he dispatched Speer to act as an envoy to the Führer. Two days later this initiative bore fruit, and Goebbels received an invitation from Hitler to visit him at his eastern headquarters in Vinnytsia.[71]

In the early afternoon of March 8, after a nonstop flight to the Ukraine, Goebbels linked up with Speer and proceeded to his rendezvous with the Führer. Hitler had cleared his calendar for the day for the pair. While they had hoped that they might find Hitler receptive to the idea of reactivating the Council of Ministers for the Defense of the Reich, this component of their agenda was quickly derailed. When Goebbels began the afternoon meeting with a report on the March 1 air raid on Berlin, Hitler launched into a tirade against Göring, and both visitors felt the moment was not opportune to propose expanding the Reichsmarschall's power. Later in the day Hitler dismissed Speer so that he could speak in private to his Propaganda Minister, Berlin Gauleiter, and chairman of the national Air Raid Damage Committee. There, according to his diary, Goebbels was more open about his concerns with the ossification of the Party's domestic leadership, though he avoided direct attacks on the Committee of Three since he was not yet ready to offer his alternative. He did manage to gain approval for his more flexible approach to the Church. He noted, after recounting his visit to St. Hedwigs Cathedral, "[Hitler] definitely approves of my tactic of treading carefully now in the Church question."

Following his one-on-one conversation with Goebbels Hitler retired to rest, but an hour later Goebbels along with Speer returned to him for dinner. Speer, reminiscing on the evening, recalled "Hitler had a fire made in the fireplace; the orderly brought us a bottle of wine, and Fachinger mineral water for Hitler. We sat up until early morning in a relaxed, almost cozy atmosphere." This intimate environment facilitated open discussion of more sensitive matters, and the conversation soon turned to the issue of Berlin's Jews. They agreed that the Jews posed a potential threat to the city, particularly if they were to begin cooperating with disaffected foreign workers, and Hitler agreed to dispatch Sepp Dietrich's *Leibstandarte* to Berlin if the use of force became necessary. Still, Hitler firmly supported Goebbels's judgment in politically delicate situations that required a quick response. "He confirms to me once again," Goebbels wrote,

> that in such cases [air raids] only I am in command of the Reich capital city. The ministries also have to obey my orders here. All of public life is subordinate to me. Only one can command in catastrophes. In the Jewish question he approves of my approach and expressly instructs me to make Berlin completely free of Jews. I will take care that no concubinage coalesces between the Berlin Jews and foreign workers.[72]

A Conclusion to the Escalation of Persecution of Intermarried Jews

Though Goebbels returned from Vinnytsia with his authority in Berlin affirmed and with Hitler's renewed blessing to remove all Jews from the city, in the wake of the releases of the intermarried Jews from Rosenstrasse the momentum towards deporting intermarried Jews had subsided. Jews in mixed marriages remained very much at risk, but the constellation of forces that had come together to precipitate their arrest in the first place would never again fully align. The RSHA gradually retreated from its embrace of escalating persecution of intermarried Jews. On May 21 RSHA director Ernst Kaltenbrunner laid out the RSHA's position, ordering that intermarried Jews held in the concentration camps for anything but criminal offenses should be released. He issued further instructions that "there may also be protective custody arrests and deportations only when they have committed real offenses," effectively blunting the Gestapo's tactic of proceeding generously in manufacturing charges in order to justify the arrest of intermarried Jews.[73]

Despite his previous commitment to see the complete removal of Jews from Berlin through "all the more thoroughly," Goebbels also backed away during that critical moment. His immediate imperative for casting Berlin as a model city cracked when, on April 12, Göring betrayed his still unconsummated alliance with Goebbels and instead fell in with the cadre of party leaders behind Bormann and Lammers. This effectively eliminated Goebbels's prospects, in the short term, of leveraging his mastery of Berlin into control of domestic matters from the entirety of the Reich.[74] Though no further deportation actions had been carried out, on May 19, 1943, Goebbels finally simply declared the city "free of Jews." The following March, four months before Hitler named him Reich Plenipotentiary for Total War, he was still looking for an opportunity to deport Berlin's intermarried Jews: "There are still 6,000 Jews living in Berlin, some privileged, some tolerated. I will look for the chance to still indeed try to shove them out at the first best opportunity."[75] It never happened, and these 6,000 intermarried Jews likely survived.

Notes

1. Joseph Goebbels, *Die Tagebücher von Joseph Goebbles*, Part II, vol. 7, March 11, 1943 (Munich: K.G. Saur, 1993), 528.

2. Intermarriages as a percentage of total Jewish marriages were 14.4 percent in 1901 and nearly 44 percent in 1933. Intermarriage continued at a much slower rate until 1935. In 1939, following the incorporation of Austria into the Reich and the establishment of the Protectorate of Bohemia and Moravia, some 20,000 intermarried couples remained. Bruno Blau, "Mischehe im Nazireich," *Judaica* 4 (April 1948): 46–7; Eric Garcia McKinley, "Reclaimed Pasts: Intermarriage and Remembrances of National Socialist Racial Stigmatization by Jewish and Non-Jewish Spouses and Mischling Children," *Leo Baeck Institute Year Book* 61 (December 30, 2015): 183–98, esp. 186.

3. George Messersmith's Report to the State Department on the "Present Status of the Anti-Semitic Movement in Germany," (September 21, 1933), German Historical Institute. https://ghdi.ghi-dc.org/sub_document.cfm?document_id=1522, April 30, 2020.

4. Karin Orth, *Die NS-Vertreibung der jüdischen Gelehrten. Die Politik der Deutschen Forschungsgemeinschaft und die Reaktionen der Betroffenen* (Göttingen: Wallstein, 2016), 268.

5. The law prohibiting *Rassenschande* is printed in Alexandra Przyrembel, *"Rassenschande": Reinheitsmythos und Vernichtungslegitimation im Nationalsozialismus* (Göttingen: Vandenhoeck & Ruprecht, 203), 128.

6. Lothar Gruchmann, *Justiz im Dritten Reich 1933-1940: Anpassung und Unterwerfung in der Ära Gürtner* (Berlin: Oldenbourg Wissenschaftsverlag, 2009), 189–90.

7. Bruno Blau, *Das Ausnahmerechte für die Juden in Deutschland 1933-1945* (Düsseldorf: Verlag Allgemeine Wochenzeitung der Juden in Deutschland, 1954), 30.

8. "[Göring's] political influence would never again be as high after Munich," wrote Ian Kershaw in *Hitler, 1936-45: Nemesis* (New York: Norton, 2001), 89.

9. Blau, "Mischehe im Nazireich," 46, 49.

10. Hilberg, *Destruction of the European Jews* (New York: Octagon Books, 1978), Vol. 2, 443–4; Uwe Adam, *Judenpolitik im Dritten Reich* (Düsseldorf: Droste Verlag, 1972), 235.

11. Stoltzfus*, Resistance of the Heart: Intermarriage and the Rosenstrasse Protest in Nazi Germany* (New York: WW Norton, 1996), 194, 336n7.

12. Hilberg, *Destruction of the European Jews*, Vol. 2, 444; Adam, *Judenpolitik im Dritten Reich*, 225–6.

13. Hilberg, *Destruction of the European Jews*, Vol. 2, 437, 445–6; Adam, *Judenpolitik im Dritten Reich*, 226–8. Letter from Schlegelberger to Lammers, April 5, 1942 regarding contemplated anti-Jewish measures, Nuremberg Document PS-4055. On forced annulments, Leugers, 148.

14. "Gauamtsleiter der Gauleitung von Groß-Berlin [Gerhard] Schach berichtet mir über die Lage in Berlin. Aus einer Zahlenübersicht entnehme ich, daß wir immer noch 46 000 Juden in Berlin haben, die außerordentlich schwer zu evakuieren sind. Wenn man bedenkt, daß Köln nur noch 200 Juden so ist die Zahl für Berlin enorm. Ich gebe Schach den Auftrag, mit allen Mitteln besorgt zu sein, diese Zahl schleunigst herunterzusetzen und für einen absehbaren Termin Berlin gänzlich judenfrei zu machen."

15. Goebbels, *Tagebücher*, September 22, 1942 and October 3, 1942.

16. Goebbels, *Tagebücher*, September 22, 1942.

17. Goebbels, *Tagebücher*, October 4, 1942, Vol. II/6, 63–4.

18. Peter Longerich, *Wannseekonferenz: der Weg zur "Endlösung,"* (Munich: Pantheon, 2017), 138; Stoltzfus, *Resistance of the Heart*, 193, 336n6.

19. Goebbels, *Tagebücher*, December 6, 1942.

20. Goebbels, entries for December 6, 1943, April 18, 1943.

21. Antonia Leugers, "Der Protest in der Rosenstraße 1943 und die Kirchen," in *Berlin, Rosenstraße 2–4: Protest in der NS-Diktatur. Neue Forschungen zum Frauenprotest in der Rosenstraße 1943*, ed. Antonia Leugers (Annweiler: Plöger, 2004), 63–4.

22. Reich Minister of Justice to the Chief of Security Police and SD, Berlin, December 9, 1942, Political Archives of the Auswärtiges Amt, R 100857, 137, cited in Hans-Christian Jasch, *Staatssekretär Wilhelm Stuckart Und Die Judenpolitik: Der Mythos Von Der Sauberen Verwaltung*, 354.

23. Albert Speer, *Inside the Third Reich* (New York: Macmillan, 1970), 254–6.

24. Goebbels, *Tagebücher*, January 29, 1943, Vol. II/7, 224.

25. Goebbels, *Tagebücher*, January 30, 1943, Vol. II/7, 230.

26. Goebbels, *Tagebücher*, January 30, 1943, Vol. II/7, 220.

27. Goebbels, *Tagebücher*, January 31, 1943, Vol. II/7, 229–30.

28. Goebbels, *Tagebücher*, February 1, 1943, Vol. II/7, 235.

29. Goebbels, *Tagebücher*, February 3, 1943, Vol. II/7, 253.

30. Goebbels, *Tagebücher*, January 30, 1943, Vol. II/7, 223–4.

31. Goebbels, *Tagebücher*, February 3, 1943, Vol. II/7, 253.

32. Goebbels, *Tagebücher*, February 2, 1943, Vol. II/7, 244.

33. Speer, *Inside the Third Reich*, 257, 259.

34. Goebbels, *Tagebücher*, February 8, 1943, Vol. II/7, 283–4.

35. Goebbels, *Tagebücher*, February 8, 1943, Vol. II/7, 295–6, 297.

36. Goebbels, *Tagebücher*, February 13, 1943, Vol. II/7, 334–6.

37. Goebbels, *Tagebücher*, February 18, 1943, Vol. II/7, 367–9.

38. Goebbels, *Tagebücher*, February 18, 1943, Vol. II/7, 369.

39. Hilberg, *Destruction of the European Jews*, Vol. 2, 459.

40. Geoffrey Megargee, ed., *The United States Holocaust Memorial Museum Encyclopedia of Camps and Ghettos, 1933-1945* (Bloomington: Indiana University Press, 2009), Vol. 1A, 215–16.

41. Transport of these Polish prisoners began on March 10, 1943. Because they would have been quarantined for no less than three weeks before departing, the decision to remove them from Auschwitz must have come on or before February 17. Neander, "Auschwitz und die Berliner *Fabrikaktion* Februar/März 1943," http://universaar.uni-saarland.de/journals/index.php/tg/article/viewArticle/76/84.

42. Neander, "Auschwitz und die Berliner *Fabrikaktion* Februar/März 1943."

43. Ibid.

44. Goebbels, *Tagebücher*, February 18, 1943, Vol. II/7, 369.

45. Stoltzfus, *Resistance of the Heart*, 206–7.

46. Ibid., 203–4.

47. Ibid., 237, 253. See also 43: Jews were taken into protective custody for sexual relations with non-Jews.

48. Public Decree of the State District Administrator of the Calau District, February 25, 1943, translated in full in *Protest in Hitler's "National Community,"* 229–32, original found at Brandenburgisches Landeshauptarchiv Potsdam, Rep. 41 Großräschen Nr. 272, 84–5. It is notable that Gruner, arguing that the document proves that no intermarried Jews were to be deported at all (whether from Frankfurt/Main or Berlin), cites only p. 84 of this document while omitting p. 85, an accompanying note from the office of the Landsrat in Calau. This is critical because the Calau note "set the direction for the interpretation" of the entire document by emphasizing that officers have a blank check for arresting intermarried Jews by accusing them of "uppity behavior," as Leugers has pointed out along with a number of other errors Gruner makes in interpreting Gestapo documents. Antonia Leugers, "Widerstand gegen die Rosenstrasse: Kritische Anmerkungen zu einer Neuerscheinung von Wolf Gruner," *theologie.geschichte* 1 (2006): 131–205, here 187ff.

49. H. G. Adler, *Der verwaltete Mensch. Studien zur Deportation der Juden aus Deutschland* (Tübingen: J.C.B. Mohr, 1974), 198–200.

50. Goebbels, *Tagebücher*, February 27, 1943, Vol. II/7, 428.

51. Speer, *Inside the Third Reich*, 257–9.

52. 2608-PS, *Trial of the Major War Criminals: Proceeding* Volumes, Vol. XXXI, 22; *Nazi Conspiracy and Aggression* (Washington, DC: U.S. Government Print Office, 1946), Vol. 2.

53. Goebbels, *Tagebücher*, February 27, 1943, Vol. II/7, 430; Speer, *Inside the Third Reich*, 257–9; Peter Longerich, *Goebbels: A Biography* (New York: Random House, 2015), 563–5.

54. A court witness remembered in 1955 that the SS-men wore field gray army uniforms with a small band carrying the script "Leibstandarte SS Adolf Hitler." Two were officers, some war medals marking valor on the battlefield. Statement of Karl Hefter, October 28, 1955, in the trial of Josef ("Sepp") Dietrich, I P Js 3767.65.

55. Mosse specifically identified the *Leibstandarte* as the spearhead of the deportation action. H. G. Adler, *Theresienstadt 1941-1945, das Antlitz einer Zwangsgemeinschaft* (Göttingen: Wallstein Verlag, 2018), 782–5. Wolf Gruner casts doubt on the involvement of the *Leibstandarte* in the February 1943 deportation of Berlin Jews, pointing out that the outfit was active in the Soviet Union at the time. He does concede that a smaller detachment from the unit or new *Leibstandarte* replacement troops training in the city could conceivably have participated. This would be consistent with Sepp Dietrich's promise from February 1, 1943, to provide Goebbels with a single company to put down unrest in the city. Wolf Gruner, *Widerstand in der Rosenstraße: Die Fabrik-Aktion und die Verfolgung der „Mischehen" 1943* (Frankfurt am Main: Fischer Taschenbuch Verlag, 2005), 61, n101.

56. Goebbels, *Tagebücher*, March 1, 1943, Vol. II/7, 444–5.

57. Goebbels, *Tagebücher*, March 2, 1943, Vol. II/7, 449–59; Speer, *Inside the Third Reich*, 259.

58. Goebbels, *Tagebücher*, March 2, 1943, Vol. II/7, 449, 454.

59. Longerich, *Goebbels*, 567; Stoltzfus, *Resistance of the Heart*, 204–5.

60. Goebbels, *Tagebücher*, March 3, 1943, Vol. II/7, 459–61, 463.

61. Goebbels, *Tagebücher,* March 3, 1943, Vol. II/7, 459–61.

62. Gruner, *Widerstand in der Rosenstraße*, 99–101.

63. Stoltzfus, "Protest and Aftermath," in *Protest in Hitler's "National Community,": Popular Unrest and the Nazi Response*, 2015, eds. Nathan Stoltzfus and Birgit Maier-Katkin (New York: Berghahn Books), 187.

64. Statement of Max Reschke, a Jewish orderly, of May 4, 1959, in supporting document #30 (Dr. Wolfgang Scheffler Collection), Otto Bovensiepen et al Trial, I Js 9/65 in Stoltzfus, *Resistance of the Heart*, 247.

65. Stoltzfus, *Resistance of the Heart*, 256.

66. Ibid., 244.

67. Stoltzfus, "Protest and Aftermath," 185; Gruner, *Widerstand in der Rosenstraße*, 115.

68. Stoltzfus, *Resistance of the Heart*, 237, 242.

69. Goebbels, *Tagebücher*, March 6, 1943, Vol. II/7, 487.

70. Gruner, *Widerstand in der Rosenstraße*, 115.

71. Speer, *Inside the Third Reich*, 261–2.

72. Goebbels, *Tagebücher*, March 9, 1943, Vol. II/7, 502–17; Speer, *Inside the Third Reich*, 262–3.

73. Stoltzfus, *Resistance of the Heart*, 255–6.

74. Speer, *Inside the Third Reich*, 264–5.

75. Goebbels, *Tagebücher*, March 16, 1944.

CHAPTER 7
GARIWO'S PHILOSOPHY

EDUCATE TO OPTIMISM AND RESPONSIBILITY
THROUGH THE MEMORY OF THE RIGHTEOUS
Gabriele Nissim

Memory as Education

Gariwo (Garden of the Righteous Worldwide) is a unique organization. Officially formed in 2001, it is dedicated to honoring the Righteous, derived from The Righteous Among the Nations, a designation coined by Yad Vashem, Israel's Holocaust memorial and museum. The Righteous Among the Nations are non-Jewish individuals recognized for risking their lives to aid Jews during the Holocaust. For Gariwo, the label of the Righteous is a little bit different. Gariwo defines the Righteous as such.

The term Righteous comes from the Talmud, which states that "whoever saves a life saves a whole world," and it was applied for the first time in Israel with reference to those who rescued Jews from Nazi persecution in Europe. The concept of Righteous has been used again to recall the attempts to stop the extermination of the Armenians in Turkey in 1915 and by extension to all those, anywhere in the world, who have tried or are trying to prevent crimes of genocide, to defend human rights—first of all human dignity—in extreme situations, or that struggle to safeguard memory from the recurring attempts to deny the truth about the persecutions.

The organization's goal is to highlight the stories of those considered righteous. In 2012, Gariwo successfully petitioned and helped found a European Day dedicated to the Righteous of all genocides, which takes place on March 6 of each year. This was chosen by Italian Parliament in 2017 as well. This date was also the day when Moshe Bejski died. Bejski was a Holocaust survivor, aided in his survival by Oskar Schindler, and Chairman of Yad Vashem's Righteous Among the Nations Commission. In addition to Yad Vashem, Gariwo also plants gardens, or Gardens of the Righteous, across Europe in symbolically important locations such as Milan, Italy; Yerevan, Armenia; Warsaw, Poland; and Israel.

In the last few years, Gariwo has publicly proposed a new culture of responsibility in Italy and Europe in regard to the memory of the Holocaust and other genocides of the twentieth century. This was a new approach to the memorialization of the Holocaust that had not yet been sufficiently developed with regard to the victims and perpetrators of evil that prevailed in public debates. But Gariwo felt that this undervalued the moral mechanisms of those who resisted. The starting point to developing this new culture was to question a deterministic view of history that did not recognize the active role of individuals, considering them completely powerless before political evil. The Righteous however, defended human dignity in dictatorships, tried to prevent the mechanisms of hatred that lead to the conditions for extreme hatred and abuse to flourish, committed themselves to behaving and preserving dignified conduct even when the world was heading in the wrong direction, and unequivocally showed that human beings can always make a choice. Their actions show how in any crisis, persons who stand up to indifference, to complicity with perpetrators, voluntary servitude, or decisions made by responsible men, can always change the course of events and more importantly, they can win. Even though people often contemplate catastrophes of the past, and study the actions of those who tried to defend human dignity, people can realize that evil is not inevitable at all, if only we all take a stand. The Righteous are important because they saved ideas of hope and because they showed that human beings, though fragile, can become the arbitrators of their own destinies. Thus, an optimistic message can be taken even in the face of extreme evil. If every human being takes responsibility, situations can be overturned, even if the outcomes are not quantifiable and immediate.

Through their approach of honoring the Righteous, Gariwo has given a new ethical dimension to the concept of memory and has tried to convey to young people a new perspective when interpreting the past. First of all, it is a matter of regarding the Shoah and genocides by not only having compassion for the victims, but focusing on the choices people made. Evil often appears to be a battlefield where the grey areas of complicity and responsibility oppose each other. Gariwo seeks to remind that history can take a different direction at any moment, starting from the judgment and behavior of human beings. If one grasps the mechanism of choice through exemplary actions of the Righteous, then it becomes possible to imagine that confronting evil is not only a concern of the past, but of the present as well. It encourages people to act now, since they can actively thwart the evilness they encounter. Understanding the past allows people to become responsible citizens in their current conditions.

Many historians as well as members of the public are convinced that remembering means only preserving past events against forms of oblivion and revisionism. This is considered the most important proof of solidarity vis-à-vis the victims, and this preservation was the greatest desire of the Holocaust survivors who demanded justice. In so many European countries, complicity is what led to the extermination that erased and silenced the Jewish identity of the victims of Nazism. But remembrance is only one part of preserving the past. There is a higher form of memorialization that allows contemporary generations to bring memory back to life and to engage in responsible behavior, which is to act now so that methods of hatred and the dehumanization of human beings are not repeated. This is the most meaningful commitment that those who survived genocide and other hardship or those who were lucky enough to be born in peacetime can maintain vis-à-vis the victims. Etty Hillesum, a Dutch diarist who was murdered in the Auschwitz concentration camp, understood this very well, claiming in Westerbork prison camp (where she had been confined before) that the final victory against Nazism could only be the birth of a world without any hatred or enemies. Without the hope this dream for the future, Nazis would have corrupted the world even after the end of the war. Remembering the events of the past and how such evil was allowed to take root and flourish can be disturbing. Yet, the feelings that are evoked by such events require a positive re-emphasis, otherwise revisiting the past does not make a deep enough impact. Without guidance, learning about the past can do nothing more than become melancholic memory, which can lead to resignation and distrust in the world. In other cases, it becomes an alibi to justify indifference and selfishness at the present time. For example, those who take part in Remembrance Days claim they are against anti-Semitism and on the side of Jews, but then have no qualms about building barriers against Muslims and migrants.

The Plurality of the Righteous

How does Gariwo convey an optimistic vision of the future and the freedom and ability of choice through the message of the Righteous? First of all, it does so by extending the idea of the Righteous to those who made the choice to help others from events like the Holocaust and including all genocides and crimes against humanity. We made it possible for the message of Moshe Bejski, who was the most passionate creator of the Jerusalem Garden of the Righteous, to become a universal idea.[1] At the end of his life, dedicated to research and appreciation of those who saved Jews, Bejski came to this staggering conclusion: there was no place during the Second World War where someone had not tried to save Jews, be it concentration camps, factories, or even parliaments in the hands of fascists. This shows that there was always the possibility for action, but very few made this choice. The choice to do what is good or what is right is therefore a possibility within the reach of every person, especially when history moves in a bad direction. The contexts may be different, but the mechanism of choice and responsibility is similar in all dictatorships, genocides, and totalitarian regimes, just as it was in the Shoah.

Choosing and making a decision between complicity or what is right, is an act of individual freedom that allows all human beings to use their body as a barrier against evil. Even if they do not succeed, their actions impact and inspire others to action, leading them to become examples beyond their own era. The outcome of a choice is not always quantifiable and ensured, but it is a personal defeat when individuals give up thinking and decide to keep quiet, turning a blind eye to the evil occurring around them. Reinterpreting the stories of the Righteous in the dark moments of human kind has a therapeutic effect in that it can show what many consider to be the foundation of hope. Those who acted managed to preserve dignity of the past combined with the moral references for the present, something for those in difficult situations to rely on when they have to make their own choices. Many tragedies throughout history could have been avoided if there had been more responsible individuals, institutions, and states.

Choosing, as Hannah Arendt argued in *Life of the Mind*, means feeling uneasy when individuals around us are dehumanized and made dispensable for political and economic reasons; choosing means thinking independently and judging by putting oneself in the shoes of others and challenging well-established ideas of the majority and unfair laws that justify oppression; choosing means acting with an act of will that defines, as Heraclitus argued, the character of someone who decides to be involved and to bring about a resolve to act.[2] But how can a young person or a citizen of today understand the mechanism of choice views against the history that has preceded us? Activating knowledge, memory, and imagination is the prerequisite, but it is not sufficient if individuals are not used to making comparisons not only in different contexts, but also between past and present. For example, it may seem that it is sufficient for youngsters to visit the Auschwitz death camp or Platform 21 in Milan, from where trains transporting Jews left, to understand the depths of the past and then tell the stories of the few Righteous who tried to resist. It is the first step of knowledge, but it is not enough because it is always the relationship with reality and with people in flesh and blood that makes us touch and better understand the past. This is why Gariwo recommends that students, after visiting Auschwitz, go and see refugee camps in the Mediterranean countries, enter prisons in Lampedusa or, as suggested by Marek Edelman, deputy commander of Warsaw ghetto revolt, spend a whole night in an emergency room to see contemporary suffering firsthand.

In this way a virtuous path is created where the past illuminates the present, allowing us to suggest questions on the current condition and our direct relationship with suffering, which leads to better understanding of what happened yesterday. Through this approach, in the Gardens of the Righteous, Gariwo shares the stories of moral individuals who saved lives during the Holocaust and the other genocides of the twentieth century, along with more contemporary individuals who saved lives in Rwanda, and in Syria; those who committed to helping migrants at sea or worked hard to protect people during terrorist attacks. Showing every generation the direct testimony of those who made risky decisions in emergency situations allows them to understand the universal mechanism of choice and opens up a completely different perspective of the interpretation of the Righteous during Shoah or, for example, the Armenian genocide.

Through this methodology, Gariwo strives to show that what makes a person Righteous is not static but changes depending on the challenges of the present situation. The collective inherits the examples of the Righteous who acted in the past, but beyond this, people must think for themselves because good and evil always take on new dimensions and are never the same. It is like the flow of a river, as Heraclitus suggested. The course of water follows the same path, but the water is always different. This is what the poet René Chair said in an aphorism that perfectly describes the condition of human beings facing a new beginning: "Our inheritance was left to us by no testament."

This is why the interpretation of the present and the assumption of responsibility are a risky leap in a largely unexplored territory, where those who side with evil often use misleading cultural references. For example, Soviet totalitarianism used the flag of anti-fascism, the fight against anti-Semitism (at least at the beginning), and equally with the intention to create new despotic regimes. We know in hindsight and under the surface that these were false claims, platitudes to sway the masses. Those who understood the semantic deception then had to struggle against well-established prejudices and often faced almost impossible battles in solitude. Those who helped the newly persecuted were indeed stigmatized as traitors of a just cause. It was difficult to be a Righteous when an act of humanity and responsibility was considered to be an action against the very idea of justice, therefore an illegal action against the laws of the newly instituted political morality.

To facilitate the path of choice in our time, Gariwo constantly tries to ask questions on unsolved problems: climate change, immigration, hospitality, the fight against terrorism and fundamentalism, and hatred on social media, in political debate, and in sport. As has always happened in the past, those who stood up in the past can help those facing difficult decisions in the present, anticipate possible solutions, and indicate new ways so that the past can be emulated positively. This is why Gariwo tries to foster and make younger generations aware of those who can be called the Righteous of our time as well. Scientists who investigate and work towards attaining environmental protections for the planet, those who promote peace and hospitality in a hostile environment, and those who insist on imagining a world without walls are forerunners of the great future battles that await human beings. As it happened to the Righteous of the Shoah or of Soviet dissidents, today these do-gooders are often forgotten. But through their example they show us that it is possible to make our own choices in the world of the present and make people today understand the existing battlefields as well as give them the opportunity of a new beginning in morality.

Goodness Is Not Sacrifice

How can one convey realistic hope and explain the concept that every human being can count in the world and always make a difference? Through the reinterpretation of much testimony by the Righteous, young people can be educated to understand that acting for the good of others does not have to be accompanied with sacrifice or privation, but instead can make life more fulfilling, richer, and more beautiful. Happiness is found by doing good for others, because doing good for others is good for oneself. This is the fundamental message of the Righteous. It is important that Gariwo's mission be clear as it is not educational to claim that self-sacrifice is a value or the mandatory path to a better world. The idea that good is renunciation paves the way for declining responsibility. "Who makes me do it, why should I suffer for goodness?" is the common reaction to this type of request. Behind this concept is the idea that earthly life is only transitional and that our sacrifice will be truly awarded in afterlife. Therefore, human beings are condemned to suffer in order to find glory in another world. Moreover, if virtue is associated with deprivation and renunciation of one's life, goodness becomes possible only for saints and heroes; in other words, a metaphysical option beyond human dimension.

Being righteous can take different forms and help potential Righteous to put themselves in other people's shoes and gain new perspectives. Acting for the justice of others means cultivating one's character and personality. Keeping one's word or promise means standing publicly behind it and knowing that doing so involves risk. It always takes character and determination to act. It is not sufficient to have the right opinion or to post on social media for a cause, as one might do today. Active decisions are always leaps into the void, because the results are never ensured. However, if we look at the genesis of the behavior of those who acted in extreme conditions under both past and current dictatorships and genocides, we realize that the starting point leading to courageous actions is always the protection of one's personal humanity and moral well-being. We put ourselves at risk to save another human being, to safeguard our own happiness.

This is how Hannah Arendt explains the secret of the Righteous, pushing them to resist and act:

> The non-participants (to Nazism) . . . were the only ones who dared judge by themselves; and they were capable of doing so not because they disposed of a better system of values or because the old standards of right and wrong were still firmly planted in their mind and conscience. . . . They asked themselves to what extent they would still be able to live in peace with themselves after having committed certain deeds; and they decided that it would be better to do nothing, not because the world would then be changed for the better, but simply because only on this condition could they go on living with themselves at all. Hence, they also chose to die when they were forced to participate. To put it crudely, they refused to murder, not so much because they still held fast to the command "Thou shalt not kill," but because they were unwilling to live together with a murderer—themselves.

The Potential Goodness of Human Beings

To always keep hope of the potential goodness within every person's reach, one must not fall into the mistake of sanctifying the Righteous and telling their stories as if they were the work of perfect individuals. We have to get used to thinking that someone who is a swindler in life, someone who has embraced the most absurd ideology, someone who helps others without giving up their small and big vices, those who live in the most disorderly way, those who apparently look like the worst selfish individuals, can still become righteous. The way they behaved previously does not matter. What actually matters is how they changed. It is wrong to seek absolute consistency: one must look humbly at fundamental decisions made by individuals in crises of humanity. No pure good exists on Earth, but there always exists a fragile and contradictory good. One must accept the ambiguity of goodness because it is not the work of a God, but of human beings who, throughout their limited life, struggle first of all for their survival and can never achieve a state of absolute goodness. Even those who have the best intentions will make mistakes and will never live up to an absolute categorical imperative. Human beings can ideally embrace the world, but cannot help all those who suffer.[3] And even when they do their best, taking care of people around them, they will leave someone behind and therefore their deed appears inadequate.

Emperor philosopher Marcus Aurelius wrote in his Meditations that recognizing, without any rhetoric, that most human beings can be responsible only by doing small things is not the sign of the impotence of human beings before extreme evil, but instead their actual opportunity to take a small step that can change the world in every situation.[4]

Moshe Bejski observed that the great moral let down during the Holocaust did not fall on the shoulders of those who feared for their lives and did not sacrifice themselves to save Jews, but instead on indifferent individuals who, despite the opportunity to make small gestures, only watched and did not act. Culprits were therefore those who could do something without risking too much and who, on the other hand, turned their heads away and did not do the right thing. The worst things in history do not happen because saints, great heroes, or individuals who are aware of everything beforehand are missing in action but because of individuals who prefer to do nothing than anything at all. What is missing is therefore not an absolute and impossible goodness, but a fragile and imperfect goodness.

This is why it is pedagogically wrong, when stories of the Righteous are told, to emphasize unattainable heroism. This paradoxically removes responsibility of those who are prone to indifference. The truest and most sincere answer would be: "Why should I do it if I have to give up my pleasure, my family, my own life to help someone in danger? Sorry, but I do not feel like being a hero. You are asking of me something that is out of my human reach. I'm not superman." In order to be effective, sharing the memory of the Righteous must therefore humanize these individuals and make clear all their contradictions, ambiguities, and even smile at all their flaws without censoring them.

Examples of flawed individuals who count among the Righteous include Giorgio Perlasca, who pretended to be a Spanish diplomat and saved many Jews in Budapest— but he did so only because he allegedly fell in love with a beautiful Hungarian girl.[5] Another example is how the German writer Armin Wegner, who after denouncing the persecution of Jews in a letter to Hitler and was arrested and tortured in prison, wrote a defensive plea in which he said he was willing to work for the Third Reich in an attempt to save his own life.[6] He was freed, but he lost the opportunity to work in Germany and emigrated to Italy. The shorter the distance between a normal individual and a virtuous individual, the more it is possible to show the potential good within everyone's reach because the Righteous are not beyond the human dimension: they are just as fragile as the rest of us.

The Function of the Gardens of the Righteous in Society

What is the function of the Gardens of the Righteous in society? Why do we suggest expanding them into schools, in every city of Europe, and eventually across the whole world as a new experience in the framework of memory and education to responsibility? First of all, Gariwo believes that the stories of good individuals and righteous acts should not remain closed in the hidden vault of a museum but rather become obtainable for the whole of society as a constant source of example and emulation. No one would hide a work by Raphael or Michelangelo from people's sight. The same should apply to the actions of the Righteous who have taken responsibility during the darkest moments of humanity. They give us pleasure and joy like a beautiful work of art does. We know that those who do good actions do not do it for recognition but for their well-being instead.

This is emphasized by the stoic Marcus Aurelius[7] and by the New Testament Matthew,[8] who warn that good should never be done to seek reward, but rather for the sake of it. And yet, it is the awareness of the fragility of human beings that should make us understand that those who perform an act of humanity, taking all their personal risks, should never be forgotten. Even the best individual with the strongest and most determined character gives up or succumbs when he feels neglected and forgotten.

Those who do good are not gods or supermen. They need to feel the warmth of gratitude to move forward. This is why Gariwo believes that planting trees in the Gardens dedicated to the Righteous fosters the public to constantly give thanks. Indeed, there is not only indifference vis-à-vis victims, but also vis-à-vis those who have come to their rescue. Thus, educators who foster the Gardens turn into pearl fishermen who, as Walter Benjamin observed, bring back to light fragments of humanity that would remain hidden in the depths of history. Such visibility not only breaks the wall of oblivion, but also conveys to society the importance of remembering goodness and the value of gratitude. The discovery that acts of good and responsibility give relief and convey hope for the future often leads to the conveyance of gratitude: the pleasure of knowing and admiring the beauty of good individuals creates a new mechanism of emulation. The Righteous can cause a sense of amazement and greater trust in human kind, thus inspiring a need to value and take care of those who are committed to goodness and human dignity. The Gardens encourage gratitude not only because society feels it as a moral obligation, but because people experience the moment of appreciation as an existential pleasure enriching their human experience. This is why the creation of the Gardens in different cities leads to a new civil phenomenon: hundreds of requests to plant new trees arrive to Gariwo as municipalities and their populations feel the need to keep alive the stories of the Righteous that would otherwise be forgotten.

The Method of Indirect Communication

The Gardens are not meant to be just a place of commemoration. Their purpose is to foster moral consciences and responsibility. The method is indirect communication. In the Gardens visitors do not listen to sermons, but to stories pushing them to reflect. Pierre Hadot explains this well when recalling Kierkegaard's teaching, as he speaks of the educational value of indirect message encouraging free and never imposed choice.[9] Nothing is less effective than a moral appeal looking like a peremptory order or an absolute truth. If one is commanded what to do, conduct is dictated with a tone of false certainty. Instead, by hearing the experiences lived by others, one can let an attitude be glimpsed and suggested, let a recall be grasped that one can accept or refuse. It is up to this individual to decide. They are free to believe or not to believe, to act or not to act.

The whole architectural structure of the new Garden of the Righteous of Milan was designed with this purpose in mind. First of all, visitors are encouraged to compare the various stories of responsibility under the different genocides or totalitarianisms. Those who walk among the trees and the plaques are inspired to have a universal vision of the human condition and not only to stop in front of a story touching them closely, as for instance fascism in Italy. They learn several stories of moral resistance concerning other countries and different historical contexts. The following step is to introduce a comparison between past and present, because alongside the stories of the Righteous of the Holocaust, of the Gulags, or of the Armenian genocide, they find examples of moral responsibility concerning our time. This way, visitors receive the message that throughout history, evil is always present even though it manifests itself in different ways and that people must always make the choice between right or wrong. They better understand the present because they read it through the memory of the past and, reflecting on difficult decisions made by their contemporaries (for example, those who risk their lives today to save migrants or fight against terrorism or for women's freedom in religious fundamentalism), they become more empathetic vis-à-vis the Righteous of the past, who no longer appear to them as if they lived in a tragic film that does not concern them.

At the end of their journey they find themselves in two squares. The first, a smaller and more personal square, where they can sit on a bench and meditate, alone or with a friend. The second square hosts a larger amphitheater, designed to foster collective debate for a school, an association, a neighborhood group. Visitors are able to leave their solitary reflection and question themselves before a small polis, where they can publicly express their opinions. They get involved and, after their visit, promise to take responsibility: their discovery of the stories of the Righteous allows them to begin to narrate their own story. It is a sort of spiritual exercise that begins that day, but continues on and is extended to their active and daily life.

Consequently, the Gardens have a Socratic function. Through the stories of the Righteous, visitors wonder and perhaps even question themselves. They must face their own prejudices without any constraints, which Socrates called frozen thoughts. The Gardens also play an important role in sharing and creating a dialogue between the majority and minorities living in metropolitan cities with different experiences, religions, and cultural references; for Jews, Armenians, Rwandans who survived a genocide; migrants from Eastern Europe who lived in communist totalitarian regimes; women who experienced religious obscurantism in Africa and Asia; as well as Muslims in Bosnia and Thailand who suffered ethnic cleansing. All of them experience good and evil differently. Even the very concept of Righteous and responsibility have different values.

Muslims who visit the Gardens learn the condition of Jews and the importance of those who fought against anti-Semitism, and in turn, Jews learn about those who tried to save lives in the Armenian or Rwandan genocides. Even Western Europeans who are linked to the historical experience of anti-fascism can open up to the knowledge of resistance to communist totalitarianism, the understanding of which is still difficult today and leads to many delays in the political and cultural construction of Europe. Too often the academic debate on those who have suffered the greatest evil is likely to cover up evil with another evil. When dealing with crimes against humanity, the concept of lesser evil can never apply.

Through this universal approach, Gariwo tries to show that a genocide or a crime does not only concern the minority that has suffered it, but must become the memory of all human kind. Gariwo, however, still faces obstacles. Sometimes misconceptions occur, for example in sharing the stories about the Righteous, visitors were only concerned with the memory of people who were oppressed, rather than connecting it to a larger dimension. Instead, the idea must be affirmed that every time a genocide occurs, the whole world is hurt. For this reason, a Righteous who comes to the rescue of an individual of a persecuted minority always becomes a guardian of all human kind. And the Righteous do not exist for a single historical context since in every circumstance there are courageous and responsible individuals who act to defend human dignity.

The Gardens also indicate that ethical and responsibility decisions taking place in different contexts have a common moral matrix. There is indeed no difference between those who helped an Armenian, a Jew, or a Muslim. There is common humanity in all gestures of solidarity. When elaborated upon, the memory of goodness allows bridging gaps and prejudices: the beauty of good individuals plays an extraordinary function because it allows for understanding to belong to the human race rather than to individuals. A Righteous no longer has a homeland in particular, but rather belongs to the whole world and has the strength to inspire others.

The Experience of Charter '77 and Education to Responsibility

How can the Gardens of the Righteous stimulate great decisions made by individuals?

It is crucial for them to always be surrounded by a collective thought process that can convey thorough information the time in which we live. Its task is not to suggest *a priori* solutions, but to indicate areas in which human beings have to choose in historical conditions in which they have been thrown as existing beings.

Gariwo has taken as a reference the historical experience of Charter '77, which in Prague during the years of resistance to communism led people of different cultures and backgrounds to come to terms with their own time, indicating possible itineraries and virtuous behaviors.

To be good and virtuous it was necessary to understand the context, because all citizens in their small circles of possibility, as Shakespeare wrote in Hamlet, had to correct their times. Moreover, this task never ends in history and repeats itself from generation to generation.

This is why Jan Patocka and Vaclav Havel, the founders of the Charter, proposed for the citizens of Prague to document their thoughts; they were encouraged to reflect and think.

With the same spirit, together with philosophers, thinkers, scientists, scholars, Gariwo draws up from time to time Charters of responsibility on the important issues of today.

Currently the great challenges that no responsible individual can escape concern defense and protection of the planet threatened by global warming; the choice between global responsibility and closure under dangerous nationalism; defense of political democracy against policies of populism and illiberal democracy; preservation of peace and nonviolence in wars and terrorist threats.

Knowledge is therefore necessary to act, as Havel realized, which good teachers must be able to convey to society.

Education to thinking as a spiritual exercise, which Pierre Hadot indicated in some practices taken from the classical world[10] (the ability to look at the world from above and to views fellow humans from a universal point of view, the willingness to always put oneself in other people's shoes, the awareness of the fragility of life that unites human beings that should push them to cooperate and to be friends, the exercise of will leading to the good behavior and freedom of individuals), must therefore be complemented by knowledge of the dynamics of the world.

An example among all: if at the time of Shoah information on concentration camps and Nazi politics had been disseminated in a much clearer way, societies would have been more likely involved in the rescue of Jews. Many governments were responsible for such forgetfulness, such as the American and Soviet governments, which did not alert public opinion, and so the Jews themselves did not realize the danger they were facing.

As Anatoly Kuznetzov wrote in Babi Yar, a book censored during the years of communism, Jews in Ukraine at the time of German invasion did not realize the danger they were facing because Soviet newspapers after the Ribbentrop Molotov pact "did nothing else than magnify and exalt Hitler, the best friend of the Soviet Union, and gave no news of the condition of Jews in Germany and Poland."[11]

This is why the task of the Gardens of the Righteous, by the highlighting of positive individuals, is to warn citizens about decisions they are all called to make in new and current emergencies. How to be Righteous in our time? This is the question that educators promoting the Gardens ask Gariwo.

The method, as Vaclav Havel explained is not, however, of the Enlightenment type with abstract indications coming from above, but rather consists in indicating positive practices that everyone can follow in their daily life.

The playwright, inspirer of Charter '77, understood that knowledge is to be conveyed so as to create alternative life forms through which totalitarian power could be eroded from the bottom. The awareness of negative time, in which Prague inhabitants were crushed, had to stimulate citizens to create a parallel society that implemented experiences of virtuous life.

It was not a matter of attacking power and pointing out enemies, once again proposing a totalitarian logic according to which the Jacobin conquest of the Palace was the solution to all issues, but rather of building good practices that changes the ways of living of people. The strength of this perspective lies in the creation of a collective emulation movement that educates even the worst individuals to repent and change course. This is why, though resisting a totalitarian power, like in the example of Etty Hillesum, Havel never fell into the logic of a final showdown between us and them (at the basis of the enemy's culture), but always set out to create collective self-education movements.

With this same spirit, Gariwo has tried to give an answer to the mechanisms of hatred and contempt that we see today in social media and politics and that can become, unless properly addressed, dangerous germs of evil and generate dangerous conflicts.

Today two phenomena are occurring, correlated to each other at the level of power, but also in widespread customs of society. The first one is how politicians use social media for campaigns that generate contempt and create enemies among people.

Once dictators like Hitler, Mussolini, and Stalin manipulated individuals through an innovative technique that galvanized people through mass gatherings and direct communication where tyrants from a balcony addressed the crowd directly and presented themselves as their absolute representatives; conversely, today, the worst politicians have created new balconies to influence people through unscrupulous use of social media and the dissemination of fake news on the web.

Through specially designed systems, they disseminate political campaigns that bypass traditional institutions and media, and from time to time create enemies against whom people should thrust. A tweet that speaks to people's guts and triggers the worst instincts against migrants or political opponents can have the same impact as a speech by Mussolini in Piazza Venezia against Jews and the Masonic Jewish power in banks.

This mechanism of communication leading to contempt and insults does not only concern the worst politicians, but has also become a negative practice in the way of speaking in the social media. Today there are so many people who present themselves as the bearers of an absolute truth and stigmatize those who have different opinions, pushing the tribe following them to insult and isolate these individuals, and using very harsh words. Everyone can say what they want without having any competence in the matter, but only by hearsay. So often people almost unconsciously get used to looking for enemies on all sides, ready to receive the worst political messages and to integrate them in their daily life.

This is why we have proposed a Charter of Responsibilities in Social Media that encourages people to create a parallel society (according to Havel's teaching), watching over hatred and fake news and in which people speak gracefully and respectfully with others. If one gets used to this virtuous behavior, it will be easier to isolate professional haters and stop the line of personal contempt in politics. We need to create a web of friends and not of enemies.

The second theme is of encouraging good competition in sports, as the Greek poet Hesiod stated, which fosters respect of the opponent and friendship in competition, in support and in the narration of sporting events. Agonism in sport that involves a relationship in which human beings compete with each other, for better or for worse, indicates the advance of civilized behavior among human beings.

It can be used by dictatorships to convey the message of superiority of a race or of a nation and become an ideological propaganda tool for totalitarian regimes; or it can become the expression of moral wealth of a democratic society enhancing equality in sport competition and the purpose of which is always exalting individual or collective performance in a spirit of friendship.

In recent years the most significant experience of good agonism has come from South Africa, where, after the years of apartheid, President Nelson Mandela wanted the national rugby team to become the vehicle for reconciliation of white and black people, the symbol of possible integration in his country.

Conversely, the football match of May 13, 1990, at Maksimir stadium between Dinamo Zagreb and Red Star Belgrade unleashed a bloody guerrilla war between the relevant supporters that recalled the civil war in former Yugoslavia. Supporters in that stadium did not cheer for sport, but rather considered the sport competition as the fight against an enemy that had to be destroyed. That match, exploited by nationalists, therefore laid the foundations for the imminence of war. Opposing footballers were hated and the ball was to be replaced by weapons. Today, in a dangerous time where hatred and nationalism are coming back, where in the name of a religion massacres are committed, where black athletes are insulted in stadiums, where an Arab athlete is prevented from competing and shaking hands with an Israeli athlete, it is necessary to bring back the values of good and positive competition in sports.

As history taught us, sometimes sport can save the world, because the behavior of athletes, supporters, and even sport journalists can positively impact the democratic life of our societies. For this reason we have drawn up a Charter of Responsibilities in Sport signed by great Olympic champions, by athletes of all sports and by well-known journalists, since current hatred in society is fed by degeneration in sport cheering, similar to the worst communication practices on social media.

What is at stake is collective awareness of the culture of the enemy and of hate speech in our fragile democracies. The Gardens of the Righteous of our time have a task that nobody would have ever imagined: to raise awareness of the Righteous who have understood that protecting the planet is crucial to safeguarding the future of humanity, as is the creation of a movement fostering collective responsibility that can break all barriers.

In this case, the Talmud principle should be updated. It is no longer sufficient to say *those who save a life save a whole world*, but *we must all together save the whole world*.

Notes

1. Gabriele Nissim, Il tribunale del bene, la storia di Moshe Bejski, l'uomo che creò il giardino dei giusti, Milan, Mondadori, 2003.

2. Heraclitus. "A man's character is his fate."

3. "Responsibility for others begins with those with whom we are truly united by bonds of mutuality and reciprocity, and expands towards those with whom we may enter into this relationship. As for all the others with whom we share this earth, we can do much for them, we can hold them in the embrace of charity and solidarity, but we do not necessarily take responsibility for them." Agnes Heller, "An Ethics of Personality, the Other and the Question of Responsibility," in Agnes Heller, *La bellezza della persona buona* (Diabasis: La Ginestra, 2008).

4. "Do not wait for Plato's Republic, but be happy if one little thing can lead to progress and reflect on the fact that what results from such a little thing is not, in fact, so very little."

Marcus Aurelius quoted in Pierre Hadot, *What Is Ancient Philosophy?* (Turin: Einaudi, 1998), 270.

5. Gabriele Nissim, *Il bene possibile, essere giusti nel nostro tempo* (Milan: Utet, 2018), 5.

6. Gabriele Nissim, *La lettera a Hitler, storia di Armin Wegner combattente solitario contro i genocidi del Novecento* (Milan: Mondadori, 2015), 175.

7. "What would you more, when you have done a man a kindness? Is it not enough for you that you have acted in this according to your nature? Do you ask a reward for it? It is as if the eye were to ask a reward for seeing, or the feet for walking . . . . So man, formed by nature to do kindness to his fellows . . . whenever he acts kindly, has fulfilled the purpose of his creation, and has possession of what is his own." Marcus Aurelius, *Ricordi* (Turin: Einaudi, 2015).

8. Beware of practicing your righteousness before other people in order to be seen by them, for then you will have no reward from your Father who is in heaven. Thus, when you give to the needy, sound no trumpet before you, as the hypocrites do in the synagogues and in the streets, that they may be praised by others. Truly, I say to you, they have received their reward. But when you give to the needy, do not let your left hand know what your right hand is doing, so that your giving may be in secret. And your Father, who sees what is done in secret, will reward you. Saint Matthew, *Gospel* (Milan: Edizioni San Paolo, 2008).

9. "If you say directly 'Do like this or like that', conduct is dictated with a tone of false certainty. Instead, thanks to the description of a spiritual life lived by another, it is possible to glimpse and suggest a spiritual attitude, let catch a call that the reader has freedom to accept and reject. It is up to the reader to decide. The reader is free to believe and not to believe, to act or not to act." Pierre Hadot, *Philosophy As a Way of Life* (Einaudi: Turin, 2008).

10. Pierre Hadot, *Spiritual Exercises and Ancient Philosophy* (Einaudi: Turin, 1981).

11. Anatolij Kuznecov, *Babij Jair* (Milan: Adelphi Edizioni, 2019), 104.

CHAPTER 8
WOMEN AND RESISTANCE
NEW PERSPECTIVES FROM GERMANY AND FRANCE
Anne Nelson

Introduction

For decades following the end of the Second World War, the popular image of the resistance movements in wartime Europe involved bands of daring men engaged in executing German officers, blowing up trains, and other paramilitary activities. Popular culture offered little to amend or broaden this depiction, whether it was dealing with the Gaullist resistance in France (such as the 1969 film *L'armée des ombres*) or the Jewish resistance in Poland (such as the 2008 film *Defiance*). Resistance was depicted as a mirror image to the military operations of the enemy. Just as the National Socialist command structure was mapped in hierarchical organigrams, the Gestapo zealously but mistakenly drew parallel hierarchical pyramids for resistance groups such as the *Rote Kapelle* network, whose fluid interconnecting subgroups bore little resemblance to military organizations with their capacity for command and control.

But over the years both the definition and the depictions of resistance to Hitler began to shift. The collective work of historians showed that rather than resembling a monolith, Nazi Germany was a patchwork of zealots, passive accommodationists, collaborationists, and beneficiaries of the regime. Active clandestine resisters such as the members of the *Rote Kapelle* network constituted a small fraction, but left their mark nonetheless.

Postwar scholarship also revised the concept of a hierarchical command structure in many resistance movements. German historians introduced the idea of the *Querverdindung*, a term that is not easily translated into English. *Quer* suggests a crosshatch; *Verbindung* a network or set of interconnections. *Querverbindung* suggests an interlocking set of relationships, governed by collaboration among overlapping groups rather than a hierarchical command. So a member of a singing society who joined a network might recruit a friend from a sporting club, who then recruited a fellow member of a church group, and so on: Members recruited from different circles were often unaware of each other's involvement. When the Gestapo brought in scores of activists from the *Rote Kapelle* for interrogation, friends and neighbors passed each other in the hallways with surprise, unaware that their acquaintances were also involved.

The great majority of resistance figures in Europe were male, and many worked within military-model hierarchies, either because they originated with military organizations, such as the German 20th of July plot or because they developed paramilitary models, such as the French Francs-Tireurs et Partisans. But the updated concept of Resistance also includes an array of activities that counter and oppose the abuses of the regime and its supporters. In this regard, rescue operations come to the fore. If one prime objective of the Third Reich was to eliminate Europe's Jewish population, actions to preserve Jewish lives can be considered an act of resistance, whether openly, as a consequence of intermarriage, or clandestinely, through providing hiding places, forged documents, and necessities such as ration cards. One could also make a case for including those who risked their own safety to harbor victims of political persecution and other endangered individuals, such as downed Allied flyers.

Once these new approaches are adopted, another new field opens up: a reevaluation of the role of women in resistance. This subject, too, has been ripe for revision. The initial postwar perspective brought three sets of blinders to the understanding of women's resistance activities, all three related to actual events, but limiting the field of vision to the tropes of the time. The first was a narrow focus on military and paramilitary operations. For example, a vibrant body of literature emerged to describe the heroic French and British women in the UK's Special Operations Executive (SOE) who parachuted into France, often as radio operators, and frequently paid the ultimate price for their courage. One early example was the 1958 feature film "Carve Her Name with Pride," depicting Violette Szabo, a young Anglo-French SOE agent who was executed at Ravensbrück in the final weeks of the Nazi regime. British military historian M. R. D. Foot was among the first to recognize the women of the SOE in his many writings on the organization, which spanned several decades. But these operations involved women who worked at the bidding of male strategists and officers. On the ground, they interacted with the French resistance, but were themselves agents of a foreign military intelligence agency rather than an indigenous resistance operation. And however great their valor, they generally acted in a support capacity.

The second set of blinders involved the literary conventions of the period. Fictional representation of women in the resistance tended to represent them as recruited and directed by their romantic partners. The feminist Simone de Beauvoir took this route in her novel of the French Resistance, *Le Sang des autres* ("The Blood of Others"), written between 1941 and 1943 and published in 1945. Beauvoir's heroine, Hélène Bertrand, is a curiously passive and self-indulgent character. Over the course of the novel she attaches herself to first to a boyfriend, then to a group of German officers, and finally to a résistant, always carried along by the winds of whim, self-interest, and attraction. De Beauvoir writes dismissively, "Gauthier was a pacifist. Paul was a communist. Hélène was in love."[1] Eventually her résistant lover enlists her in an operation that goes wrong. As she lies on her deathbed, she reassures him that she undertook the mission of her own free will, but he is left wondering whether she had fully understood what she was undertaking.[2]

As historian Claire Gorrara writes, "It would appear that Beauvoir could envisage no other ending for her female resistance protagonist than physical breakdown or death." It is hard to escape the idea of Hélène as a victim, of either her lover's manipulation or her own naïveté. Perhaps Beauvoir was distancing herself from her character to justify her own distance from the resistance over a critical period of the Occupation. As biographer Carole Seymour-Jones shows in her book *A Dangerous Liaison*, both Beauvoir and her partner Jean-Paul Sartre kept a safe distance from the resistance over the period she was writing the novel, and only sought an involvement with the final days of the Occupation.[3]

Beauvoir wrote *Le Sang des autres* between 1941 and 1943. (It was published in 1945.) Lacking heat in their apartments, she and Sartre did their writing in the Café de Flore on the Left Bank (occupying their respective spots in the front and the back so as not to distract each other). Beauvoir, who had no involvement in resistance activities herself, wrote a fantasy of the eroticized and ineffectual woman in the resistance. Ironically, over the same period the existentialists were imagining the resistance at the Café de Flore was also the favored location for Suzanne Spaak's colleagues from the Jewish resistance, Léon Chertok. There the handsome young physician from Vilnius (nom de guerre "*le Bel Alex*") enlisted supporters for their resistance efforts among his swarms of female admirers. Two of his recruits, the Catala sisters, carried out the heroic task of infiltrating the *Vel d'Hiv* stadium after the mass arrests in July 1942. Presenting themselves as French social workers, they provided one of the first and very few eyewitness accounts of the horrific conditions suffered by the nearly 13,000 Jewish immigrant children, women, and men detained there as a waystation to Auschwitz. Spaak's and Chertok's movement subsequently published the sisters' testimony in their underground *tract*.

They would like us to be silent about this appalling crime. But no, we cannot permit ourselves. People have to know. Everyone needs to know about what happened here.[4]

But it is Beauvoir's fantasy of resistance that has lived on in popular literature, while the valiant and effective undertakings of Suzanne Spaak, the Catala sisters, and their networks—many of them "composed" at the same café—have been long obscured.

Clearly, the active female resister was not easy to place in the mainstream occupation narratives of the late 1940s and early 1950s.[5] One could point to a parallel process in fashion: wartime women donned utilitarian factory overalls, uniforms, pants, and suits. After the war, Christian Dior (whose sister Catherine was a notable résistante) retrofitted them into the "New Look," constraining them in wasp-waisted dresses and heels, just as the postwar literature of the resistance constricted them in roles as romantic foils and sidekicks to the male leading characters.

The third set of blinders resulted from Cold War interpretations of wartime movements. Resistance movements can be the ultimate illustration of the adage "Politics makes strange bedfellows." Throughout Germany and much of Occupied Europe, these movements assembled Royalists, Socialists, and Communists, and Catholics, Protestants, and Jews, in common cause against the German occupiers and their local proxies. These factions may have been bitter enemies before and after the war, but desperate conditions united them against a common enemy.

But many postwar historians inflated the role of the Communist Party, and portrayed these coalitions as purely communist organizations and instruments of the Soviet Union, even if party members constituted a minority, and the groups repeatedly defied Soviet instructions.[6]

The Cold War interpretation also distorted the record of women in the resistance. It was legitimate, but not conclusive, to see ties between communist front organizations and some women's organizations. In the decades before the war, women entered the European labor force in record numbers, many impoverished by the economic upheavals following the First World War. In France, Belgium, and Germany these included émigrés who responded to the egalitarian message of Marxism, and benefited from communist-backed trade unions' struggle for higher wages and improved working conditions. Marxist study groups and mutual support organizations eased the hardships of their daily life, especially for women in low-wage and cottage-industry jobs, such as the garment industry and the fur trade.

These groups were extinguished or driven underground in Nazi Germany in the 1930s, but they were thriving in Paris at the time of the German invasion. As the repressive measures of the Occupation increased, the groups in France also dissolved or went underground, but their social ties often remained, serving as a lifeline to their members and an organizational template for resistance and rescue activity.

The influence of leftist organizations spread to women beyond the working class. Female intellectuals and upper- and middle-class reformers were also influenced by the strains of socialism that gathered momentum alongside first-wave feminism. In the pre-Stalinist era of the 1920s, the boundaries that divided different brands of socialism were not yet hardened. Visitors to the Soviet Union saw unprecedented reforms in action, as granting women paid maternity leave, legalized abortion, a minimum wage, and equality under the constitution. Western European women formed clubs and discussion groups in support of such goals—if not the communists' violent paths to power.

Most of the women of the anti-Nazi resistance were women of a very specific time. Most were born in the early twentieth century, a period marked by sweeping ideas of reform—feminism, socialism, rebukes to anti-Semitism—which touched many of them at a formative stage. They came of age under the influence of new voices such as Rosa Luxembourg (in the case of Greta Kuckhoff) and Belgian Senator Marie Spaak (in the case of her daughter-in-law Suzanne Spaak). Nazi ideology constituted a harsh reversal of these reformist values. In many ways, the actions of the women resisters represented a reassertion of female agency and reform, as well as a rebuke of Nazism.

Greta Kuckhoff and Suzanne Spaak shared many of these values, but there were also important distinctions. As a Belgian national living in Occupied Paris, Spaak is easy to place within the context of resisters against a foreign occupier—all the more so because her brother-in-law, Paul-Henri Spaak, was a ranking member of the Belgian-government-in exile in London. Over the course of the Occupation, an increasing portion of the French population adopted this position, as Vichy's complicity with the Germans was revealed and the Occupation grew more brutal.

Kuckhoff and her associates, on the other hand, were German nationals working against their own government, and thus subject to accusations of treason. They argued that true patriotism required them to try to end the regime that was destroying their country—an argument that has been debated to this day

The Women of the Rote Kapelle: Berlin

In recent years, closer looks at anti-Nazi movements have revealed many important influences and patterns in the "women's work" of resistance. One of the best known examples is Sophie Scholl, the brave young student from Munich who worked alongside her brother Hans and other youth in the Weisse Rose resistance movement. The group studied Nazi crimes and attempted to alert the public through a series of pamphlets, until most of them were detected and executed. Sophie Scholl and her companions have been justly celebrated for their courage and the nobility of their vision, but they were of limited effectiveness.

There was a lesser known group, with a much larger number of women, that the Nazis judged to be a far greater threat to the regime. This was the set of interlocking networks that German military intelligence and the Gestapo labeled the *Rote Kapelle*, or "Red Orchestra." These groups began with anti-Nazi activities in Berlin in the mid-1930s, and extended to Paris and Brussels under the Occupation.

For years, historians followed the Gestapo's lead in portraying them as principally intelligence operations, inasmuch as they shared varying levels of contact with Soviet master spy Leopold Trepper. But further study has revealed that Trepper recruited the Berlin and Paris groups for intelligence work years after they were established and engaged in resistance activities, including the production of underground publications and providing humanitarian aid to victims of the regime. Both the Berlin and the Paris circles devoted considerable effort to Jewish rescue operations, against the express wishes of the Soviet intelligence service.

Finally, both the German and French/Belgian *Rote Kapelle* circles were overwhelmingly nationalist in nature, seeking to liberate their countries from the National Socialists rather than deliver them to the Soviets. Both the German and the French/Belgian groups were formed by members of the non-Jewish intellectual and economic elite—people who could have bargained with and benefited from the regime had they so chosen. While the groups included some members of the Communist Party, these were in the minority and played subordinate roles. Trepper sought out these groups precisely because they were already organized and had access to important contacts, information, and resources. The surviving evidence, based on their leaders' writings and conversations, shows that they agreed to work with the Soviets because they saw an Allied victory as the quickest route to defeating Hitler, ending the bloodshed, and restoring their countries' democratic autonomy.

To understand the role of women in the *Rote Kapelle* German resistance network, it is useful to start with one of the earliest members, Greta Lorke Kuckhoff. She illustrates one common characteristic of women's resistance networks: their expansive range of contacts woven through social ties rather than rooted in institutions such as business or the military. In 1927 Greta Lorke, a twenty-five-year-old woman from Frankfurt-an-der-Oder, set off for America to pursue graduate studies in sociology. Her original goal was Columbia University, but an American friend pointed her to go to the University of Wisconsin as a more affordable alternative. Lorke (who later went by her married name of Greta Kuckoff), found Madison to be a vibrant laboratory for social reform. In her memoirs, *Vom Rosenkranz zur Roten Kapelle*, she recorded her enthusiastic reactions to progressive movements taking shape around her. She befriended African American students engaged in the struggle for civil rights, and visited a Ford factory to witness the harsh working conditions that trade unions were fighting to improve. Throughout her time in Wisconsin, feminism was a constant theme. She noted that in Germany, professors declined to even shake hands with female students, whereas the American professors welcomed her perspective. Her social circle was replete with strong, accomplished women who had set out to change the world; one of them was Elizabeth Brandeis, whose father was the first Jewish justice on the US Supreme Court, and who became a member of Roosevelt's Brain Trust a few years later. Her roommate, PhD student Elsie Glück, would become a prominent labor economist.

But the female friend who would have the largest impact on Greta's life was Mildred Fish Harnack, the American wife of another German student. Arvid Harnack belonged to a family of prominent theologians and academics, far above Greta in social status, both in Berlin and Madison. Greta's memoirs recorded that his cerebral, austere manner could be off-putting but his wife Mildred, an aspiring literature professor, was friendly, high-minded, and unpretentious. Greta and the gentle American became fast friends, whereas Greta remained highly conscious of Arvid's superior academic standing.

Greta and the Harnacks returned to a thriving Germany—shortly before the stock market crash of 1929. It hit the US economy hard, but it hit Germany much harder. The Harnacks moved often, and work was hard to come by. Mildred, who had experienced economic hardship as a child, brought a humanitarian perspective to the crisis. She wrote home to her mother, "The situation is hardest on many children of the middle and lower classes, who don't get enough to eat and are in economic fear."[7] In 1932 the Harnacks were invited to visit the Soviet Union by an economist friend. They were given a Potemkin Village tour of the country's economic conditions; Mildred was impressed by reforms that benefited women through access to birth control and maternity leave.

The following year brought more upheaval in Germany. January 30, 1933, marked the *Machtergreifung* that brought Adolf Hitler to power. A few years earlier, Greta Lorke had fallen in love with a prominent German writer named Adam Kuckhoff. (They would marry in 1937.) Both Arvid Harnack and Adam Kuckhoff initiated resistance work early on in the Nazi period, and Mildred and Greta joined them in their anti-Nazi activities. They also took on important initiatives of their own, based on circles of female friendship. Mildred made friends with the new US ambassador's daughter, Martha Dodd, and parlayed the friendship into access to the embassy as an organizing outlet.

In 1935 Martha Dodd asked Mildred Harnack to organize a reception for visiting American novelist Thomas Wolfe. Mildred asked Greta to use the occasion to assemble possible recruits for their resistance activities. Greta wrote in her memoirs that Arvid Harnack "was concerned that in order to explore the extent of the anti-Nazi front and its possibilities for expansion, it was necessary to make acquaintances and establish contacts between different circles and groups, and increase the sources of information."[8] Martha Dodd had little understanding of the event going on around her. She found her party "a dull, yet at the same time tense afternoon"—but then, it had not been arranged for her amusement. Rather it was a deployment of women's social networks to serve resistance strategy. Both of the Harnacks had infiltrated Nazi Party organizations as part of their resistance work; Arvid won an influential position at the economics ministry and Mildred joined a Nazi women's association. Even more importantly, Mildred's US embassy contacts led to an introduction to economics attaché Donald Heath, who was secretly serving an intelligence function in Berlin. The Harnacks would provide Heath with a flow of anti-Nazi intelligence until 1941, when the US Embassy was closed and he was transferred to Chile.

Greta and Mildred watched as Hitler drove Germany ever deeper into conflict: with the occupation of the Rhineland in 1936; to the annexation of Austria and the Sudetenland in 1938; to the conquest of the rest of Czechoslovakia in the spring of 1939; and the invasion of Poland the following September. The Berlin resistance circles stepped up their activities accordingly. These included recruiting more new members, gathering and disseminating accurate information to contest Nazi propaganda, and assisting victims of persecution. The circle added an increasingly diverse assortment of members with widely varying backgrounds. Many of them—ultimately almost half—were women. Maria Terwiel, a beautiful young law student, was engaged to Helmut Himpel, a dentist, but they were barred from marrying under the 1935 Nuremberg Laws because she was half-Jewish. Terwiel and Himpel forged ration cards and travel documents for desperate Jews and hosted clandestine meetings in his dental office. Dr. Elfriede Paul was a medical doctor and a Communist Party member who offered her clinic as a clandestine print shop for flyers. Dr. Paul went the extra mile, mailing the flyers from remote locations around Berlin under the guise of making house calls.

The women of the *Rote Kapelle* were as varied in their backgrounds as they were in ideology. Hilda Coppi came from a working-class family in Berlin. She and her husband Hans, a Communist Party member, hid political fugitives and participated in anti-Nazi information campaigns. At the other end of the social scale was the most glamorous of the assembly, Libertas Schulze-Boysen, the granddaughter of a Prussian prince. She worked in the movie industry and married Harro Schulze-Boysen, the scion of a celebrated military family. He had a deep antipathy towards the Nazis and found a position as one of Goering's air force intelligence officers as a means to undermine them. The Schulze-Boysens joined the Harnack-Kuckhoff circle in 1939. After the invasion of the Soviet Union, Libertas used her position in the documentary film division of Goebbels' propaganda ministry to secretly gather documentation of German war crimes for future prosecution.

Some of the women of the Rote Kapelle had party affiliations; many did not. Libertas had no particular ideology; this was also the case with an acquaintance of hers, Cato Bontjes van Beek, an accomplished young ceramics artist. Bontjes van Beek began her resistance career with her sister Mietje, collecting ration cards on behalf of Jewish neighbors and offering friendly assistance to French prisoners of war. After she joined the Schulze-Boysens' resistance circle, Cato recruited a band of male and female art students to support the work of the movement, hiding fugitives, carrying messages, and participating in information campaigns. Two of these were Jewish art students she befriended, Katja Casella and Lisa Egler-Gervai (later known by their married names, Katja Meirowsky and Lisa Eisenberg). They were able to hide their Jewish identities, and became last known surviving members of the resistance group after the war.

The expanded group functioned for less than three years in the heart of Berlin, from 1939 to 1942. German military intelligence and the Gestapo called it the *Rote Kapelle* in reference to its attempts to use radio transmitters, or *klaviers*, to transmit information to the "Reds" in Moscow. A group of radios was called a *Kapelle*, or chamber orchestra.) The Nazi regime preferred to emphasize the group's link to foreign intelligence over its resistance activities. In actuality, only handful of its members had any knowledge of the radio operations, which were late, sporadic, and largely unsuccessful.

The resistance network grew to over 150 members, about half of them women. Women engaged in humanitarian resistance, such as Cato Bontjes van Beek and her friends, risked arrest by diffusing anti-Nazi information and providing small mercies to French prisoners of war and compulsory work gangs; actress Marta Wolter was sent to a concentration camp for hiding a political fugitive. For the most part, the men fulfilled the intelligence functions by virtue of their positions in the regime: Arvid Harnack in the Economics Ministry, Harro Schulze-Boysen in the Luftwaffe, etc. But the humanitarian resistance activities carried out by the women was also dangerous. Cato Bontjes van Beek and her friends risked arrest by participating in anti-Nazi information campaigns and providing small mercies to French prisoners of war and compulsory work gangs; actress Marta Wolter was sent to a concentration camp for hiding a fugitive from the regime.

However, the Gestapo did have reason for linking the group to foreign intelligence. For several years before the United States entered the war, Arvid and Mildred Harnack provided information to their friend Donald Heath, a foreign service officer at the US embassy in Berlin. Arvid Harnack also secretly offered his services to the US State Department on a trip to Washington in 1939. (They were declined.) In September 1940 Harnack was approached by an agent for the Soviet intelligence agency NKVD and asked to send intelligence to the Soviets. Harnack was initially wary, but he acquiesced, desperate to avert the coming catastrophe.

Soviet communications in Western Europe were coordinated through a master spy named Leopold Trepper, based in Brussels and Paris. Trepper conveyed Moscow's orders that the Berlin group should cease all humanitarian efforts on behalf of Jews and political prisoners, as well as their efforts to gather and distribute information to break through Nazi censorship. These activities, they argued, endangered their intelligence efforts. The leaders of the Berlin network flatly refused; they considered themselves German patriots first and foremost, and considered their intelligence functions for the Allies to be a means to the end of liberating their country from Nazi rule.

Ironically, when a fatal security lapse occurred, it was committed by the Moscow intelligence professionals, not the Berlin amateurs. In August 1941, an impatient intelligence officer radioed coded instructions to Trepper to make personal contact with members of the Berlin group, sending their names and addresses over the airwaves. The Germans intercepted the message; it was only a matter of time before they broke the code. In September 1942 the Gestapo began a wave of arrests: the Schulze-Boysens, the Harnacks, the Kuckhoffs; some 150 members of the network in all. (Many others eluded detection; the total number of the network has never been established.) Between December 1942 and July 1943, forty-five members of the group were sentenced to death, twenty-nine were sent to prison, and two were acquitted for lack of evidence.[9] Many of the men in the group were assigned an agonizing death of slow strangulation from meat hooks. Several men committed suicide in detention rather than give way to torture. Women—among them Libertas Schulze-Boysen, Hilda Coppi, and Cato Bontjes van Beek—were granted a swifter death by guillotine. Mildred Harnack was the only American woman executed by direct order from Hitler; Greta Kuckhoff was initially sentenced to death, but fate intervened to send her to prison instead.

Greta Kuckhoff became one of the guardians of the memory of the *Rote Kapelle*, though her memoirs, published in 1972, were harshly constrained by East German censorship. She wrote movingly about her friendships with Mildred Harnack, Libertas Schulze-Boysen, and other women in the network. She sought out Hans Coppi, the orphaned son of Hilda and Hans Coppi, and took him under her wing.

To the extent that the *Querverbindung* of the *Rote Kapelle* had a leadership, one cannot argue that it consisted of the women; in Germany the network is often referred to as the Harnack/Schulze-Boysen Gruppe after the husbands of Mildred and Greta. On the other hand, the women of the group undertook bold missions at the risk of their lives, and initiated humanitarian actions that saved lives. Their participation sent a strong message that resistance to tyranny was also "women's work" that they carried out across a number of fronts. They exploited their traditional role as conveners of social gatherings to host strategy sessions. This function took on critical importance under a dictatorship that surveilled meetings and banned public gatherings. Time and again, contacts are made and crucial information is exchanged at dinners, tea dances, and cocktail parties. These meetings initially escaped the notice of the regime because it dismissed women as inconsequential. But the brutal reprisal demonstrated that these women were effective enough to pay with their lives.

The Women of the Rote Kapelle: Paris

Another network in Paris—as in Berlin—was dedicated to resistance against the Nazis and rescue efforts on behalf of their victims, and linked to the espionage network organized by Leopold Trepper. This group was also labeled as the *Rote Kapelle* (or in French, *l'Orchestre rouge*). In the French case, the ties to espionage activity were even more limited (mostly involving attempts to shelter Trepper and other Jewish members of his espionage ring from Gestapo arrest). The Jewish rescue operations, on the other hand, were carried out on a far greater scale, and it can be argued that the leadership grew directly from women's friendships and associations. Yet, again, it has taken historians decades to peel away the misleading layers of Cold War interpretations of their work, and expand the focus from Trepper's spy network to their humanitarian operations.

It is telling that even the nomenclature of the movement presents a problem (as reflected in the Germans' awkward Harnack/Schulze-Boysen Gruppe). In Paris, the question of women's resistance networks is further complicated by the fluid nature of their organizations. As we shall see, organizations that began as ladies' charitable or mutual aid societies took on rescue and resistance roles. Women's groups that were founded as sectarian and political associations blended, merged, and cooperated to make common cause against the Occupation and its abuses.

These phenomena are amply illustrated in the Paris rescue and resistance network associated with Suzanne Spaak. She was the daughter of a Belgian financier named Louis Lorge, who had worked his way up from messenger boy to head of a major firm that provided financing for large-scale industrial projects around the turn of the century (among them the Paris Métro and the Suez Canal). Lorge doted on his oldest daughter, a delicate, gifted child named Suzanne. Suzanne had little use for her father's acquisitiveness, but she was deeply influenced by her mother's Catholic charity lunches, held to benefit the poor and disabled. She also admired one of her mother's friends, Marie Spaak, who became the first female Senator in the world. Marie Spaak was a member of Belgium's leading political dynasty and a tireless reformist, using her position to advocate for women's, workers', and immigrants' rights. As a teenager, Suzanne fell in love with Marie's youngest son Claude. They married—against her father's wishes—when the couple was barely twenty.

It was a difficult marriage from the start. Claude was the least distinguished of three brothers. The oldest, Paul-Henri, would become Belgian prime minister, while Charles, would become France's leading screenwriter. Claude achieved only modest success as a playwright, and took his frustration out on his wife. Suzanne turned to political activism, and joined a coalition of feminists and pacifists called the *Comité mondial des femmes contre la guerre et le fascism* (Women's World Committee against War and Fascism), founded by the Communist International but whose chapters included many non-communists.

The 1930s saw the flight of a number of Jewish refugees from Germany and Eastern Europe, and Belgium was a frequent destination. Suzanne met and assisted a number of Jewish émigrés, some of whom she met through the committee in Brussels. One of them, Mira Sokol, became her closest friend. Sokol, a diminutive, dark-haired exile from Vilnius, had a PhD in social science, while Suzanne's education had been restricted to the ladylike pursuits of poetry and needlework. But the two women shared a love of literature, a commitment to social justice, and a madcap sense of humor. Mira's husband Harry, a communist physician from Bialystock, was less cordial; his uncompromising militancy led to political problems.

In 1937 Claude Spaak moved his wife and two children to France, hoping it would benefit his writing career. The following year the Sokols appeared on their doorstep. They had been granted residency in Belgium on the condition that they abstain from political activity, and Harry's insistence on delivering Marxist lectures led to their expulsion. Suzanne helped the couple settle in France, offering financial and emotional support. She devoted additional efforts to fund-raising on behalf of the refugees from the Spanish Civil War who were flooding into France without shelter or provisions.

When the Germans invaded France in 1940 the Spaak family joined the mass exodus to the south, but failed to escape the country. They returned to Paris and found new lodgings in the Palais Royal just north of the Louvre. Suzanne continued to look out for her friend Mira, especially after her husband was arrested and sent to the Pithiviers detention camp. He was freed with the Spaak's help. Soon after, he and his wife were recruited by Leopold Trepper as part of his radio operations. It's not clear whether the Spaak was aware of this arrangement at the time; Suzanne only knew that as the anti-Jewish regulations grew more onerous, her friends had gone into hiding and were harder to assist.

At some point, apparently in late 1941, Suzanne Spaak found her way to a Jewish underground organization called Solidarité. (The introduction may have been made through Harry Sokol, who had served on the Resistance Committee members of the group in Pithiviers.) The organization had its roots in the communist-backed Jewish trade union, the Yiddish-MOI, but as conditions for Jews degenerated, they expanded their reach. Solidarité took on the tasks of offering provisions for prisoners and support for their families, as well as gathering and disseminating information to counter the lies promulgated by the official news media. Suzanne Spaak was among very few non-Jews to take an interest in the organization, and its leaders were initially unenthusiastic about her. They regarded her elite pedigree as a security risk, and she lacked the skill set of a resistance fighter. But she quickly won them over, and her wealth and status became important assets.

Suzanne Spaak didn't realize it at first, but her involvement in Solidarité connected her to other extraordinary figures whose resistance work originated in women's associations. Sometime over the winter of 1941–2, the leadership of Solidarité decided that they needed to win support from the non-Jewish population in France and founded an offshoot called the *Mouvement national contre le racisme* (the MNCR, or National Movement Against Racism). Suzanne Spaak was the only recorded non-Jewish founder of the group. There she joined forces with Sophie Schwarz-Micnik, an undocumented Jewish immigrant from Lodz. Before the war, Sophie had worked with a women's association supporting the impoverished Jewish refugees pouring into France. They set up a day-care center for working mothers in Belleville, and fed their minds with book clubs and discussion groups. When the arrests of undocumented Jewish immigrant men began, her association turned to activism and emergency relief for the families left behind. In 1941 Sophie led a women's march on the Jewish men's detention camp at Pithiviers, in a failed attempt to deliver messages and supplies to the detainees. Her own husband Lazar was deported to Auschwitz in July 1942; she would later learn that he died in the gas chambers three days after his arrival.

The men and women of the MNCR embarked on a broad range of resistance activities, though few of them fit the traditional image of French Resistance operations. This is because they were almost entirely devoted to rescuing and sustaining persecuted Jews. The Jewish immigrants were culturally and socially isolated. Living in enclaves, many of them didn't speak fluent French. Suzanne Spaak worked with male leaders of the network, including Jewish lawyer Charles Lederman and physician Léon Chertok.[10] Jews were prohibited from owning radios, typewriters, and presses, and the community was in desperate need of information to warn them of coming arrests and inspire support from the broader population. Suzanne Spaak joined forces with the intellectuals to produce a series of *tracts*, or flyers, to break through the walls of censorship and disinformation. She also took part in the related activities of forging and delivering identity papers and ration cards, doctoring some of them in her own kitchen with the help of her teenage daughter Lucy.

The initial arrests primarily affected Jewish immigrant men, rounded up and detained, country by country. In early 1942 the French police began to arrest immigrant Jewish women in limited numbers. When the deportations began that March, French citizens were informed that the prisoners were conveyed to work details, similar to those of French prisoners of war. But on July 16, 1942, an event occurred that destroyed that illusion. At the behest of the German occupiers, French police fanned out across Paris with orders to fill a quota of arrests. Within a few days, nearly 13,000 men, women, and children were arrested—only 3,031 of whom were grown men. The idea of small children participating in work details was clearly absurd, and boded something far more ominous.

The event galvanized Suzanne Spaak, Sophie Schwartz, and their respective networks. Many of their activities pivoted to rescuing and hiding Jews threatened with deportation. The French authorities went to some length to defend French Jews; the Germans agreed to start the deportations with the immigrant populations. Many of the adult immigrants were already in detention, but hundreds of their children remained in their neighborhoods and in orphanages, effectively stockpiled to fill deportation quotas when needed.

For the rest of 1942, Suzanne Spaak, Sophie Schwartz, and members of their networks redoubled their efforts on behalf of the immigrant Jewish population. These acquired even more urgency in October, when the first credible reports of the gas chambers in Poland trickled back to Paris. There was a slight pause in the convoys in the fall, but in January 1943 the Germans demanded another delivery. On February 9 another convoy departed for Auschwitz. Of the 1,000 prisoners, 126 were children.[11] The MNCR learned that arrests of more Jewish children warehoused in the orphanages were imminent.

On February 13, 1943, Suzanne Spaak and Sophie Schwartz carried out one of the most audacious mass rescues of the Occupation. They recruited women from every trusted circle they could identify. Sophie recruited fifteen Jewish women from her community circle. Suzanne approached the Protestant church near her home, the Oratoire du Louvre, and enlisted twenty-five women from the congregation and members of its girl scout troop, as well as her own teenaged daughter. On the morning of February 15, 1943, the women made their way to the Jewish orphanages and departed with children, who were escorted to a church facility, then hidden in the city until they could be taken to the countryside. Within two days, some ninety children were extracted from the institutions and spirited into safety.

The rescue network hid Jewish adults as well, but children were easier because they tended to be less conspicuous and to speak fluent French, allowing them to be placed in rural homes under false identities. The February operation was the largest of many to come. Suzanne Spaak and Sophie Schwartz built out an impressive network to implement them, composed largely of women. They came from all walks of life. Suzanne

Spaak's famous neighbor at the Palais Royal, the novelist Colette, contributed significant funds and names of additional contacts—as well as hosting Jewish resistance meetings in her apartment. Valiant girl scouts shuttled Jewish children to the countryside on the train. Seamstresses reoutfitted the children, ridding them of their yellow stars, and Marie Marteau, the manager of the humble Hotel Stella, offered rooms where members of the network could hide and change clothes. Additional assistance came from Entr'aide Temporaire, an interdenominational aid society founded by lawyer Lucie Chevalley, the daughter of a Protestant pastor.[12] (Entr'aide included members of the Parisian elite, including the young Jewish diarist Hélène Berr, who would die in a concentration camp at the end of the war.)

At least fourteen members of Suzanne Spaak's rescue network have been recognized by Yad Vashem as Righteous Among Nations; it is telling that ten of the fourteen (including Suzanne Spaak herself) are women.

Suzanne Spaak, the financier's daughter, handled many of the financial aspects of the operation. This was a major business operation. It was estimated that some 500 children were hidden by the network, and their host families needed monthly stipends for room and board. These costs ran about 750 francs per child hidden in the countryside and 1,000 francs in Paris. Suzanne and her network maintained careful ledgers recording contributions and disbursements, which were often delivered by girls and women in the movement, riding the rails. Suzanne Spaak acquired a fashionable suit and hat, and solicited funds in the wealthy areas of Paris, shaming businesspeople and aristocrats into offering a contribution. Her brother-in-law, the screenwriter, paid on a subscription basis, and a member of the Oratoire delivered regular installments from the congregation to her apartment in the Palais Royal.

There is no complete history of the rescue operation; the records that were kept were often clandestine, coded, and hidden. Much of what we know about the activities comes from materials that were painstakingly assembled after the war by grown Jewish children who were rescued: notably, Sami Dassa, Jacques Alexandre, and Larissa Gruszow.[13] Their research indicates that the rescue network achieved an astonishing level of success; of some 500 children taken into its care, there is no record of any falling prey to arrest and deportation.

Very few members of the rescue operation were detected and arrested based on their work with the network. When disaster struck the network, it came from a different source entirely. In June 1942, a stranger appeared at the Spaak's apartment to tell them that their friends Mira and Harry Sokol had been caught and arrested in the act of sending a radio message to Moscow. They had given the Spaak's contact information to their handler, Leopold Trepper, and now he turned to them for help. In September 1943 he returned, just escaped from Gestapo custody. Suzanne and Claude Spaak not only took him in, they asked other members of the children's rescue network to assist them. In the Gestapo dragnet that followed, it didn't take long for the trail to lead back to the Spaaks. Claude escaped to a Paris suburb and hid out there with his mistress for the remainder of the war. Suzanne and the children fled to her family in Belgium, but Gestapo arrested her there and took her children into custody for interrogation. The Germans obliged her to write a letter to her husband, reporting that they would free her if he turned himself in. In contrast to his wife's valor, he made no response, nor did he inquire about the safety of his children. Many other members of the rescue network were arrested in relation to Trepper.

Suzanne Spaak underwent long interrogations by the Gestapo. She convinced them that she was merely a frivolous housewife who had ingenuously stumbled into Trepper's orbit, and avoided any mention of the rescue network. (Her interrogator reported that she "was above all an artist, with a very modern taste in painting, which [her] pictures ... indicated"—referring to the priceless collection of Magrittes and Delvauxes that hung on her apartment walls.)

The Germans attached more importance to her prominent family than to her infractions. As the Allies advanced on Paris, the Gestapo focused on her hostage value. But things went horribly wrong. In the final chaotic days of the Occupation, Suzanne Spaak was executed in the courtyard of the Fresnes prison, apparently in error.

Until recently, the record has minimized Suzanne Spaak's story. Cold War histories list her among Trepper's Soviet agents, while art histories describe her merely as the "wife of Claude Spaak." Her counterparts in the Protestant and Jewish sectors of her rescue network paid tribute to her leadership in their own institutional histories, yet for decades her story went untold because her network of loose affiliations didn't have a name.

The eight major French resistance organizations made up the Conseil National de Résistance were largely affiliated with political parties and movements. There is an expansive vocabulary for these military and paramilitary groupings, but none that applies to the informal networks of women who assembled through social connections: day-care centers, charity lunches, book clubs, church circles. For the most part, they had no secretaries to file their correspondence, and their papers were abandoned to family attics or lost to time. But the evidence is clear: these associations were present, they were active, and they mattered.

In modern-day America, the term "Resistance" has been popular among opponents of the Trump administration. But would Greta Kuckhoff or Suzanne Spaak approve? When these women lived under democratic governments, their actions were governed by the principles of citizenship, not resistance.

Americans enjoy the benefits of many instruments of democracy: a free press, an independent legal system, free elections, however flawed and challenged those institutions may be at the present. Germany lost its free press and free elections in 1933, when Hitler took power, and the legal system was compromised soon after. Women in France didn't have the right to vote during Suzanne Spaak's lifetime, and she wasn't permitted to open a bank account with her own money without her husband's permission. They turned to deeds of resistance as acts of last resort, when no legal or political remedies were possible. Women were limited in their scope of action by their status, but sometimes they became more effective because they were underestimated.

The tools of fascism have not vanished from the earth. Disinformation and hate speech travel faster via new technologies, and the Big Lie didn't die in the bunker with

Joseph Goebbels. Immigrants and minorities are still scapegoated, and their children still suffer barbaric cruelties. Suzanne Spaak's mantra in the face of Nazi savagery was "*Il faut faire quelque chose.*"—"Something must be done." Then she acted on it.

Those who seek to uphold the legacy of Greta Kuckhoff and the Rote *Kapelle* should start with a spirited defense of the institutions they sacrificed so much to restore: human rights, a vibrant, free press, and democratic elections. The spirit of Suzanne Spaak can be honored by opposing the inhumane treatment of immigrants and minorities. The expanding history of women in resistance demonstrates that civil courage comes in many forms, across many social networks, proclaimed in many voices. It is up to us to recognize, record, and act on their inspiration.

Notes

1. S. Beauvoir, *The Blood of Others* (London: Penguin Books, London, 1948), 26.
2. Ibid., 240.
3. Carole Seymour-Jones, *A Dangerous Liaison: A Revelatory New Biography of Simone de Beauvoir and Jean-Paul Sartre* (New York: Overlook Press, 2009).
4. Anne Nelson *Suzanne's Children: A Daring Rescue in Nazi Paris* (New York, Simon and Schuster, 2017), 93.
5. Claire Gomarra, *Women's Representations of the Occupation in Post-'68 France* (New York: St. Martin's Press, 1968), 19.
6. See Heinz Höhne's Codeword: Direktor (1971) and The Rote Kapelle: the CIA's history of Soviet intelligence and espionage networks in Western Europe, 1936-1945 (1986).
7. Anne Nelson, *Red Orchestra: The Story of the Berlin Underground and the Circle of Friends Who Resisted Hitler* (New York: Random House, 2009), 38.
8. Ibid., 92.
9. Ibid., 282.
10. See Céline Marrot-Fellag Ariouet, *Les enfants cachés pendant la seconde guerre mondiale aux sources d'une histoire clandestine*. https://www.lamaisondesevres.org/cel/cel3.html.
11. Nelson, Suzanne's Children, 136.
12. See Céline Marrot-Fellag Ariouet, *Les enfants cachés pendant la seconde guerre mondiale aux sources d'une histoire clandestine*.
13. See Nelson, Suzanne's Children and Sami Dassa, *Vivre, aimer avec Auschwitz au Coeur*. Mémoires du XXe siècle, 2002.

CHAPTER 9
JEWISH WOMEN RESCUERS OF JEWS
Mordecai Paldiel

During the Columbia University Conference of October 4–5, 2018 on the Rosenstrasse women's protest, in Berlin, in February–March 1943, many participants spoke of the role of women in various clandestine and rescue operations in German-occupied European countries. Presently, I should like to describe some of the rescue acts done by Jewish women in saving their brethren; rescuers who acted at great risk to their personal safety, on top of their already dangerous status as targets for elimination for being Jewish.

It took many years for Jewish institutions dedicated to Holocaust remembrance to highlight the role of Jewish rescuers of fellow Jews. The standard response often advanced was that a Jew helping a fellow Jew was merely doing what he or she was obligated to do; hence, there was nothing remarkable in such a type of behavior. By contrast, gentiles helping Jews were acting in ways not consistent with normative human behavior, especially in light of the personal risks to themselves, and therefore merited special recognition. There was, however, something intellectually absurd in such an argument. As noted by Marion Pritchard-van Binsbergen, a celebrated non-Jewish rescuer in the Netherlands, and recipient of Yad Vashem's Righteous title, who, in a private communication to me in 1997, wrote: "Not recognizing the moral courage, the heroism of the Jewish rescuers, who if caught were at much higher risk of the most punitive measures than the gentiles, is a distortion of history. It also contributes to the widespread fallacious impression that the Jews were cowards, who allowed themselves to be led like 'lambs to the slaughter.'"[1]

One possible explanation, in light of Yad Vashem's creation by Israeli law, was the Zionist ethos to minimize, dilute, and even dismiss the significance of Diaspora Jewry that evolved throughout the eighteen centuries of exile and dispersion. It was explained that in order to survive the ongoing persecutions, Jewish leaders encouraged submissiveness, in the hope of weathering the passing storms, coupled with the avoidance of any self-protective aggressive steps or countermeasures, since that would provoke even greater threats to Jewish survival. According to this interpretation of Jewish history, this viewpoint is best exemplified by the record of Jewish behavior during the Holocaust that, with a few exceptions, such as the Warsaw Ghetto uprising and Jews in various partisan units in Eastern Europe, was exemplified by a mixture of confusion, helplessness, and submission to a bitter fate, over which Diaspora Jews at the outset conceded they had little or no control.

This trivialization of Jewish life in the Diaspora also received support from the conditions accompanying the creation of Israel that came to birth in a bloody confrontation and a military stand-off with neighboring Arab countries, and which continued with additional military struggles for decades afterwards, that necessitated a constant military preparedness to avoid a second Holocaust. This emphasis on the heroic record of military successes against more numerous and powerful enemies, bent on the destruction of Israel, went hand in hand with minimizing Jewish self-assertion in the Diaspora. Educators felt no need to give positive marks to Diaspora Jewish noncombat assertiveness, by mentioning, let alone highlighting, the unusual role of Jewish rescuers who exerted superhuman efforts in efforts to save their Jewish brethren, in which they solicited the help of non-Jews—many of whom were hailed and celebrated by the state of Israel, through Yad Vashem.

Even the very idea of erecting a memorial for the Holocaust in Israel was not initially viewed with favor, to say the least, and the leaders of the new-born state did not see it as a high priority. As pointed out by Israeli diplomat Eliahu Eilat: "Nations are in the habit of erecting monuments not to the memory of failures or sufferings but rather to victories and acts of glory."[2] That is why Mordechai Shenhabi, the originator of the Yad Vashem monument idea, proposed to include in the coming museum a greater emphasis on "heroism" (*gevurah* in Hebrew), in the sense of Jewish military activism during the Holocaust, such as displayed by the Warsaw Ghetto uprising, or Jews who militarily engaged the enemy in the various Allied armies. It took many years for this Maccabean "heroic" concept viewed against the background of the Holocaust to translate into a more realistic perception of what actually took place. The Eichmann trial in 1960–2 was a milestone in the rise of a new thinking that gave special attention to other forms of Jewish resistance in the ghettos and camps, as well as outside them, including rescue attempts by Jewish individuals and organizations.

We should remember that when speaking of Jewish rescuers, we do not have in mind the rescue of one or a handful of Jews by individual rescuers, as is the case of non-Jewish rescuers of Jews, honored as Righteous. Such individual rescue acts, almost without exception between people closely related or known to each other, were prompted mostly in last-ditch attempts to avoid capture or death at the hands of the Germans, and they are probably too numerous to count. We have here in mind carefully calculated constructed efforts by Jewish rescue activists to save as many Jews possible, as part of specially designed clandestine operations, created for that single purpose—not necessarily combat, but the saving of lives. Where they consequently succeeded, the number of persons saved runs into many dozens, even hundreds, and in some case—especially in France and Belgium, into the thousands. In this chapter, we concentrate on Jewish women rescue activists who were part of these vast rescue efforts and took a lead in helping Jews avoid apprehension, followed with deportation to the concentration camps. In recent years, indeed, more attention is gradually being placed on the role of Jewish women as rescuers of fellow Jews in distress during the Nazi period.[3]

* * *

We begin with the story of Recha Freier, wife of a rabbi, in Berlin, who soon after Hitler's assumption of power, created a movement, later known as Youth Aliyah, to get teenage Jewish boys and girls out of Germany, with their parents' consent, for work in Palestine in Jewish settlements, mostly kibbutzim, or private homes. At first dismissed by mainline Jewish organizations who believed the Nazi phenomenon would not last, and scoffed at the idea of a "children's crusade," in their words, she persevered—even facing a challenging confrontation with Adolf Eichmann, the SS officer in charge of Jewish deportations—and was able to get thousands of children out of the country in time. The creation of her rescue network for Jewish youth, on January 30, 1933, coincided with Hitler's assumption of power on that very day. As Freier's newly formed group left a notary's office and turned into *Unter den Linden* boulevard, they could not help witnessing the torchlight procession of thousands of Nazi Storm Troopers (SA) celebrating Hitler's accession to power. The bell of doom had just rung for German Jews.[4] Fearing arrest, after the Nazi staged Kristallnacht pogrom, of November 1938, she fled to Yugoslavia, and continued to Palestine via Turkey, together with a group of Jewish youth who left Europe in time before the outbreak of the war.

In German-occupied Poland, Feigele Peltel, better later known as Vladka Meed, belonged to the Jewish-Socialist Bund organization. Incarcerated with other Jews in the Warsaw Ghetto, in light of her non-Jewish facial appearance and fluency in Polish, she was chosen as a secret courier to help Jews leaving the ghetto to find safe hiding places, and supply them with false documents. It was much easier for women to act as couriers, and stroll the streets, for men could be ordered to drop their pants and the telltale circumcision sign would give them away.[5] But danger still existed, especially from criminal blackmailers from among the local population, prompted by rewards for turning over Jews on the run. In one of several such encounters with three blackmailers, they shouted at her: "You are from the ghetto. . . . If you want us to release you, let's have three thousand *zloty*—one thousand for each of us. . . . Hand over the money or else we'll go straight to the Germans." Vladka continued to deny she was Jewish and walked away, mingling with the crowd. Luckily for her, she managed to elude the blackmailers.[6] To avoid being recognized as a Jew while out on a mission to help fellow Jews, Meed was cautioned by a gentile friend: "Your eyes give you away. Make them livelier, merrier—you won't attract so much attention then."[7] Constantly on the move as a courier, and appearing several times under different identities, she is credited with having saved many Jews, while herself luckily surviving the Holocaust, but not so her parents, her sister and brother—who perished. After the war she married Benjamin Miedzyrzecki, one of those helped by her, who changed his name to Meed, and both moved to the United States. Together with her husband they established a registry and database of Jewish Holocaust survivors and their families.

Turning to the Kraków region, in southern Poland, Miriam Hochberg was a leading activist in Żegota, the secret rescue organization created by the Polish underground to help Jews in hiding, while she assumed the non-Jewish name of Marysia Mariańska. Only her closest leadership confederates knew of her Jewish identity; otherwise, she appeared as a Christian Pole, while visiting and affording aid to many Jews in the Kraków region. Before joining up with the Żegota organization, Miriam-Marysia devoted herself to helping Jews on the run, in collaboration with her associates in the Polish Socialist

Party. She was blessed with good looks which was impeccably so-called Aryan, and an unshakable self-confidence. Even her Jewish charges did not detect her real identity and saw her as but a noble Pole.

Passing as a non-Jew remained a risky undertaking in those days as everybody knew the way Gestapo interrogations were carried out. To make sure this would never happen to her, Miriam carried with her a portion of cyanide poison in a test-tube made of very thin glass, which could be easily crunched, just in case. "Fortunately, I never had to use it."

Miriam found various ways of avoiding dangerous situations. For example, during sudden document checks, when all the train passengers would be evacuated in one of the stations and selections were made outside, women with small children were likely to be allowed to pass by. So, advancing toward the inspection point, Miriam would suddenly borrow a child from a mother who happened to lead one children. "I did not allow the woman any time to think, and would only say quickly. 'I will help you,' and I would take the child by the hand or, which was even more reliable, on my arm."

But she came very close to be discovered, during a tête-à-tête with her landlady who one day, while dusting the painting of Jesus, stated that only now the Jews were reaping the just rewards for their crime and that this should be consolation to Him who suffered so much at their hands. Miriam, or rather Marysia, promptly told her: "Do you know that if Jesus could get one leg off the cross he would kick you for what you are saying now?" "Why, the stunned landlady said?" Because, Miriam added, he proclaimed "love thy neighbor," and he probably meant the innocent Jews who are being murdered now. "I can see that you are on the side of the Jews," she responded. "No," I said, "I am on the side of Jesus Christ." The landlady had no suspicion of her interlocutor's belonging to this "vile" people. But Miriam felt it safer to move out elsewhere. [8]

In another story, Miriam had to coach a Jewish woman in the Catholic religion, to prepare her for her undercover appearance as a housekeeper, including how to behave during Christian holidays so as not to reveal her Jewish origin.[9]

> "I told her to remember that Good Friday was a day of fast and of visits to church; that on Saturday the food was taken to church to be blessed and on Easter Day there was a special service in church and then everybody returned home for an equally special and big meal during which a 'blessed egg' was shared."

The woman then said, "I know all this, just tell me about breaking the wafer with others . . ." Miriam cut her short very sternly: "Heaven forbid that you should get religious holidays mixed up. A wafer is broken on Christmas Eve, not at Easter. Such a mistake may have dire results." To which the woman angrily shot back, not knowing of Miriam's Jewish identity: "All you have told me is not that important. If I started teaching you about our celebrations of Passover, you would never learn it!" Miriam had to quietly swallow this retort, without disclosing her own Jewish affinity.[10]

Miriam Hochberg was probably the sole Jewish person in the Kraków branch of Żegota, an identity only known to her closest associates.[11] While Miriam obtained all of her aid addresses from Żegota, she sometimes attempted to make contacts based on self-initiated instincts. One day, while riding the tram she noticed two women, probably a mother and daughter judging by their appearance. "They both seemed 'suspect' to me. Both were clearly depressed and it was their behavior rather than their external appearance that indicated to me that they were Jewish." When they got off the tram Miriam decided to follow them. Catching up with them, she said: "Excuse me, is there anything I can do to help you? Perhaps you need . . . " The younger one would not let Miriam finish. "Why are you picking on us?" she shouted in fear. "What do you want from us? Leave us alone!" At that moment a passerby turned and stared at them. There was a danger that this incident could have a completely different ending from the one Miriam intended and that she could be exposing these two women to immediate danger instead of helping them. She immediately turned around and went off in the opposite direction. "I was devastated when I thought that these two people perhaps thought me a blackmailer and were probably glad that they got rid of me so easily."[12]

After the war, Miriam cared for the surviving children under the aegis of the reconstituted Jewish Committee; she then left for Israel in 1949, where she appeared as Miriam Peleg (the Hebraized family name of her husband, the former Mordecai Kurz). I knew her well when she worked as a member of the Tel Aviv branch of the Commission for the Designation of the Righteous, whose meetings I regularly attended during the 1980s. There, she worked assiduously to have as many of her non-Jewish colleagues within Żegota honored with the Righteous title by Yad Vashem, but never spoke of her own wartime ordeals and heroic rescue activities. She remained a self-effacing woman, never asking honors for herself, until her passing, in 1996.

In Slovakia, a fascist and anti-semitic country, closely allied to Nazi Germany during the war years, Gisi Fleischman headed a clandestine Jewish group, known as the Working Group, that helped Jews on the run in many ways; such as, escape to Hungary, when it was still safe there, but was no longer so in Slovakia, and helping Jews flee Poland to Slovakia, when deportations ceased there. Intensely of Zionist persuasion, she was affiliated with WIZO, the women's section of the Zionist movement. During the war period, Gisi also assumed the leadership of the Slovak branch of the American-based Joint Distribution Committee.[13] Before the war, in 1938 and 1939, Gisi Fleischmann sent her daughters to Palestine. Care of her own husband, Josef, as well as her ailing mother prevented Gisi from joining her daughters, no less than her sense of responsibility toward her fellow Jews, as the dark clouds gathered over Slovakia. Her brother, Dr. Gustav Fischer, succumbed to injuries sustained after a brutal beating by a group of antisemites; his wife, Lilly, commiserating the loss of her husband, committed suicide by jumping from her third floor window.[14] These personal family tragedies did not deter her from her work on behalf of fellow Jews in need but, on the contrary, reinforced her commitment and determination.

Throughout her wartime activity, Gisi kept busy organizing parcels, medicines, and money, all dispatched with the help of paid emissaries to deportees in Poland. She also kept her sources outside Slovakia fully informed of the fate of the Slovak deportees in Poland.[15] Thanks to her efforts, and her colleagues of the clandestine Working Group,

3,000 to 5,000 Jews found solace in the three main labor camps established by the Slovak regime in lieu of deportations—Sered, Novaky, and Vhyne—lasting for over two years, until late summer 1944.[16]

In all these efforts, she collaborated with her distant cousin, Rabbi Michael Dov-Ber Weissmandl, also of the Working Group, especially in the fantastic idea, known as the Europa Plan, to ransom European Jewry with money and avoid their deportation to the death camps in Poland—an idea that was for a time met with favor by Heinrich Himmler, head of the SS, via his SS representative in Slovakia, Dieter Wisliceny. Historians dispute the reasons for the failure of this plan, although all underline the courage of Gisi Fleischmann during the months-long negotiations period with Wisliceny.[17] To the pleadings of her sister-in-law, Lilly Fischer, for Gisi to leave for Palestine and rejoin her daughter there, she firmly responded: "My whole being is bound up with saving the Jews. I must do what my conscience tells me."[18] While others in her family went into hiding, Gisi Fleischmann refused to join them. "I have work to do," she told them.[19]

After the German takeover of Slovakia, in the fall of 1944, to help the regime put down a local uprising, she tried to negotiate with SS officer Alois Brunner, known as a notorious Jew hunter, who had arrived in Bratislava to take control of the renewed deportation of the remaining Jews. Brunner offered her life if she would reveal the hiding places of her friends, which she categorically refused. Her fate was sealed, as Brunner ordered her deported to Auschwitz, with a note to the camp commander that her return was not desired (*Rückkehr unerwünscht*)—a code word for immediate elimination. She left on the convoy of October 17, 1944, and arrived in Auschwitz-Birkenau the following day, and was led away straight to the gas chamber.[20] In the words of historian Yehuda Bauer, she was "a brave woman, a brave leader"; a person who "chose to stand at the head of a group that tried to save a community. I don't know of any other woman who did something similar during the Holocaust or, indeed, before it."[21]

Turning to the Netherlands, Mirjam Waterman joined a group of Jews who searched and found hiding places for Jewish youth on the run, members of a Zionist pioneer group, known as the Loosdrecht Hechalutz group, led by Menachem Pinkhof, whom she later married. Born in 1916, Mirjam grew up in an assimilated Jewish home, and knowing little about Judaism. Her mother, born Lopes Cardozo, was of Portuguese Jewish descent. With her four siblings, Mirjam moved from Amsterdam to Loosdrecht. There, she learned of a special school in nearby Bilthoven, called Children's Community Workshop (*Werkplaats Kinder Gemeenschap*), and Mirjam taught there too. When, before the war, Jewish youth began arriving from Nazi Germany and were admitted in the *Werkplaats*, Johannes (Joop) Westerweel, one of the school's most charismatic teachers, asked Mirjam, because of her Jewish origin, to teach this particular group.

In mid-1941, bowing to German pressure, the school dismissed Mirjam Waterman, and she returned to her parents' home in Loosdrecht, where, in the fall of 1941, she opened a school for the local Jewish children who could no longer attend public schools. There, she also became acquainted with the Loosdrecht Hechalutz center. She had never given much thought to Zionism before the war, Mirjam admitted. "But when Hitler invaded Poland in 1939, I began to think about it. When the Germans occupied Holland in '40, I became a Zionist. It was only then that suddenly something inside told me I belonged to the Jewish people. . . . I joined the Zionist youth movement. Like most people starting something new, I entered it with a great deal of enthusiasm."

Closing ranks with the Loosdrecht center, and her future husband Menachem Pinkhof, and with the help of Joop Westerweel, the group prepared a list of persons willing to hide them. "We searched all over Holland," Mirjam recalled. When a worker at the *Joodse Raad* (the Dutch version of the Judenrat), in Amsterdam, secretly informed the group, on August 15, 1942, of a soon-to-be German raid of the Loosdrecht center, they had already devised plans for escape, so when the Germans appeared on August 18, 1942, the Loosdrecht home was empty, except for two stray dogs.

Sophie Yaari, born Sophie Nussbaum, 1925, in Emden, Germany, and her ten-year-old sister Ruth were among the youngsters aided by Mirjam Waterdam. The two sisters were hidden in eighteen different homes in Amsterdam, Rotterdam, Doorn, and other towns and villages in the country; and in Doorn, for instance, Mirjam Waterman sometimes came to visit them. "She brought us life and hope. . . . She wanted to know how the people were treating us. . . . I'll never forget it. Mirjam was blond and didn't look Jewish. She had so many non-Jewish friends, she could have easily left and made a life for herself. But she didn't do that… She worked with the non-Jewish organizers as if she were not a Jew—with false papers. It greatly endangered her life."

In March 1943, Mirjam's parents were picked up, as well as her younger sister and brother, and dispatched to the Westerbork transit camp in northeast Holland. Mirjam was able to bribe the Gestapo to have her relatives released and she found for them a hiding place, where they stayed safely until the end of the war. A total of 150 other youths were helped by her underground confederated to be spirited into France, and seventy of them crossed safely into Spain and were even able to make it to Palestine during the war.

In Mirjam's words, "When I came to a house I never knew if I could trust the people or not. The only way to figure it out was to have a talk with them. I always looked them straight in the eye and asked myself, can I trust you?" During this phase of her clandestine life, Mirjam Waterman slept every night in a different place. Then tragedy struck, when she and Menachem were arrested in a failed attempt to free their non-Jewish fellow rescue activist Joop Westerweel from Nazi imprisonment. In April 1944, both were sent to Bergen-Belsen camp, where they stayed for a year until the camp's liberation. After the war, Mirjam and Menachem Pinkhof married and moved to Israel.[23]

In nearby Belgium, Ida Sterno worked before the war as a social worker, helping refugee children of the Spanish Civil War. Born in Bucharest, Romania, in 1902, Ida Sterno (code-named "Jeanne") left for Belgium in 1914, where later during the early period of the German occupation, she was a social worker in the Charleroi region for a gas and electricity firm, until her dismissal because of her Jewishness. She stated that in solidarity with her fellow Jews, she had registered as Jewish, as required by the Germans, although she could have avoided this, taking advantage of the marriage of her brothers with non-Jewish spouses. She then accepted the offer of the Jewish Yvonne Jospa, whom she knew from before, to work in the rescue of Jewish children, under the direction of Maurice Heiber, head of the clandestine Jewish Defense Committee's children section.[24]

As part of her work, she arranged for children to be placed with families for safekeeping. Records of all these hidden children were kept in two locations, in Brussels. She recollected: "I hid the list of the sheltered children, with the names of their hosts, under a rug in my apartment, rue de Belle Vue—an illegal residence that I shared with [the non-Jewish] Andrée [Geulen]."[25] These comprised separate notebooks with valuable information, each with a different indication of a child's data. One would bear the child's true name, plus a code letter; another would have the child's borrowed name; then, another notebook with the previous address; finally, one with the new sheltering address. Also noted were payments that had to be made, and anything of particular concerning each child.[26]

Often, it was necessary to transfer the children to new locations, due to various reasons; such as danger of denunciation; the host not deemed appropriate to keep the child; better conditions for the child in another location; or the child having advanced to the age where he needed to frequent a school.[27] As recalled by Ida Sterno: "One day, for instance, I was informed that two small children of 3 and 4 years, placed in an orphanage at Huy for approximately a year, were taken back by their parents. They were covered with scabs, infected, lice-ridden and clearly feeble. That is why we struggled to arrange a system of inspections, since similar cases were possible."[28] When absolutely necessary, parents or relatives were allowed to see their hidden children, but only from a distance. "Such as when one day, we showed, between two trains, a child and its grandmother. . . . The old woman was overwhelmed with joy. She had seen again her grandson, the only child that was left her of a large family."[29]

Ida Sterno was on May 31, 1944, arrested, and confined in the Mechelen/Malines transit camp. Luckily for her, her arrest was just months before Belgium's liberation, in early September, 1944. Her arrest came as a result of her meeting with a certain lady at the café Beau Séjour, in Brussels, in broad daylight. They took precaution by choosing to sit, not inside, but on the terrace, where they could observe the comings and goings on the outside street. Ida carried in her bag compromising documents, including the names of a dozen children needing to be placed. The two women failed to notice the appearance of the infamous Jewish informer, surnamed "Fat Jacques," who was the terror of any Jew circulating on the streets. Presently, he appeared in the company of a Gestapo agent, and immediately began to interrogate Ida's lady companion.[30] However, since she had an official employee card by the German controlled *Judenrat* in Belgium (*Association des Juifs en Belgique*), and momentarily exempt from deportation, she was let go.

During that tense interval, Ida had silently removed the documents from her bag and slipped them on the next chair whose seat was covered by the tablecloth and, consequently, it remained unseen. Then came Ida Sterno's turn to be interrogated. "I explained that in my capacity of social worker, I dealt with Jewish children, like the Spanish children that I dealt with previously." But she adamantly refused to give any information on the Jewish children in her care. Fat Jacques promised that no harm would befall the children, since they would be placed in a children home. "If I did not speak, it would be Breendonck [a notorious camp for mainly political prisoners] . . . [Jacques] pushed me to a corner and pointed a revolver on my chest."[31] She stood her ground, and was taken away—not to Breendonck, with its infamous torturing chambers, but the relatively less harsh internment and transit camp of Mechelen/Malines. All this time, she had only one thing on her mind—the incriminating papers left on the chair in the cafeteria. She was relieved to learn later, that her lady companion had noticed them, and taken them to a safe location. The lists of the hidden children were later recovered from Sterno's home by Andrée Geulen with the help of a trustworthy colleague.

Ida was placed in a cell with twelve or fifteen other people. During her incarceration, awaiting deportation, she met many arrested parents whose children she had arranged sheltering places, but since they had known her under her codename of Jeanne, she preferred not to disclose her true identity. On the morrow of September 4, 1944, the Germans suddenly left, due to the swift approach of Allied armies, thus precluding the deportation of Ida and other interned Jews.[32] After the war, Ida Sterno went back to her social work, aiding Jewish survivors.

Turning to France, the list is long of Jewish women active in various rescue operations, either inside the country, or across the borders into Spain and Switzerland—especially involving children. Beginning with Andrée Salomon, she was active in the Jewish children's organization known by its initials OSE (*Oeuvre de Secours aux Enfants*), where she was principally involved in organizing volunteers to penetrate the French internment camps where foreign-born Jews were kept, such as Gurs, Rivesaltes, and Les Milles, with the permission of the Vichy regime. Working in tandem with other welfare organizations, non-Jewish and Jewish, she smuggled children out of these camps, and then organized their secret passage into Spain, across the forbidding Pyrenees mountains.[33] For instance, in March 1944 Andrée Salomon arranged up to 134 children to take the Spanish route. Seventy-nine of them were then able to board a boat, in October 1944, and sail to Palestine.[34]

In her constant travels, in Lyon, Marseilles, Toulouse, Montpellier, and Limoges, while on train rides, she made notes on her manual typewriter, while often falling asleep due to fatigue. She wore a red ribbon in her hair as a recognizable sign to her friends. In her words, "I have acquired the habit, from these many kilometers across France, to sleep at the start of a vehicle's movement, the only means to recover from the fatigue." This habit apparently stuck with her in the postwar years, for it is told that, when visiting the cinema, she would fall asleep during the whole screening, and awake when the movie flashed the sign "end," and would then exclaim, "What a beautiful film."[35]

Madeleine Dreyfus was also a principal fieldworker in the OSE children's network. Born Madeleine Kahn, in 1909, to French assimilated Jewish parents, and mingling in the Parisian surrealist milieu, Madeleine Dreyfus rubbed shoulders with literary circles, such as Jean Cocteau, André Breton, and corresponded with famed public figures—Pierre Mendès-France, Roger Martin du Gard, Robert Aron, and Claude Lévi-Strauss, while working as an English-French bilingual secretary in an import-export firm. After the French defeat in 1940, Madeleine's family moved to Lyon, in the Vichy zone, where she enlisted in the OSE. She began by dispersing children in various parts outside the city, as well as distributing false identity and ration cards. She was especially adept in canvassing religious and lay institutions in the Lyon area. Several times a month, she would take the train from Lyon to Saint-Etienne with a group of children, while counseling those who had only recently arrived in the county not to speak any other language save French, if they knew it, while on the train ride.[36]

Madeleine Dreyfus's trips benefited over 100 children, whom she often visited in their new sheltered homes, bringing them much-needed clothing, medicine, food tickets, and letters from their loved ones.[37] Recalling one such search for a sheltering place:

> I remember one day when there remained for me to find a place for two fourteen-year-old boys—a very difficult business. I went from place to place through the area around Chambon. . . . Nobody wanted the two boys. I came up to a rather old couple, the Courtials, and told them my "fable"; city children who are hungry and need the fresh air of Le Chambon. . . . The Courtials' answer was friendly but firm: it was not possible for them to take them in. They themselves were too old, and these boys were too big. Having thrown out a feeler, I decided to disclose the secret: "The truth is that these are two young Jewish boys whose parents have been arrested and whom the Germans are looking for everywhere to imprison with their parents." No more hesitation. "But you should have said that before! Of course, bring them, your two boys."[38]

Luckily, for Madeleine Dreyfus and the boys, the Courtials were part of the Protestant community of Le Chambon, who, taking every word in the Bible literally, considered the Jews God's still chosen people, who needed to be saved.

Tragedy struck for Madeleine, when on November 23, 1943, she received a phone call from the father of a child she had hidden in a deaf-mute institute in Villeurbanne. The father was alarmed since he was informed of a soon-to-be Gestapo raid on that home. Then came a woman's voice: "you must come very quickly," as she was being held at gunpoint. Madeleine suspecting the worse, decided on the spot to go there, and was immediately arrested.[39]

She was kept imprisoned for two months in Fort Monluc, Lyon, and in Drancy for four months. From there, she managed to get a letter out to her mother with a coded message to urge her husband Raymond to have their sons Michel and Jacques taken to Switzerland. The message read, "The boys must stop eating ham." In French, the word ham, *jambon*, sounds like Chambon (where the boys were in hiding), and the family understood. Raymond immediately arranged to have the two boys smuggled over into Switzerland. Deported to Bergen-Belsen, in May 1944, Madeleine Dreyfus survived for eleven months the afflictions and tortures of the camp, and lived through liberation. Returning to France on May 18, 1945, she eventually resumed her work with the OSE.[40]

Her colleague, Marianne Cohn, was not so lucky. Born in Germany, when the Nazis came to power, she first immigrated to Spain; then during the Spanish Civil War, she moved to Paris. In early 1944, Marianne volunteered to take up the dangerous work of surreptitiously guiding Jewish children across the border into Switzerland. Carrying identity papers that listed her name as Colin instead of Cohn, she smuggled groups of children across the border from January through May 1944. On May 31, while leading a party of twenty-eight children ranging in age from four to sixteen years old, they were all apprehended and imprisoned by the Germans in Annemasse. Undergoing severe interrogations, accompanied with brutal beatings, to make her reveal her associates in the children escape operation, she remained silent. To the cruel interrogator, she would respond: "Yes, I have saved the lives of more than 200 children, and if I were freed now, I would continue. Nothing could keep me back." In the meantime, the children were fetched by Annemasse mayor, Jean Deffaugt, who used ruse and subterfuge to extract the children from the hands of the Germans, and they remained safe until the liberation, a short time later. From her cell, Marianne Cohn penned the following moving poem: "Tomorrow, I will betray, not today. Tear out my nails today, I will not betray. You don't know how long I can hold out but I know. You are five rough hands. . . . You have hobnailed boots on your feet. . . . Today I have nothing to say. Tomorrow, I will betray.[41]

On the night of July 7–8, 1944, she was taken out of prison to a nearby wooded area and brutally tortured, and killed. In 1982, French President François Mitterand, during his official visit to Israel, dedicated a garden at Yad Vashem to the memory of Marianne Cohn. Two schools, one in Annemasse, France, and the other in the Tempelhof section of Berlin, also bear her name.[42]

In Switzerland, which remained neutral during the war, Recha Sternbuch helped Jews cross illegally into the country from nearby Germany and German-annexed Austria, with the help of Swiss non-Jewish helpers; such as police commandment Paul Grüninger, responsible for the St. Gallen section of the Swiss-German border. In one of her feats—when she learned that a group of Jews had been apprehended on the German-Swiss border, and were about to be turned back to Germany, she rushed to the border point by motorcycle, then proceeded on foot, when she was accosted by a German uniformed man who took her to his chief, in a border house, where the hapless Jews were also held. She was asked: "What do you want?" She responded: "I am Swiss. These Jews came upon my initiative. I am responsible for them. I would like to ask you to turn them over to me. I am taking them into Switzerland." The officer's eyes reddened with fury, and he shouted back: "I'll send you away with these dirty Jews! You cursed Jewish woman! I'll rip up your Swiss passport if you don't disappear from here this minute!" Recha stood her ground, and there was a fearful silence. Then: "Take your twelve Jews and be gone immediately," he shouted; "but at once! Otherwise, I'll change my mind." Undauntingly, she had saved a group of twelve Jews literally at gunpoint, for whom she later arranged a temporary stay in Switzerland.[43]

She then expanded her illegal rescue activities, which landed her in Swiss jail. On trial, she refused to disclose her non-Jewish Swiss confederates in smuggling Jews into the country. On the witness stand, in May 1941, she stated: "I have financed these immigration transports out of my own means; when these refugees didn't have the money, I paid their debts to chauffeurs and others." In an earlier letter to the District Attorney written from prison, Recha stated:

> If I deserve punishment, I want to bear it, because I have respect for the law and I do not fear it. . . . You demand, however . . . that I should denounce human

beings that haven't harmed anyone, and for the most part are poor, decent workers who could not bear to suffer a punishment, be it financial or a loss of their employment for a few months, bringing extreme hardship to their wives and children, this I cannot do![44]

Impressed by her courageous stand, the Swiss authorities eventually released her. She later enlisted the aid of former Swiss president, Jean-Mary Musy, a man known for his pro-fascist sympathies, to contact SS leader Himmler to convince him to release imprisoned Jews, in a gamble that both he and Musy hoped would lead to negotiations with the Western Allies. These intricate negotiations, too long to recite here, led to the release of 1,200 Jews from Theresienstadt camp who arrived safely in Switzerland, on February 7, 1945.[45]

A final word in this short résumé of women rescuers is due to Hadassah Rosensaft (nee Bimko), who helped Jewish prisoners, first in Auschwitz, then Bergen-Belsen camp with medical needs. Although trained as a dentist, while in Auschwitz, SS officer Joseph Mengele told her that as there were already two dentists, she would have to work as a doctor. The Jewish infirmary (*Revier* in Nazi camp terminology) was a small barrack where two women doctors and four nurses lived and worked. Each had her own bed, and their task was to attend to Jewish women patients, ill with abscesses, furuncles, and wounds inflicted by the dogs and whips of the SS guards. Short on medicaments, the medics had only some paper bandages, which looked like rolls of toilet paper, and very few pills, mainly aspirin, as well as a little bit of ointment which resembled Vaseline.[46]

In November 1944, she and others were transferred to Bergen-Belsen camp, which soon degenerated into a state of chaos, with a typhus epidemic at its height.[47] There, Hadassah was appointed by SS camp doctor, Dr. Schnabel, to supervise the camp clinic, while outside an epidemic plague raged, with hundreds of people dying daily (including the diary-famous Anne Frank and her sister Margot).[48] In two of the barracks that once held Russian prisoners of war, Hadassah and her colleagues established a hospital and an infirmary; a third block was set aside for the children. They had their own beds, and Hadassah's group lived with them and attended to their needs, day and night. "We talked to them, played with them, tried to make them laugh, listened to them, comforted them when they cried and had nightmares. When they were sick with typhus, we sat beside them telling fairy tales. I sang songs to them in Polish, Yiddish, and Hebrew—whatever I remembered—just to calm them until they fell asleep."[49]

When Bergen-Belsen was liberated by the British army, on April 14, 1945, there were some 60,000 prisoners in the camp, most of them in critical condition. Hadassah was asked by British officers to head a medical team from among the survivors. Eight doctors and 620 still-convalescent men and women answered Hadassah's call for help. Only a few were certified nurses. They all worked with great devotion together with the British army doctors, nurses, and other personnel to save as many of the recently liberated inmates from dying due to the debilitated state of their bodies.[50] After marrying Josef Rosensaft, also a Holocaust survivor, a boy named Menachem was born to them in the Bergen-Belsen DP camp. Eventually, moving to the United States, Hadassah died in 1997 of liver failure resulting from malaria and hepatitis she had contracted in the Auschwitz-Birkenau camp.

* * *

In conclusion, we have listed some of the heroic Jewish women, who each sought ways and means to save Jews on the run, and succeeded in rescuing many lives. Some of them are currently honored by the B'nai B'rith organization, under a special program designed to make their deeds known to the public at large. In most of these stories, let us remember, while already at risk of apprehension due to their Jewishness, these courageous women rescuers, instead of seeking ways to save themselves, initiated rescue operations, thus increasing manifold times the dangers to their personal safety. The role of women in launching superhuman rescue endeavors still suffers from a lack of due recognition, as such undertakings are still considered the reserve of persons of the opposite sex. This gender prejudice is in need of a major revision, so as to give women initiators of altruistic acts their due merit—as also exemplified by the courageous behavior of the Rosenstrasse protesting women, on the streets of Berlin, in February–March 1943.

Notes

1. Dalia Ofer, "Linguistic Conceptualization of the Holocaust in Palestine and Israel, 1942-1953." *Journal of Contemporary History* 31, no. 3 (July 1996): 567–95.

2. Tom Segev, *The Seventh Million* (New York: Hill & Wang, 1993), 429–30.

3. See, for instance, Dalia Ofer and Lenore J. Weitzman, eds., *Women in the Holocaust.* (New Haven: Yale University, 1998); and Marion Kaplan, *Between Dignity and Despair: Jewish Life in Nazi Germany* (New York: Oxford University, 1999).

4. Recha Freier, *Let the Children Come: The Early History of Youth Aliyah* (London: Weidenfeld and Nicolson, 1961), 20–1.

5. As confirmed by Warsaw Ghetto historian, Emanuel Ringelblum, writing in May 1942: "These heroic girls. . . . In mortal danger every day. They rely entirely on their 'Aryan' faces and on the peasant kerchiefs that cover their heads. . . . They accept and carry out the most dangerous missions. . . . Nothing stands in their way. Nothing deters them. . . . How many times have they looked death in the eyes." Emanuel Ringelblum, *Notes from the Warsaw Ghetto* (New York: Schocken, 1974), 273–4.

6. Vladka Meed, *On Both Sides of the Wall* (New York: Holocaust Library, 1993), 113, 115, 117–18, 214.

7. Meed, *On Both*, 245–6.

8. Miriam Hochberg added in her book: "I thought . . . about all the Poles with whom we worked and who put their own lives in danger. Was it possible that these people belonged to the same nation; that they grew in the same land?" Miriam Peleg-Mariańska and Mordecai Peleg, *Witnesses: Life in Occupied Kraków* (London and New York: Routledge, 1991), 10–11.

9. Peleg-Mariańska, *Witnesses*, 61–2.

10. Ibid., 63.

11. Ibid., 82–5. The following were awarded the Righteous title by Yad Vashem: Stanislaw Dobrowolski, YVA-M31.2/1681 (1979); Anna Dobrowolska-Michalska, YVA-M31.2/2909 (1984), Tadeusz Seweryn, YVA-M31.2/2230 (1982); Wladyslaw Wojcik, YVA-M31.2/1613 (1963); and Jerzy Matus, YVA-M31.2/2229 (1982).

12. Peleg-Mariańska, *Witnesses*, 111–12.

13. Joan Campion, *In the Lion's Mouth: Gisi Fleischmann and the Jewish Fight for Survival* (San Jose: toExcel, 2000), 4–5, 9–10, 13, 19.

14. Ibid., 23–5, 37–8. Oskar Neumann, *Gisi Fleischmann: The Story of a Heroic Woman* (Tel Aviv: WIZO, 1970), 16.

15. Campion, *Lion's*, 62–5. Neumann, *Gisi Fleischmann*, 19–20.

16. Campion, *Lion's*, 78. Throughout much of the war, Saly Mayer, of the Joint, Alfred Silberschein, representing the World Jewish Congress known as RELICO (Committee for Relief of the War-Stricken Jewish Population), and Nathan Schwalb of Hechalutz, were Fleischmann's principal contacts in Switzerland. Her contacts with rescue activists in Turkey were with Chaim Barlas, of the Jewish Agency, and other delegates of various Palestinian Zionist organizations, such as Venia Pomerantz (later Zeev Hadari), of the kibbutz movement.

17. Campion, *Lion's*, 83, 87; Neumann, *Gisi Fleischmann*, 25–6.

18. Campion, *Lion's*, 102–4, 107, 110–11. Gila Fatran, "The Working Group," *Holocaust and Genocide Studies* 8, no. 2 (Fall 1994): 164–201.

19. Campion, *Lion's*, 114–15.

20. Ibid., 117, 119–20, 123. Neumann, *Gisi Fleischmann*, 35. Livia Rotkirchen, *The Destruction of Slovak Jewry: A Documentary History* (Jerusalem: Yad Vashem, 1961), xxvi.

21. Yehuda Bauer, *Rethinking the Holocaust* (New Haven: Yale University, 2001), 184.

22. http://www.sorrel.humboldt.edu/-rescuers/book/Pinkhof/ yaari/sophie1.html. "Sophie Yaari Tells Her Story."

23. Joop Westerweel was executed by the Germans on Dutch soil; his wife, Wilhelmina, also arrested, survived the hardships and torments of the Ravensbrück concentration camp. Both were honored by Yad Vashem with the Righteous title, in 1963; YVA-M31.2/32.

24. Ida Sterno, "Hiding of Jewish Children in Belgium," *Yad Vashem Archives* 02/571, 1–3.

25. Sterno, "Hiding," 1–3.

26. Sterno, "Hiding," 1–3.

27. Sterno, "Hiding," 1–3.

28. In her postwar account, Ida Sterno noted that a medical report of July 1945 found that among 539 children living with their families or with hosts, there were fifteen cases of pre-tuberculosis; sixty-one—bowed legs due to vitamin D deficiency; ninety-six—much loss of weight; thirty—serious physical weakness; and six—abnormal curvature of the spine. Sterno, *Yad*, 36.

29. Sterno, *Yad*, 14.

30. Ibid., 28.

31. Ibid., 29–30.

32. Ibid., 32–4.

33. Lucien Lazare, *Rescue as Resistance: How Jewish Organizations Fought the Holocaust in France* (New York: Columbia University, 1996), 165–6, 194, 201–2.

34. Haim Avni, "Interview with Andrée Salomon (Paris), June 8, 1963." *Hebrew University, Dept. of Contemporary Judaism; Oral Testimony Section.* Jerusalem, 1963, 15, 18–19.

35. Georges Weill, "Andrée Salomon et le Sauvetage des Enfants Juifs (1933-1947)," in *French Politics, Culture & Society*, ed. Chapman Herrick, 30, no. 2 (Summer 2012): 89–112.

36. Henry Patrick, "Madeleine Dreyfus: Righteous Jews." *Author's Collection*, 13–14, 16–17, 32.

37. Ibid., 17. In Chambon, Madeleine Dreyfus was in close touch with Magda Trocmé, wife of the town's pastor, André Trocmé, and many non-Jewish rescuers of Jews, especially Léonie Déléage and daughter, Eva (today, Phillit). Mrs. Déléage was her chief link in Chambon. The two would leave the children at the Hotel May and then make the rounds from farm to farm. Patrick, *Author's*, 18. They were both honored by Yad Vashem with the Righteous title. YVA-M31.2/3835 (1988).

38. Vivette Samuel, *Rescuing the Children* (Madison: University of Wisconsin, 2002), 95. Eugene Paul and Celie Courtial were awarded the Righteous title by Yad Vashem, in 2012 (YVA-M31.2/12367).

39. Patrick, *Author's*, 20–1.

40. Ibid., 24–5, 30–1, 33.

41. Anny Latour, *The Jewish Resistance in France (1940-1944)* (New York: Holocaust Library, 1981), 65.

42. Nancy Lefenfeld, "Marianne Cohn," *Mishpocha*, Summer 2003. Frédéric Chimon Hammel, *Souviens-Toi d'Amalek: Témoignage sur la lutte des Juifs en France (1938-1944)* (Paris: CLKH, 1982), 451. Raphael Delpard, *Les Justes de l'Ombre* (Paris: J. C. Lattès, 1995), 180.

43. Joseph Friedenson and David Kranzler, *Heroine of Rescue: The Incredible Story of Recha Sternbuch who Saved Thousands from the Holocaust* (Brooklyn: Mesorah Publications, 1984), 253.

44. Ibid., *Heroine*, 38–9, 42.

45. Ibid., 124–30; Yehuda Bauer, *Jews for Sale* (New Haven: Yale University Press, 1994), 225.

46. Hadassah Rosensaft, *Yesterday: My Story* (New York, Jerusalem: American Society for Yad Vashem & Yad Vashem, 2004), 33–7.

47. Ibid., 41–2.

48. Ibid., 43.

49. Ibid., 44–5.

50. Ibid., 52, 59.

CHAPTER 10
IS FOOD PROTEST POLITICAL?
WOMEN'S DEMONSTRATIONS IN OCCUPIED FRANCE
Paula Schwartz

The question may seem disingenuous in an era when a good part of the world's population does not have enough to eat and when the eruption of food protest is not only not common, but expected and feared. Few today would argue that food and eating have nothing to do with politics, yet women's food protest in Second World War France has rarely been credited as "resistance," or even viewed as political. Some have qualified the most menacing of those conflicts as uprisings or riots, terms that imply that food protest was spontaneous, unruly, and devoid of political intent. However, the women's underground press, memoirs, interviews, and police reports show that food protests not only disturbed the peace, they also disturbed prevailing notions of what it meant to demand enough to eat. Protesting women were not merely seeking the satisfaction of a basic material need. They were denouncing the rationing and distribution systems controlled by the French, and the penury of foodstuffs created by the Germans.

Hundreds of food protests took place all over France, in occupied and unoccupied areas, from late 1940 until after the Liberation. In German-occupied Paris and the surrounding region, food protests ranged from brief incidents involving only a few protagonists, to large-scale demonstrations like the one on the rue de Buci, a market street in central Paris.[1] Hunger was a one-size-fits-all issue, but it was mostly women who scrounged for food, waited in long lines in front of food shops, and managed meals for their families. Many of these incidents—demonstrations, delegations of women to town halls demanding better rations, the presentation of petitions calling for the release of warehoused goods—were organized by the underground French Communist party in an effort to bring housewives, mothers, and other women into a broad-based resistance movement.

The invisibility of food protest as political work is not a new phenomenon. The urban and rural uprisings of *ancien régime* France were characterized as spontaneous riots, despite the proclamations of the rioters invoking the responsibility of public authorities, be they king or government.[2] That hunger arouse anger, frustration, and resentment seems natural, but empty bellies do not inexorably lead to protest action. Is the path from hunger to protest a straight line, or is it mediated by something else, namely, political consciousness?

In this chapter, I will show that women's food protests in wartime France were quite explicitly political in origin, nature, and intent. I will then speculate on the reasons for the failure to see women's food protests as actions that were motivated by concerns that transcended bodily sustenance.

Food Demonstrations in France

The French Communist party (PCF) created women's popular committees in towns and neighborhoods for the explicit purpose of building a broad-based resistance movement comprising every element of the population. By reaching into the homes and kitchens of French women, the party sought to mobilize women by appealing to their roles as mothers and housewives. Their objective was to harness this groundswell of anger and frustration into meaningful collective action. Food scarcity was a universal concern but women were uniquely situated as shoppers and cooks. That women spearhead such actions was a way of legitimizing public protest, which had been banned by the Vichy government. But it was precisely the central role of women in these protests that obscured their deeply political nature. One the one hand, the presence of women conferred legitimacy on such actions. One could hardly call them terrorists. But the other side of the coin is that protest activity by women was also invisible to scholars and contemporaries as part and parcel of the battle to free France, precisely because women were not viewed as political actors.

Just as the presence of women lent camouflage to the political nature of food protest, so too did the presence of children effectively "cover" the political work of their mothers. In some areas, children of all ages joined their mothers at street protests. It was an age-old and clever tactic. For one, police were less likely to intervene or to make arrests. For another, the authorities could see for themselves the women's charges, with their withered bodies and wan faces. Lucette Abada remembered accompanying her mother to food protests in Nice. Her family was already in the French Communist party orbit, and while her mother wanted to engage in politics, her father strictly forbid it. By bringing her eleven-year-old daughter to the demonstrations, Lucette's mother was able to circumvent her husband's orders.[3] The presence of the daughter effectively depoliticized the mother's activity, at least in the eyes of her husband. Protesting for food was an extension of her private role. It did not qualify as political engagement.

Women took to the streets all over France, in all of the five zones created under the armistice of June 1940.[4] In Paris and the surrounding area (what is now the department of the Ile-de-France), there were hundreds of women's food protests, according to police reports, but establishing reliable figures on a national, departmental, or even local level is challenging for several reasons.[5] Official reports by police and prefects do not necessarily include small-scale, lightning-strike actions that were short-lived, precisely to avoid police detection. Some incidents that are mentioned by witnesses in oral testimony or reported in the underground press were unknown to the authorities. On the other hand, the clandestine press also noted protest activities that never took place, over-reported attendance, or announced planned demonstrations that apparently failed to materialize. The purpose of illegal underground newspapers was not only to inform but also to mobilize the public, and such mobilization efforts could and did include false claims.

By the fall of 1944, it was possible to stage a large-scale protest in some areas where food restrictions remained dire but the risks of repression had diminished. In the southern department of the Alpes-Maritimes, food protests rallied crowds ranging from as few as ten to as many as several hundred in the summer of 1944.[6] Moreover, the liberation and the end of the war did not signal the end of women's food protests, which continued in some areas until 1947-8. These protests took different forms and posed different risks, depending on locality and timing.

According to the scholars who report these figures, many but not all of these food protests were organized by the French Communist party. However, the signal identifying features of a PCF-led protest—singing the *Marseillaise*, the distribution of flyers to accompany the demonstration, the language and references of such flyers—were often present. If these events were not sponsored by the party, then demonstrators availed themselves of a familiar template. In that case, communist-led women's demonstrations, either in the same locale or elsewhere, may have served as models for food protests organized by other entities or individuals.

Protests in the occupied or northern zone, including the Paris region, were overwhelmingly if not exclusively the work of the underground Communist party. Their activity was heavily concentrated in working-class neighborhoods and towns where organizers had the greatest successes forming popular committees to spearhead local initiatives. At the time it was forbidden to assemble; to sing the *Marseillaise*; or to criticize the regime, in word or in print. Moreover, the presence of the Germans made such activities all the riskier. This in turn affected the forms, duration, and frequency of highly public activity that exposed protesters to arrest, detention, and even deportation to concentration camps.

Communist women organized public demonstrations in markets and market streets in hopes of sweeping bystanders and shoppers into the movement. These events did not resemble what we think of today as a demonstration; they were not formal processions of women carrying banners and shouting slogans. The outlawed French Communist party was in the crosshairs of both French and German authorities. Under the circumstances, what qualified as a "demonstration" for food could be a furtive assembly of a handful of women lasting only a few minutes. For the most part, in the occupied capital and surrounding region, food protests reportedly included anywhere from a several or several dozen women, to several hundred. A good many of these events are recorded in police files and prefects' reports; others are recounted in the underground women's press and in the postwar testimony of organizers and participants.

Such protest was usually peaceful, if strident, and took various forms: delegations of women marched to town halls, prefects' offices, warehouses, and food distribution centers, where they pressed authorities to release stockpiled foodstuffs. They signed petitions and presented them to mayors and prefects. Sometimes their demands were met with limited but nonetheless satisfying success: a one-time release of potatoes, or rice, or lentils. News of protests that resulted in the distribution of extra ration tickets or warehoused goods circulated by word of mouth among shoppers and neighbors, which in turn encouraged others to do the same. Indeed, authorities were loath to meet protesters' demands because they feared a "snowball effect."[7] Some officials were sympathetic to the protesters. Others feared the consequences if protesters' demands were not met. The propaganda value of this activity was twofold: there was the spectacle itself, and there was the report of a favorable outcome in the women's underground press.

Clandestine party activists produced and distributed newspapers and broadsheets addressed exclusively to women. Many were homemade, mimeographed flyers with collective signatures such as "a group of women," "the women's committee of the 15th arrondissement," or "the mothers of the 6th arrondissement." *La Voix des femmes* was one newspaper among many that invited women to participate in demonstrations for food, directing them to convene at particular sites at a given time.[8]

Conditions were different in the southern, or "free zone," which was not occupied by the Germans until November 1942. Food scarcity was particularly dire in the south where agricultural production was more specialized. Moreover, these areas had a heavier dependence on imports from the colonies, which had been cut off under the terms of the armistice. The department of the Alpes-Maritimes suffered from food scarcity in the extreme. Famine accounted for an increase in mortality rates among older people, babies, and children under the age of five. In Marseille and Nice, food protests were frequent at war's end until 1947, when most rationing measures were finally lifted. Police reported hundreds of protesters at these events, most of them women.[9]

The departments that shared a border with Belgium, the Nord and the Pas-de-Calais, were in a unique situation. They constituted the "forbidden zone," an area that was administered by German authorities based in Brussels. It was an industrial and mining area with a heavy concentration of working-class party members, sympathizers, and activists. Cut off from the Occupied zone, the population suffered severe food scarcity on account of its isolation from the rest of France. Women's food protests were common, especially in the harsh winters of 1940–1 and 1941–2.[10] Although the forbidden zone was technically part of France, protesting women faced the German military police, not their French counterparts. In 1943, they had succeeded in dismantling the women's committees connected to the underground newspaper *La Ménagère du Nord* and imprisoning the leadership. It was not until the summer of 1944 that women resumed such activity.[11]

Reading Women's Protest

Collective actions that bring food concerns into a public forum have a long history in France. The French women who organized and participated in food demonstrations from 1940 through the immediate postwar era drew on historical precedent as a means both to explain and to legitimize their demands. Protests did not erupt in a void; be they planned or triggered by conflicts on site, protesters addressed their complaints and demands to public authorities. They targeted the German occupiers but more often the Vichy government: French mayors, departmental prefects, and the Ministry of Food Supply (*Ministère du ravitaillement*). The audience to whom protest was addressed and the discourse of that protest make it abundantly clear that protesters identified food supply as a deeply political issue.

One might argue that no food protest that confronts public authorities can be truly "spontaneous" in that such action must be prepared over time by the assimilation of ideas of equity, hierarchy, and human rights, acquired either informally, through the transmission of political culture from generation to generation, or by way of institutions such as schools and the media. The action may be unplanned but the basis and justification for that action derive from a cultural disposition. In France, such a cultural disposition is part of national identity, itself forged from centuries of conflict among eaters, producers, sellers, and regulators. It includes the right to sustenance and the responsibility of public authorities to make food—be it bread or butter or meat—available and attainable.

The discourse and performance of women's food protests reveal their explicit political character. Organizers produced flyers to distribute to the public, sometimes to announce a future event and elicit support, and sometimes to interpret an event after the fact. Some of these documents were collected by police patrols on duty at markets, in the subway, and along city streets. Police duly recorded where and when such materials were found. Articles in the underground women's press showcased successful protest actions and encouraged housewives and mothers to take up the fight in their own neighborhoods. In many cases these amateur productions featured drawings alongside text to convey their message.

Protesters drew on a commonly shared vision of the past in order to elicit support, encourage participation, and justify their actions. At their disposal was an extensive historical repertoire of words, signs, and stories from Joan of Arc to the Paris Commune of 1871, but it was the French revolution that had pride of place. A recurring theme in the women's clandestine press is the women's march to Versailles in October 1789, when the people of Paris, led by an avant-garde of market women, marched to the king's palace to demand bread. The "October Days," as the event was known, figure prominently in the underground women's press of the period.

For Josette Dumeix, a women's organizer and French Communist party activist, the underground was both school and proving ground. Her *responsable,* or party supervisor, Danielle Casanova, had been a leading figure in the women's and youth section of the party since the Popular Front period of the 1930s. She remembers Casanova directing her to Michelet's iconic nineteenth-century tome, *Les femmes de la Révolution.*[12] The story would serve as inspiration, example, and template for Dumeix's articles in the women's clandestine press.[13]

In homemade, single-page newspapers and broadsheets, the authors of the underground press held up revolutionary women as models for mothers and housewives plagued by hunger. The women's edition of the PCF newspaper, *L'Humanité,* which circulated in different versions throughout France, addressed women of the capital in April 1941:

> Women and mothers of Paris, we must put an end to these criminal machinations and resolve the bread problem like the women of '89 did. The time has come to take action. From now on, our motto is : 500 grams of bread per day for everyone.[14]

In *L'Appel des Femmes* of September 1943, an appeal to the women of Toulouse. urges them to take their grievances to local authorities and invokes the political legacy of French revolutionary women.

> Let us remember the October days, the 5th and 6th of October 1789 when women went to Paris to demand bread. Let us remember how they brought Louis XVI back to Paris. In 1943 women have lost none of the ardor and courage of their forebears.[15]

Subsistence issues are also linked to the historic inequities between rich and poor, masters and slaves in the excerpt below.

> Housewives! Mothers! You who are unable to obtain anything to feed your children, demand better provisions, denounce privileges and injustices, because the <u>rich have it all while the people are dying of hunger</u>. Go en masse to town halls and prefectures, demand your due. [. . .] *Femmes à l'action!* The women of France played a glorious role in all periods of the history of our country. In 1793, the women who formed a club in Lyon swore "to teach their children and all others over whom they have authority, to prefer death to slavery." In Paris, on May 1, 1793, a delegation of women asked the Convention "to control basic foodstuffs."[16]

An original feature of women's food protests was the collection of grievances to present to town authorities in the form of *cahiers de doléances*. The practice was adopted in pre-revolutionary times when peasants inscribed their complaints and demands in the famous "notebooks" to present to local nobility or the king. In the underground press, French housewives and mothers were incited time and again to follow the example of their forebears by circulating their own *cahiers*. Delegations of women were charged with presenting them to local authorities, be they mayors or departmental prefects.

Echoes of revolutionary propaganda that pilloried the excesses of the haves at the expense of the have-nots appeared frequently in the women's underground press. German soldiers were said to use cooking oil or "real French butter" to lubricate their vehicles. The wife of Otto Abetz, the chief of German occupation troops in Paris, allegedly bathed in milk while French children went hungry. This colorful image brings to mind the apocryphal words of Marie-Antoinette who mockingly advised the poor of Paris to eat brioche (cake) if they had no bread. However fanciful the claims of the underground press may have been, such metaphors are unambiguous allusions to the revolutionary past, and they display the political sentiment that drove women's protest during the war.

The performance of food protests often included the singing of the banned national anthem, the *Marseillaise*. Witnesses, police reports, and articles in the underground press note the use of the *Marseillaise* as a rallying cry. Organizers skillfully deployed it to identify and legitimize food protests as part of a shared historical past. It signaled to the public that despite some appearances, demonstrating for food was not a bread riot but a patriotic act.

Women protesters did not confine their attacks on public officials to historical allusions. On June 27, 1942, Georgette Wallé organized a food demonstration at the open-air market on the avenue Ledru-Rollin in the 12th arrondissement of Paris.

According to Wallé, party leadership had assigned her the task of "motivating" women for protest actions in late 1940 or early 1941.[17] In a report made to her supervisor, Wallé accounted for some thirty-four recruits, women whom she had gathered from cities and towns in the red belt surrounding Paris.

At the Ledru-Rollin market stood a statue, which was melted down in late 1942 for its bronze. But the statue served one last purpose before meeting its demise: Wallé used it to string up a hand-made effigy of Prime Minister Pierre Laval, which she then set aflame. This unusual feature of the demonstration, a clear denunciation of the Vichy authorities, was her own personal touch. It is a detail she mentioned in an interview, but there is no indication of it in her report.[18]

Such allusions, both historical and contemporary, in text, discourse, and performance, signaled to the public—and later, to some historians—the unambiguous political character of women's food protests in this period.

Food Politics

If public protest that targets governmental authorities using a repertoire of historical references and symbols may be considered a political act, what about the object of that protest, food itself? To borrow a concept made famous by anthropologist Marcel Mauss, food is a "total social phenomenon": it expresses and reflects every aspect—social, political, economic, cultural—of human life.[19] Second World War Europe, and France in particular, demonstrates this most clearly. German military planners wielded food was a weapon of war in all of the occupied countries and in their savage conquest of the eastern territories.[20] In occupied France, the quest for food and fear of hunger shaped national and local politics, social relations, and the culture of everyday existence.[21] By 1942, hunger and scarcity were slowly but surely eroding popular support for the Vichy regime. Yet French authorities were slow to acknowledge the profound and multilayered significance of food.

The minister of food provisioning and agriculture, Jacques Le Roy Ladurie, believed that provisioning the people could be isolated from the policies and practices of a criminal regime. This is what the agronomist-farmer told himself when, in April 1942, he agreed to accept a portfolio in Pétain's government.[22] Joining the Vichy government carried a risk, but, he insisted, his own role would be a purely *technical* one.[23] The management of food supply (or as resister and writer Edith Thomas cleverly called it, the "organization of dearth"[24]) was a noble and respectable undertaking in the service of his fellow citizens, wholly separate and apart from politics. How could feeding the people be anything other than honorable?

But there was no escaping the political import of food, as Le Roy Ladurie was eventually forced to concede. By the time he resigned his post after five months in office, it had become abundantly clear that food and food supply were as deeply imbricated in the politics of the regime as anti-Semitic measures, the repression of resisters, or the eradication of Republican freedoms.

While the police viewed food protest as menacing and disruptive, they did not deem it inherently political—at least not at the outset. Public protest did, however, expose women to the risk of arrest. For precisely this reason, Communist party organizers found it difficult to mobilize neighborhood women for highly visible protest activities. No one wanted to risk arrest for a chance at a few potatoes. But food protest did not initially qualify as a criminal or political offense. Disturbing the peace and looting were against the law, but they were not political acts that called for political repression.

After the first massive round-up of food protesters, however, it became clear that demonstrators were not just demanding food; they were targeting the regime itself. On May 31, 1942, women staged a demonstration on the rue de Buci, a central market in the sixth arrondissement of Paris. Some forty people were arrested in the first of several round-ups. Initially, prosecutors qualified the protest as a civil offense. However, when investigators uncovered the multilayered backstory and the involvement of the underground French Communist party, the affair escalated in severity from a civil case to a criminal, political one. Demonstrators were subsequently tried by the *Tribunal d'état*, a new "exceptional" court specifically created for the purpose of expediting the large caseload of political crimes.[25]

The politics of food that played out in Laval's cabinet or the police and justice systems of the Vichy government were equally present in family life. Women's role in the distribution of food among family members was explicitly articulated by the state as a way to manage food scarcity. Wives were urged to serve their wage-earning husbands the meat and to take the vegetables for themselves. Mothers were expected to skip meals so that growing children had enough to eat.[26] Such admonitions were deeply rooted in relations of power and the role of women in the family economy, where the nurturance of others takes precedence over women's own needs. No doubt wives and mothers did this regardless of whether they read and heeded the suggestions of the state-controlled press. Such gestures were no less altruistic or selfless, nor were they any less political. Food in all its manifestations—finding and preparing it, sharing and serving it—lay at the very heart of the politics of everyday life.

Conclusions

How does a riot differ from a demonstration, and what is at stake in distinguishing one from the other? A bread riot erupts. It is unplanned and therefore "spontaneous." In this scenario, hunger leads inexorably to demands for food—there is no intention other than the fulfillment of a basic want. Rioters are motivated by desires, not ideas; their actions are prompted by reflex, not reflection. A bread riot may have political implications, but it is not always a political act.

As we have seen, however, women's food protests in Second World War France were neither spontaneous nor apolitical. The imagery and language of the women's press, the staging of protest against the backdrop of the *Marseillaise*, the *cahiers de doléances* or books of grievances: these signs and symbols make it unambiguously clear that women's food protests in wartime France were fully political in nature.

However, the real litmus test in distinguishing a spontaneous bread riot from a food protest, in this period and perhaps at other times in other places, is the intended interlocutor of the protesters. The archival record makes it clear that women addressed their concerns to the public authorities. They did not target individual shops, market stalls, or shopkeepers.

This is not to say that the frustrations, resentments, and animosities that seethed in the long lines outside food shops did not spill over into conflicts with merchants. Sellers were often accused, not without reason, of hoarding, favoritism, fraud, and dealing on the black market. But protesting women targeted state officials and civil servants, not small proprietors. This was fully in keeping with Communist party policy. The PCF's *Front national,* the mass movement that aimed to group every sector of the population—workers, students, members of professions—extended to small shopkeepers as well. Although the party's plans to recruit small shopkeepers were doomed from the start, there was certainly no point in antagonizing them. Articles in the clandestine press portrayed them as victims of Vichy's ineffectual policies and German depredations, alongside French mothers, housewives, and their families.

For decades after the end of the Second World War and even now, women's food protest has been invisible as "resistance" or even political activism. Eating and not having enough to eat are problems of daily life, however iniquitous and pervasive, but for many observers they do not rise to the level of *haute politique.* Moreover, because food protest has been women's work, it has suffered from the same invisibility that plagued women resisters in general, especially until the 1980s.[27] Finally, food protest under the auspices of the underground French Communist party has long been overlooked as resistance and dismissed as rabble-rousing. Some commentators even surmised that the party was using unsuspecting women to stir up trouble and promote civil unrest.[28] Such claims deny the possibility of women's own agency. It was politics all right—but politics of the wrong kind. In short, women's protests have been visible as "food riots" but invisible as "demonstrations."

Although food protest is now more readily acknowledged as political activity and as resistance, one or more of these factors continue to influence the way scholars, teachers, writers, and citizens think about women's food protest in this period.[29] A training ground, a baptism of fire, an education: taking to the streets in wartime to demand that the authorities provision the people lay the groundwork for women's participation in the new republic, when women belatedly got the vote in April 1944. Henceforth, they would express their politics not only with their bodies, but also with the ballot.

The transition from food scarcity to food sufficiency was a protracted one. Although food protests had subsided by the end of 1947, rationing of some goods would remain in effect until 1949. Did involvement in wartime food protests effectively politicize women, as the French Communist party had hoped and planned? It is hard to know what lasting effects participation may have had on the housewives and mothers who took to the streets for the first time. In any event, the women who initiated and organized many of these protests had already been politicized in party-sponsored women's and youth groups of the interwar period. They brought their experience to bear in the vastly different context of war and German occupation.[30] In this instance as in others, protesting women were acting like political subjects long before they were accorded the full rights and obligations of citizenship.

Notes

1. Paula Schwartz, "The Politics of Food and Gender in Occupied Paris," *Modern and Contemporary France* 7, no. 1 (February 1999): 35–45.

2. The *entraves* were rural protests by peasants, mostly men, who blocked roads. *Émeutes* were riots or uprisings in towns or cities that were more often dominated by women. Cynthia A. Bouton, "Gendered Behavior in Subsistence Riots: The French Flour War of 1775," *Journal of Social History* 23, no. 4 (Summer 1990): 735–54.

3. Interview with Lucette Abada, Paris, November 6, 1985.

4. Originally there were seven zones, the borders of which evolved over the course of the occupation.

5. According to historian Danielle Tartakowsky, there were 239 "housewives' demonstrations" in France from 1940 to 1944, but this figure is surely an undercount. Tartakowsky, *Les manifestations de rue en France (1918-1968)* (Paris: Presses de la Sorbonne, 1997). In the department of the Var alone, there were 100 such demonstrations. Jean-Marie Guillon, "Les manifestations de ménagères: protestation populaire et résistance féminine spécifique," in *Les Femmes dans la Résistance en France*, eds. Mechtild Gilzmer, Christine Levisse-Touzé, and Stefan Martens (Paris: Tallandier, 2003), 107–33. See especially, 115–17.

6. Guillon, «Les manifestations de ménagères.»

7. Jean-François Condette, «Les manifestations de ménagères dans le département du Nord de 1940 à 1944: Révolte frumentaire ou résistance?,» in *Femmes et Résistance en Belgique et en zone interdite*, ed. Robert Vandenbussche (Lille: Publications de l'Institut de recherches historiques du Septentrion, 2007), 125–64.

8. Ibid.

9. Jean-Louis Panicacci, "Le temps des penuries (1939-1949) dans les Alpes-Maritimes," *Cahiers de la Méditerranée* 1, no. 48 (1994): 191–209.

10. Condette, «Les manifestations de ménagères.»

11. Ibid.

12. Jules Michelet, *Les femmes de la Révolution* (2è édition, revue et corrigée) (Paris: Adolphe Delahays, 1855). See especially chapter V, «Les femmes du 6 octobre (89),» 26–56. Michelet qualifies the event as «necessary and legitimate, natural . . . spontaneous, unforeseen, truly popular . . .» He states: "The revolution of October 6 . . . belongs to women, as that of July 14 belongs to men. Men took the Bastille, and women took the king." (56).

13. Interview with Josette Dumeix, Paris, June 5, 1978.

14. *L'Humanité de la femme*, April 23, 1941, presse clandestine, Archives of the Musée de la Résistance nationale, Champigny-sur-Marne, France (Underlining in the original).

15. *L'Appel des femmes: organe du comité féminin de Toulouse*, Septembre 1943. Res. G 1470 (10), Bibliothèque nationale, Paris, France.

16. *Sauvetage de la Famille française: Organe de combat des Femmes Françaises dans le Front National*, March 1943. Res. G 1470 (351), Bibliothèque nationale, Paris, France. (Underlining in the original).

17. Interview with Georgette Wallé, Paris, November 22, 1985.

18. Collection Musée de la Résistance nationale, Champigny-sur-Marne, France. Fonds Lise London-Ricol, note, «Manifestation 27 juin 1942.»

19. Mauss originally coined the term in reference to gift-giving in his 1923 work, *Essai sur le don*. For an English-language version of his essay, see Marcel Mauss, *The Gift: Forms and Functions of Exchange in Archaic Societies* (New York: W.W. Norton, 1967).

20. Lizzie Collingham, *The Taste of War: World War II and the Battle for Food* (New York: The Penguin Press, 2013). Originally Allen Lane, 2011.

21. Ken Mouré and Paula Schwartz, "'*On vit mal*': Food Shortages and Popular Culture in Occupied France, 1940-44," *Food, Culture & Society* 10, no. 2 (summer 2007): 262–95.

22. Jacques Le Roy Ladurie, *Mémoires, 1902-1945* (Paris: Flammarion/Plon, 1997), 304. In peacetime, the minister of agriculture was a cabinet post of secondary importance. However, during the war it acquired new status when food supply became critical. Even Prime Minister Pierre Laval remarked how exceptional it was that Le Roy Ladurie have a seat at the conference table alongside the higher-ranking ministers of justice and interior. Le Roy Ladurie, *Mémoires*, 330.

23. Le Roy Ladurie quotes his colleague, justice minister René Bousquet: "Agriculture is neither left nor right. [. . .] There is no reactionary wheat, no socialist wine." Le Roy Ladurie, *Mémoires*, 368.

24. "Food provisioning [*ravitaillement*]" is merely a euphemism for "the organization of scarcity." Edith Thomas, "La Relève," in *Contes d'Auxois (Transcrit du réel)* (Paris: Éditions de Minuit, 1943), 18.

25. Paula Schwartz, *Today Sardines Are Not for Sale* (Oxford: Oxford University Press, 2020).

26. Archives nationales, AB XIX 4020, folder 5. Unlabeled news clipping from the "legal," or government-censored press.

27. Paula Schwartz, "Résistance et différence des sexes: bilan et perspectives," in *Les Femmes dans la Résistance en France*, eds. Mechtild Gilzmer, Christine Levisse-Touzé, and Stefan Martens (Paris: Tallandier, 2003), 71–86. For an early discussion of how women got left out, See also Paula Schwartz, "Redefining Resistance: The Activism of Women in Wartime France," in *Behind the Lines: Gender and the Two World Wars*, eds. Margaret Randolph Higonnet et al. (New Haven: Yale University Press, 1987).

28. Danielle Tartakovsky makes this claim in *Les manifestations en France*.

29. According to Éric Alary et al., women's food protests were driven merely by hunger: "These women [were] not motivated by patriotism or political ideals." Éric Alary with Bénédicte Vergez-Chaignon and Gilles Gauvin, *Les Français au quotidien, 1939–1949* (Paris: Perrin, 2006), 216.

30. For the political antecedents of women demonstrators at the rue de Buci, see Schwartz, *Today Sardines Are Not for Sale*.

CHAPTER 11
REFLECTIONS ON ROSENSTRASSE
WITH AN EXCERPT FROM *BROKEN GLASS,*
BROKEN LIVES: A JEWISH GIRL'S SURVIVAL
STORY IN BERLIN, 1933–1945 BY RITA KUHN
Ruth Wiseman

(Excerpt from Rita Kuhn's memoir, *Broken Glass, Broken Lives: A Jewish Girl's Survival Story in Berlin, 1933–1945*, beginning with supplemental historical commentary by Professor Nathan Stoltzfus.)

The German public generally disdained German gentiles married to Jews. Some suggested that they should be "marked" by wearing the yellow Star like the Jews themselves.[1] Goebbels agreed, writing in November 1941 that there were to be no Jews in the Nazi Reich and anyone siding with them should be treated like a Jew: "Whoever wears a Jewish Star is marked as an enemy of the people. Whoever still goes around with [a Jew] privately in everyday life belongs to him and must be valued and treated as a Jew. He earns the contempt of the entire people, whom he abandons in base cowardice at the hardest moment, by putting himself at the side of his despiser."[2] Several months earlier Goebbels had convinced Hitler to force all Jews marked for elimination from the Reich to wear the yellow Star. His deputy State Secretary Leopold Gutterer chaired a preparatory meeting where officials from various agencies agreed to require Jews to wear the star as of age six.

But a suicide that month by a famous German actor, Joachim Gottschalk, and his Jewish wife and their son revealed that this could cause problems. Gottschalk, Goebbels reasoned, "could no longer find any way to escape the conflict between state and family. I will thus immediately see to it that this case . . . is not used to construct alarming rumors." (Goebbels diary, November 7, 1941). Trying to limit popular awareness, Goebbels forbade obituaries and banned anyone from attending Gottschalk's funeral. Nevertheless, a number of Gottschalk's professional associates attended the funeral. This show of defiance indicated the sympathy that Germans demonstrated for other Germans, even if they were married to a Jews. Incidents like this could erode Hitler's authority as well as the image of Hitler as a leader backed unanimously, and Hitler's popular image was the glue that held the Germans together. The regime also attempted to carry out the genocide of Jews in secret, fearing that telling the Germans, the Jews, or foreign enemies would make this more difficult.

Hitler took this into account. Two weeks later he told Goebbels that he wanted "a forceful policy against the Jews, though one that does not cause us unnecessary difficulties. The evacuation of the Jews is to be conducted city by city. It is therefore still unclear when it will be Berlin's turn; but when it has its turn, then the evacuation should also be carried out as quickly as possible. Concerning the Jewish mixed marriages, especially those in artist's circles, the Führer recommends that I follow a somewhat reserved course of action since he is of the opinion that these marriages in any case will die out bit by bit, and one shouldn't get any gray hair over this." Goebbels Diary, Nov 22, 1941

At this point, the Gestapo was ordered to "hold back" German "Aryans," married to Jews on a "temporary" basis, from the deportation of other "full Jews" headed for murder. This "temporary" exclusion of intermarried Jews could end at any time, and in fact dozens to hundreds of intermarried Jews were dispatched to the East; the temporary exclusion was lifted here and there to accommodate what the Nazis saw as their historic mission to clear Europe of Jews, once and for all, in a 'Final Solution.' In Berlin, Goebbels intended to end the temporary exclusion of Jews married to Germans with a massive arrest of the last Jews in Berlin, beginning on February 27, 1943.

*   *   *

On March 5th, [1943] a Friday, my mother, [Frieda Kuhn], went to pick up our [family's wartime] ration cards at a school nearby. She left early that day but, contrary to our expectations, returned soon after. As she entered the door, something in her demeanor held us locked [with] fear. [. . .]

"They wouldn't give them to me. You have to go get them yourselves," she said, with her eyes still averted.

"That's it," my father, [Fritz, who unlike my mother was born Jewish] said in response to the news, his voice remarkably clear and steady. "Put on some extra layers of clothes." That was all the advice he gave us and there was no need for an explanation. [. . .]

The four of us, [me, my brother Hans, my mother, and my father,] set out for the school. Once inside, my mother directed us to a room with several SS-men in it, some standing, some seated behind tables with papers piled before them which they examined with granite faces. . . . They asked us questions and checked our answers with the papers stacked in front of them. These contained our vital statistics. And that was what we were to these men—mere statistics, living or dead. They did not acknowledge us with a glance. It was all the same to them. [. . .] The SS-man sitting behind the desk snapped an order to another standing near us, "Take them away."

[The Gestapo was still rounding up the last Berliners wearing the yellow Star, in line with Goebbels declaration two weeks earlier that he was now going to make Berlin "free of Jews" by mid-March: "The Jews in Berlin will now once and for all be pushed out. With the final

deadline of February 28 they are supposed to be first collected in camps and then deported, up to 2,000, batch-by-batch, day-by-day. I have set for myself a goal to make Berlin entirely free of Jews by the middle or end of March at the latest." (Goebbels Diary, February 18, 1943) As the Nazi leader (Gauleiter) of Greater Berlin, Goebbels was in charge of deciding when to make Berlin (his region or Gau), free of Jews. A little more than a year earlier, Hitler had told Goebbels that he wanted "a forceful policy against the Jews, though one that does not cause us unnecessary difficulties. The evacuation of the Jews is to be conducted city by city. It is therefore still unclear when it will be Berlin's turn; but when it has its turn, then the evacuation should also be carried out as quickly as possible. Concerning the Jewish mixed marriages, especially those in artist's circles, the Führer recommends that I follow a somewhat reserved course of action since he is of the opinion that these marriages in any case will die out bit by bit, and one shouldn't get any gray hair over this." (Goebbels Diary, Nov 22, 1941).]

My mother made ready to join us as we followed the SS-man, but he brushed her away with a brusque, "No! Not you!" Her face changed color, looking ashen and rigid, her arms dropped helplessly to her side. The look in her eyes, full of non-comprehension and deep pain, followed me into the room which became our prison, and [it] remain[s] with me ever after. The key turned in the lock with a finality that brooked no dissension, no reversal. Without a word, we sat down on the classroom chairs. [. . .]

Images began rushing through my mind of people being loaded onto trucks, men and women separated, the hushed talk, the feeling of solidarity, the selection to the right or left, and I wondered how long it would be before we were separated and whether this time it would be our turn to go left.

My father broke the silence by saying, "I guess they realized they made a mistake when they released you a week ago, so . . . our poor Mama," he sighed.

Again, silence. My heart wept.

The key turned in the lock once more to admit more "yellow stars," people deceived like us by the thought they were coming to get their ration cards. A Jewish woman, Frau Goedicke, who had recently come to occupy one of our bedrooms, entered at one point with a hesitant step and eyes cast to the ground, but as soon as she saw us, she straightened up and gave us a smile of recognition and relief. There was little talk among those assembled; each harbored thoughts for which there were no words.

Time stopped.

We waited for more people to arrive and did not want to think beyond that . . .

Suddenly a woman's voice startled us with its piercing, desperate screams, "Let me see my children. You can't take my children from me . . . let me go with my children." We listened and could not identify the voice until my father turned to Hans and me and said, loud enough for others to hear, "*Das ist doch unsere Mama*," that is our Mama. There was a stir in the room, for my mother was known to many from helping out in my grandmother's store. Her voice, usually low and gentle, never raised even in anger, was stretched beyond recognition by a terror so great it rose above any care for herself as she faced fully armed SS-men.

Just as suddenly as it had started, the voice stopped; in its stead there were other voices, hoarse, male voices giving orders.

What had they done to my mother?

I wanted to leave the room to find out. I wanted to see her, touch her, comfort her as much as I needed her comfort.

My heart wept.

Sometime later the door opened part way and a familiar face scanned the room, until his eyes found us and he nodded ever so slightly. It was our "Onkel" Helmut, [a close family gentile friend], unable to conceal the agitation and solicitude showing in his handsome features. When we questioned him later how in the world he had gained access to our room, he told us he knew from Mama where we were and, under the pretext of having opened the wrong door, he was able to ascertain that we were still safe.

Finally, the door swung wide open and a group of SS-men entered and ordered everyone to follow them. We were walking in a file of two and were led into the courtyard. There, under a covered archway, my mother was leaning against the stone wall, motionless, her lips closed . . . her eyes . . . looked at us like those of a wounded deer.

A truck was waiting for us in the middle of the street. The loading proceeded noiselessly and in broad daylight. There was no lack of witnesses. I was the last one to get on and had to sit between two SS-men with their guns poised high. We understood that language. I had a good view of the street and, while waiting for the truck to start moving, fastened my eyes on my mother who stood there with the other relatives of those with us on the truck, among them the daughters of Frau Goedicke. My mother had turned to stone from grief. [. . .]

The moment the truck started to move, one of Frau Goedicke's daughters, Herta, cried out, "*Nehmt mich doch auch mit*," take me too, and then collapsed on the pavement. Her mother behind cried out, and I could see her hand stretched out in a futile gesture to catch her falling daughter. Just then the truck turned a corner—leaving a void where my mother had been.

Someone was comforting Frau Goedicke who had begun to moan quietly, muttering all the while, "*Meine Tochter . . . meine Herta.*" My thoughts were elsewhere, wondering how this could be happening again, and that I might never wake up from this nightmare. Just then I looked at the SS-man to my right and saw his face twitch with emotion. His eyes moistened and . . . and my hand wanted to move to rest on his shoulder. Was I going mad?

The truck came to a stop. Terse orders of "*Raus!*" told us that we had arrived at our destination. Dusk was falling. The cold was penetrating even through our double layers of clothes. A wet bleakness blanketed the place where other Jews had been collected and stood at attention before SS-men and Gestapo agents in leather coats who were making selections. I had no idea where we were and dared not ask my father, since speaking was forbidden. Someone on my left mumbled the name Levetzowstrasse, and I could make out the presence of a building known to me from pictures as a synagogue.

So they choose houses of prayer from which to send Jews to their death.

My father stood straight and stiffly before a hulk of a man in civilian clothes who bullied him to reveal our identities. "Jude Fritz Israel Kuhn; Tochter Rita Sara Kuhn;

Sohn Hans Israel Kuhn," I heard him say with a steady, clear voice, followed by another voice sizzling with contempt, "*Stinkjuden.*"

Echoes of subdued voices could be heard through the descending darkness, interspersed with obscenities which stood in lurid contrast to the stillness all around, like thunder from a cloudless sky. Someone was shoving me, "To the right!" I went, like a child's mechanical toy, in the direction toward another waiting truck where I saw my father and brother.

Thank God, we were together.

* * *

We stopped!

Another unfamiliar building for another unloading.

Once inside, the SS was separating men, women, and children after having checked everyone's papers. An SS officer, young and handsome, looked at my papers, then at my yellow star, and finally directly at me with a sardonic smile, "You're really Jewish?" to which I responded by pointing to my ID, "Rita Sara Kuhn," afraid to say anything more to this blond poison.

The inside of the building was dark; a musty smell told me it had not been used or aired for some time. It seemed like a perfect hiding place for clandestine actions and my old fears returned. [. . .]

A [Jewish] orderly with a yellow star took me up a flight of stairs to a room on the second floor. "Stay here," he said curtly in a tired voice and pointed to a straw mattress on the floor. The room was medium sized, lit by a bare bulb which gave out a feeble light. The damp mattresses explained the odor which met me when I entered. I wanted to turn around but knew I couldn't. There was nothing else to sit on so I sat down on the straw sack assigned to me. I could just make out the shape of three women lying on their mattresses opposite mine. One of them sat huddled in a corner to my left, and the other two near a window to my right. My arrival made little impression on them, no one moved and there was no exchange of greetings. Their silence and immobility only added to the gloom and sense of abandonment pervading this place, in sharp contrast to my own state of agitation and need for human contact. I seemed to be no longer in the land of the living and wanted to know how long they had been here, forgotten by the outside world. [. . .]

Hope had died here [where most had been imprisoned since February 27 or 28].

Time held no dimension for these women whose bodies seemed locked in the same position as on the day they were thrown in here, like a sack of potatoes carelessly tossed into some corner, left to rot.

Once I got used to my surroundings and the silence became increasingly oppressive, my natural curiosity asserted itself and I asked, "Where are we?" The woman to my left answered with, "Rosenstrasse 2-4, the former Jewish *Hilfsverein*," welfare agency. She fell silent again, whether from lack of energy or interest was difficult to say.

Now that I was settled on my mattress and all action had stopped for the time being, the lack of food caught up with me and I asked myself whether there might be something to eat in this tomb. It was certainly time for supper.

The same orderly who had accompanied me to this floor soon appeared with bowls of soup and slices of black bread which he placed unceremoniously on the floor. We each took our portion and I did so eagerly, but my appetite turned to revulsion at the first sight of the contents in the bowl. More to myself than to those in the room, I expressed my disgust with a very definite, "I can't eat this."

"You'd better . . ." the woman to my left warned me, "because it's all you're going to get in here."

"But it looks like dirty dishwater. What's that swimming around in it?" I asked with a slight shudder.

"Well, if you'd rather go hungry. . ." the woman shrugged and fell quiet again. Another look at the soup convinced me that I'd rather choose hunger than this toxic brew. The piece of bread will have to do, and I broke off small bits of it to make it last longer.

*   *   *

Language too had died here.

The lack of air, warmth, and energy in these languid bodies was not conducive to conversation so that, more than ever, I thought of my family and whether we would ever be together again. Stifled by the silence and gloom, I asked the more talkative of the women how long she had been in this place. She welcomed this overture to talk and entered into a dialogue with me while the other two, in all probability mother and daughter, maintained their impenetrable silence.

The woman's name was Miriam Jürgens. When I looked puzzled at the odd combination of names, she told me her story. Her husband was an 'Aryan' with whom she had a son who was not raised as a Jew. They divorced some time in 1937 when he decided to join the NSDAP for "professional advancement," he assured her, and not from conviction. "If I'm lucky and they'll consider me *arisch versippt* (kin to an Aryan), they'll send me to Theresienstadt," she said rather indifferently. She had been waiting for their decision all week long since she was taken from her factory on the first day of the round-ups, February 27th. Everyone in this building was living in some form of a mixed marriage, she told me. The Gestapo had not yet decided what to do with the different cases. Some had been deported already for reasons Miriam did not know. She then related a most incredible and unique incident that had occurred outside these walls for the entire week she had been confined to this room.

From the first day of the city-wide round-ups, there had been a demonstration, truly a protest, by the gentile wives and mothers for their Jewish husbands and children interned in Rosenstrasse. They demanded the release of their family members. It started with a small number but soon swelled to a chorus of a few hundred desperate women shouting, "Give us back our men. Give us back our men." We could hear those cries through the only window in our room. There were short intermittences when the SS succeeded in dispersing them, but a few hours later, the women would continue, and in increasing numbers. As a result of this protest many prisoners had been released, while others were deported. The logic of that escaped her because of "the crazy nature of the Nuremberg laws."

"And one day, in the middle of the protest," Miriam continued, "the SS officer in charge of this place came into our room and, standing erect and proud, his hand pointing to the window, he told us, 'Do you hear that? These are your relatives. They want you to go home. We are proud of them. *Das ist deutsche Treue* (that is German loyalty).'" [. . .]

*   *   *

She finished her story with a "Tja," and I knew we were thinking along similar lines in pondering this enigma of a man who can momentarily place his avowed values of family loyalty, long honored by Germanic tribes, over his prescribed duty of sending Jews to their deaths. Such inconsistency between morality and depravity can be more frightening than the blank hatred most SS-men expressed towards Jews. The element of unpredictability and incongruity elicited more fear than the behavior we had come to expect from such men.

And then, leaning forward slightly for fear she might be overheard, Miriam whispered audibly enough, "I don't like to think of SS-men as being human, but this man, so proud of the German tradition of fealty to family, extended even to Jews, is too human for my liking." [. . .]

*   *   *

Nighttime brought another kind of terror as the sound of sirens announced the approach of British bombers. In response to my customary reaction of jumping out of bed to head for the cellar, I heard Miriam's voice reminding me there was no shelter for those interned here. I lay down again on my mattress and when the first bombs started falling some distance away, I covered my head with the foul smelling horse blanket to lessen the noise of detonations all around us. I could no longer make a distinction between my body and that of the building shaking. The window rattled as if it would burst and I saw the two silent women move away from it.

When the "all clear" signal finally sounded, I was bathed in sweat despite the freezing temperatures.

*   *   *

The following morning brought new anxieties and more waiting. The room was quiet, the air heavy with thoughts that found no relief in talk. After last night's air raid, a general lethargy had taken over at the approach of a new day. It takes so much energy to hope, to guard one's faith in the ultimate victory of good over evil, and not be lulled into a state of mental blackout of what the next hour may bring. [. . .]

Breakfast was a slice of black bread with a hint of margarine and a cup of lukewarm *Ersatzkaffee*, which was of little help against the cold. It was our only diversion and we all lingered over this meager repast to give us something to do.

Sometime in the afternoon, the Jewish forced laborer appeared at the door to ask me to follow him. Hope and fear rose in me. I followed him downstairs into the same vestibule where we had checked in. Two lines of children were waiting, one for boys, among them Hans, the other for girls. Hans and I exchanged smiles of recognition, caught between relief and dread. I joined the line of girls as the orderly had directed me.

Somewhere to my left, the voice of a man—calm, firm, eerily warm—told us to listen quietly to his instructions. Without having seen him yet, I knew it to be the SS officer about whom I had heard so much. His measured steps moved closer to the front of the two lines until he was in view of all of us. He was indeed good looking, his features young, refined, and tinted with a confident smile. His impeccable, grey-green uniform enhanced the supple grace of his lean body. Only the death head on his cap was evidence of his sinister mission. He paced his words with deliberate smoothness.

"I am strict with the men, courteous to women, and affectionate with children." He demonstrated the latter statement by patting the dark curls of a girl in front of him. I shuddered, reminded of the talk with Miriam. His words, his face, and the death head above his forehead conveyed a contradiction too deep to comprehend. He informed us that we were allowed to go home and that we should wait for our release papers.

Standing in front of him, he told Hans and me that they had to check my father's papers more thoroughly and that he would be sent home later. I believed him, because I wanted to believe; the other alternative was too unthinkable.

[*The people gathered together in large throngs and even sided with the Jews to some extent. I will commission the security police not to continue the Jewish evacuations during such a critical time. Rather we want to put that off for a few weeks; then we can carry it out all the more thoroughly. One has to intervene all over the place, to ward off damage. The efforts of certain offices are so lacking in savvy that one cannot leave them on their own for ten minutes. The basic malady of our leadership and above all of our administration consists in operating according to Schema F* [*incapable of adapting orders to circumstances*]. One has the impression that these people, who carry out this or that measure, don't reflect one bit, but rather hang to the written word, whose main value to them is that they thus have their actions covered by orders from above. (Goebbels Diary, March 6, 1943).]

The first sight that met my eyes on leaving our prison was the lone figure of a stranger standing in the entrance way to an apartment building across the street, his right hand raised in a gesture of welcome to our freedom. Farther down the street were more figures waiting for the release of those in prison, relatives or friends.

I felt connected to these people, connected by a shared anguish, a common sorrow. Yet I had no tears left when I was reunited with my mother, even tears of joy, because joy had long ago fled from our life.

* * *

As soon as we were back in our apartment, Frau Schmidt told us what had happened to Frau Philipps. The Gestapo had come to pick her up the day of our arrest. It was ghastly to see how they pushed this eighty-two year old woman and hardly gave her enough time to pack her few belongings. [. . .] My mother's exhausted look told us all. Even her smile at seeing us return unharmed was strained, tentative, and worried at not seeing her husband.

My father did indeed arrive home the next day, a Sunday. We gave my mother a detailed account of the events of the last two anguished days and thought as well of the possible fate of my father's cousins, Tante Ilse and Tante Irene. Thinking of them and so many others caught in the net of the *Aktion* cast a gloom over our reunion.

Herta Gödicke came to my grandmother's store on that Sunday, and related her story of the protest in Rosenstrasse. She had gone there to inquire about her mother and was told that she may be released and would in the future be protected from any further arrests if the daughters pledged to have her live with them. Herta agreed to it all willingly. She had heard of the demonstration and how the women faced the machine guns of the SS to demand the release of their husbands. One woman told her that at one point they had had enough and had yelled, "*Ihr Mörder*" (You murderers) to the SS pointing the machine guns at them. The SS [did] not shoot, and lowered their guns.

"Can you imagine?" she asked us. "These women broke down the walls of silence."

We looked at one another, unable to speak, but then my father turned to my mother and said, calm and proud, "And so did you, Mama. And so did you."

*   *   *

Reflections on Rosenstrasse

By Ruth Wiseman,
Daughter of Rita J. Kuhn

Rosenstrasse, as a place, as a protest, and as a rescue did not enter my conscious mind until I was in my 20s. My mother, Rita Jenny Kuhn, rarely spoke about the war when we were children, and I say "war" here to underline the fact that she most definitely did not speak about the Shoah. I had a vague idea that she wore the yellow star, for there it sat in her box gleaming up at us with its dull yellow background and foreboding black Gothic lettering, pulling me into its grey fog of melancholy. There was also her *poesie album*, which we were instructed not to open nor would she open it for us despite our pleading. I imagine it is akin to walking in the graveyard of her murdered school friends. It was only years later when I understood that this album contained her lost friends' poems and good wishes at the end of the school year, each poem written in unique and beautiful handwriting. Ironically every word is in German; I would not have understood a single word if I'd ever managed to open it when it was forbidden to me.

It is possible—and I am guessing here—that the first time I heard the entire story of Rosenstrasse was in 1985, when my mother came to speak to my college class about the Shoah at Sonoma State University, taught by Dr. Jon Steiner, himself a German-Jewish survivor and formidable man. I was terribly distraught in his class when, at the age of 20, I was coming to grips with the enormity of what happened (if anyone can come to grips with genocide). The documentary images were the skeletons and ghosts of my childhood nightmares come to life. I frequently remained after class to speak with Professor Steiner. His unflagging honesty and patience gave me the strength to continue his class. I spoke to him about many things, most especially about understanding that my mother is indeed a survivor. I had not until then been quite sure. Whereas many survivors despise(d) Germany, my mother extolled German culture on intellectual grounds; Goethe, Mahler, Wolfram von Eshenbach, and the good Germans whom she knew during the war years. Dr. Steiner understood my mother's affection for her native country. He was compassionate.

Dr. Steiner invited my mother to come speak to our class. This was her first public speaking engagement. I was startled by her broken sentences and emotional demeanor, though grateful to hear her story from beginning to end. I did not know any survivors when I was growing up. I was ensconced in a rather idyllic life in the hills of Berkeley, CA with normal childhood activities. Nonetheless I felt chronically out of place in the world—particularly in school. I carried within me the mysterious "black box" of my mother's story. For many years I was not even sure that my mother was Jewish; in middle school I only told my first Jewish friend that my mother is German. Dr. Steiner, with his knowledge of the Nuremberg laws, was able to tell my mother that she was considered a *Geltungsjude*, hence her requirement to wear the yellow star and subsequent forced labor.

I did not understand the complexities of my mother's story until I began interviewing other survivors in 1993. Most people I speak to have never heard of Rosenstrasse. My many Jewish friends who are either children or grandchildren of survivors are stunned when they hear about it. I have always been uncomfortable to begin this conversation because it means that I need to divulge the fact that my Oma converted to Judaism.

Perhaps I've inherited my mother's survival guilt. I continuously try to find the reason she survived if she was "just as Jewish" by Nazi law as her school friends who perished. I have not only internalized the guilt but also the need to defend her Jewish identity and thereby my own. It took me years to untangle the conflict between Jewish law and the Nuremberg laws in defining who is a Jew. I still hear Jews outside the orthodox community refer to themselves as half or a quarter Jewish, as though it is a racial identity. Or perhaps they are proud of this familial connection and wish to hold onto it without the religious obligations, which are admittedly onerous. Quite honestly, I have not engaged anyone deeply on this topic. It is reasonable that the rabbis thrice turn away a prospective convert to Judaism; only a courageous depth of faith can inspire someone to interlace their history with that of the Jewish people.

My maternal grandmother, Frieda nee Krueger, was a woman of such courage. She converted to Judaism in Berlin circa 1925. She married my grandfather, Herz Fritz Kuhn, on February 20, 1926. My "Oma" did not abandon her Jewish beliefs despite the increasingly dangerous environment, and despite eventual Nazi pressure to leave both her husband and her faith. She did, however, cancel her membership to the Jüdische Gemeinde in 1941, in order to continue receiving the Tuberculosis ration cards that helped her entire family. I discovered this when doing family research. The International Tracing Service sent me a letter that my grandmother wrote to the Jüdische Gemeinde requesting to have her membership reinstated. My grandparents also decided, in 1941, to baptize Rita and Hans in the desperate hope that this might save them, as it did many Marrano Jews.

When my mother first began sharing her story she met camp survivors who minimized her trauma. They called her a "German lover" because she defended the "good" Germans who were not in lockstep with Hitler, such as the loyal family friend who risked his life to peek his head into the room where they were held at the school. Or the women of Rosenstrasse who risked their lives in protest to the SS.

As a child, I was told I am only "one-quarter" Jewish. Mutti married our talented, charismatic Methodist-raised father in 1954. Their marriage lasted 14 years, until I was three months old. The religious identity tug-of-war between my parents was subtle in the beginning. I was unaware of the Jewish maternal lineage, and when I did learn of it, I was even more confused. Did I come by my Jewish identity "honestly"? Was it erased because of my mother's baptism? Was my grandmother's conversion even "kosher," that is, orthodox? These questions tortured me as I began my own religious exploration in 1995. Thankfully I met the kind and gentle Rabbi Eliezer Finkelman, who was then the pulpit rabbi at the modern orthodox synagogue, Congregation Beth Israel in Berkeley, CA. He encouraged me to try to obtain my grandmother's conversion records from Berlin while at the same time understanding this may be impossible. As time went on, he advised me that the prudent and halachic thing to do, if I chose to live an orthodox Jewish life, would be to undergo my own conversion to "remove any doubt."

This decision, initiated a decade earlier with my mother's statements about the Rosenstrasse Protest as public interest in it awakened, impacted many of my relationships, particularly with the loving, non-Jewish man with whom I was in a relationship. I walked away from him, reluctant to continue intermarriage into a third generation. It was a painful loss. I do not stand in judgment of fellow Jews who intermarry, for it might have been me, but I also know that it is that much harder to find one's footing without a Jewish spouse. Other relationships to suffer strain were with my immediate family members.

My father knew only that I was going to the modern orthodox synagogue three blocks from his home. On one of my visits with him he expressed concern to me about my becoming orthodox. His discomfort with traditional Judaism created a painful tension between us. The more Jewishly observant I became, the more he articulated his religious beliefs to me; beliefs which I did not know he held. Yes, we celebrated Christmas with him growing up, but it was a lovely, secular holiday. Yes, his stepmother took us to church for a while when we were young. I was deeply unsettled in church, yet had no means of telling her. I believe she stopped taking me when my mother requested it. Fortunately, I believe my father and I made peace before he passed away. The last conversation we had about religion was an acknowledgement between us that neither of us can abide a fundamentalist, black and white approach to God, and that one's spiritual practice is a deeply personal experience.

On the other hand, I could not even tell my mother that I was studying with an orthodox rabbi in order to eventually immerse in the mikveh and formalize my Jewish commitment. I feared her reaction. How could I challenge her Jewish identity, that of a *stern traeger* a star-bearing, forced laborer, survivor of Hitler? Shabbat dinner before my Sunday mikvah appointment, I gathered the courage to tell her that since we cannot find the conversion records of her mother, and because I want to live an orthodox life, I must do a formal conversion to legalize my status. Her reaction stunned me. She was quiet for a moment, then said, "Do you know who would be very proud?" "No," I responded. She spoke through tears, "Your Opa." Mutti came with me the next day and together we completed the circle that was broken. My immersion in the mikvah restored the family link to Judaism that was nearly destroyed. My mother's presence there was a blessing that surely removed all doubt.

Postscript: I wrote this just days after four people were gunned down in a kosher supermarket in Jersey City. Hardly a week passed in early 2020 when we didn't hear about an anti-Semitic incident on American soil, whether in Brooklyn, Beverly Hills, Pittsburgh, or Monsey. Many Jews view these attacks as the "writing on the wall" that Jews are no longer welcome in the USA. Yet these are individual acts of harassment and terror—not government sanctioned persecution. The perpetrators are either caught or killed in gunfire exchange. Nonetheless, it once again does not feel safe to be a Jew. I cannot tell my mother about this disturbing rise of violence against Jews. I wish I could say that the bravery of the Rosenstrasse women has manifested in my own life as being a politically involved person, yet I shy away from politics. I assume the Rosenstrasse women were not motivated with our modern-day imperative of "speaking truth to power." After all, as members of the preferred "Aryan" race, they were the power paradigm. In the course of one week they reclaimed that power *for goodness* and saved hundreds of future generations. Their staggering bravery was borne out of devotion to their imprisoned loved ones. My debt of gratitude can never be repaid. The choice to live my life as a Jew of faith is the best way I have to thank them for their resistance to Hitler's madness. It has always been our faith that sustains our people through centuries of persecution and migration. It is our faith that will sustain us in these difficult times.

Notes

1. SD Report, February 2, 1942, Boberach, *Meldungen aus dem Reich*, vol. 9, 3245.

2. Joseph Goebbels, "Die Juden Sind Schuld!," in *Das Eherne Herz* (Munich: Eher Verlag, 1943), 85–91, here 87, 91.

CHAPTER 12
THE MISCHLINGE EXPOSÉ
STORIES OF ASSIMILATION AND CONVERSION
Carolyn Enger

Introduction

In February 2020, I find myself back in Wroclaw, Poland (formally Breslau, Germany), the city where my father was born. I am here to realize a longtime goal of mine: to perform my multimedia performance project, *The Mischlinge Exposé* at the White Stork Synagogue. The project combines videos and sound from my godmother and father with music composed by Mischlinge and German-Jewish converts. My family's history is interwoven with the stories of important cultural figures whose stories echo my own.

I can't believe that it is actually happening. I feel mixed emotions, some of excitement and pride for my work and perseverance, and others of fear and dread. I'm staying in the Hotel Monopol, in a room above the balcony where Hitler gave a speech in 1938. The balcony was purposely built for his visit here. I wonder if my father, who was then twenty-eight years old, knew of Hitler's visit. I wonder where my father was on that day, and how he felt. Did he think Hitler's rise to power would blow over or not? Was he afraid or anxious?

If he were here now, he would have been filled with pride and might have felt some sense of vindication to know that I was performing in his home city, Breslau. For me, it was a moment of "victory" and "restitution," to bring my talents and experiences as a Steinway concert pianist, back to Breslau, where my father had lost so much. I could bring proof of his survival and success. Before the depression and the war, my father had lived a life of comfort, with a cook, governess, chauffeur, a grand piano, etc. All was lost. In the United States, he worked very hard to acquire a Steinway grand piano for me and to support my career. Even though he was not a practicing Jew in Breslau, he was perceived and persecuted for his mixed status as a Mischling, that is, "half-Jew ." His mother was Jewish. His father was not. It was important for me to return to Breslau in a Jewish way, as a Jew, telling his story, the story of a Mischling; to be a spokesperson for a group of which many are unaware.

I have been reading and pursuing topics of the Holocaust, German-Jewry, and the Mischlinge for over thirty years. My collection of books, articles, movies, and lectures is too numerous to list. I feel the importance of speaking out about diversity, tolerance, and identity is especially needed and that I can use music as a vehicle for spreading a message of social justice. Being a pianist, I felt the best way to tell the story would be to create a film that includes the stories of my family, my godmother, Rosemarie Steinfeld, also a

Mischling 1st Degree, Grade A, and the stories of German-Jewish converts such as the Mendelssohn family, Heinrich Heine, Rachel Varnhagen, Alexander Zemlinsky, Gustav Mahler, Hanns Eisler, and Arnold Schoenberg. I perform the music of these composers while the film shows images and quotes of these artists and thinkers.[1]

My Family History

My grandmother, Charlotte Poppelauer, converted from Judaism to Christianity in 1919, after marrying my grandfather, Franz Hermann Kurt Enger. (In Germany, conversion of Jews to Christianity was, for the majority, motivated by economic and/or social status.) She passed away in 1928, from toxemia, a complication during her third pregnancy. My father, Horst Joachim (later Horace) was then almost seven; his brother Hans Dieter was two and a half. Nine years after my paternal grandmother Charlotte's passing, my grandfather remarried, a German woman, Gertrude Minkus. She believed in the racial laws of the time, and was unkind to my father and his brother Dieter, my uncle. She felt that they were inferior, having been born of a Jewish mother. My father soon moved out and found his own apartment at the age of sixteen. My grandfather's family had installed the telephone system in Breslau. My father's aunts and uncles all had jobs working for the post office, which was the government agency responsible for the telephone system. My grandfather didn't want to be a part of that; instead he chose to be an entrepreneur. However, the conditions were not so good. The economy was in shambles after the First World War. The war reparations demanded of Germany in the Treaty of Versailles and the worldwide depression created a climate where social unrest and political instability were the norm, a climate that Hitler used to his advantage. My father remembers going to his aunts and uncles on payday with a note from his father asking them for money.[2]

The Jewish community in Breslau at the time was the third largest in Germany, after Berlin and Frankfurt. Many Jewish men had fought in the First World War for their Fatherland. Many were decorated soldiers, earning the Iron Cross for their valor. German Jews were loyal to Germany and had actively assimilated into German culture, gradually secularizing after emancipation in 1871. The Ostjuden or Eastern-Jews, Jews coming to Germany from Poland, were looked down upon by German Jews. The prejudice had to do with language, socioeconomic advantage, and differences in level of religious observance. They were seen as a welfare cause. There were organizations formed to provide charity, aid agencies to fight for their basic rights and economic improvement; but most regarded the Ostjuden as a hindrance to German-Jewish social integration and many aid organizations encouraged their settlement abroad. Moving away from Traditional or Orthodox practice, both Conservative and Reform Judaism originated in Breslau. These movements had a lasting impact on Judaism. Today the Reform Movement counts one million members in the United States, making it the largest Jewish denomination.[3]

My father attended the Johannes Gymnasium. On my trip to Breslau in August 2019, I was able to enter the school and saw photos from that time. The Star of David and the

Crucifix, Jewish and Christian symbols, were pictured together demonstrating tolerance between Judaism, Evangelical Christianity, and Catholicism. My father told us that at a certain time of day, they would have religion class. The students would split up and attend the class of their faith. My father attended the Evangelical class, as that is how his family identified. We find this strange, that religion was taught in public school. In Europe, there is no separation between church and state. The students all knew who was who, who was Jewish, who was Evangelical (Protestant), and who was Catholic.

My father had feelings of inferiority due to his issues of identity, not being fully Aryan or fully Jewish. The lack of a simple racial, religious, or nationalist identity created an inherent confusion and anxiety. He had to shape his own unique identity, his own personal identity. In Germany he experienced prejudice as a Mischling. Prejudice continued to plague him in the United States. He wasn't Christian enough, wasn't Jewish enough.

Across the street lived my father's Aunt Kate and Uncle Georg Neumann, and his cousins, Heinz (Henry) and Susan, who were Jewish. They shared their governess, who was a Seventh-Day Adventist.[4] The families were close. As the laws continued to change, Heinz was able to emigrate to India and then to England. Susan was able to emigrate to Palestine.

On Kristallnacht (Night of Broken Glass) in Breslau, November 9–10, 1938, also called the November Pogrom, the Nazi SA paramilitary destroyed almost 200 synagogues. Ninety-one people were killed and Jewish property was looted and burned. German Jews living in Breslau were sent to Theresienstadt, the ghetto in the Czech protectorate, controlled by Nazi Germany. They were ordered by the Nazis to gather in the courtyard of the White Stork Synagogue.[5] By 1938, emigration was not possible. The Nazis levied heavy emigration taxes and other countries would not take in the refugees, restricting immigration to their shores.[6] There were no choices. They were in a warlike atmosphere, troops marching around regularly, rallies, speeches, propaganda, deportations, neighbors spying on each other, weapons in full view. I try to imagine how this affected my father and his family. He didn't speak about it very much. He wouldn't eat red beets; as he used to say, that's all they had to eat during the war. My uncle Helmut, the half-brother of my father and my uncle Dieter, was born in 1938. His experiences were different from my father and his brother, Dieter. He was too young to be drafted or to be part of the Hitler Youth. He remembers that the girls at the time were delegated by the government to aid new mothers, while the boys were being prepared to fight. Helmut's mother (my father's stepmother) was aided by one of these girls. New mothers were highly regarded as they were helping to create the "Master Race." After the war, he and my grandparents had to leave Silesia, annexed to Poland, and move West, with nothing. He remembers that they had to leave by train and that at the railway station, airplanes were bombing the trains. They were relocated to Goslar, West Germany.

At the beginning of 1940, the Mischlinge were drafted into the military. In April 1940, several tens of thousands were banned and discharged by the Nazis, nearly all were sent to forced-labor camps or worse. By October of 1940 the ban was strictly enforced.[7] During the Wannsee Conference, on January 20, 1942, held to discuss the destruction of the Jewish people, among the issues discussed was what to do with the Mischlinge. Were they to be considered as Jewish or not? It created a problem for the Nazis. At the conference, they were not initially able to come to a consensus. Attendees of the conference were ambivalent about harming anyone with German blood. The Mischlinge, being partially Aryan and partially Jewish, didn't fit easily into their plans for destroying the Jewish people. By the end of the meeting, after debate, they decided that the Mischlinge would have to be destroyed as well.

My father's fully Jewish Aunt Kate and Uncle Georg Neumann were deported to Theresienstadt in 1943 and then to Auschwitz. I don't know when. Their daughter, my father's cousin Susan, immigrated to Israel. Their son, my father's cousin Heinz (Henry), immigrated to India, where he was detained as a German citizen. He worked in textiles, made his way to England and then finally to the United States, where he became a successful accountant.

Initially, my father was drafted into the army, and then the laws changed and the Mischlinge were kicked out of the army. If my father hadn't been a Mischling, he would've been on the Russian front, fighting as a soldier. He faked a limp with a cane so as not to be suspected by his neighbors for not being in the army. He worked as an apprentice in textile and commercial art and worked on blueprints during the war.

In July 1944, my father was questioned and sent to a forced-labor camp (Arbeitslager) because a member of the Gestapo had found out that my father and his first wife, Ursula, were engaged to be married. He needed to know what my father's racial mix was, and if they would have to go to prison for potentially mixing pure Aryan blood with nonpure blood. The Gestapo had no choice but to let them go, instead of arresting them and sending them either to prison or deporting them to a ghetto and/or concentration camp, as they were both Mischlinge Grade A, or of the 1st Degree. Given that their "racial status" matched, they were allowed to procreate.[8] They were both ordered to the same camp, Ostlinde. As the Russians were approaching, they were transferred around, into various forced-labor camps; Görlitz, Schmiegrode, Waldenburg, and Osterrode, all subcamps of the Gross-Rosen concentration camp.

The Mischlinge were considered dangerous after the failed attempt on Hitler's life, on July 20, 1944. Hitler and many of his cronies declared the Mischlinge guilty, deemed them no longer worthy of living, and earmarked them for extermination. On August 8, 1944, my uncle Dieter was sent a letter to go to the train station to a forced-labor camp. He departed from the train station in Breslau and was sent to Schmiegrode, with other Mischlinge. The prisoners, including my father and my uncle, built tiered bunks or beds, cut trees, and dug trenches to fortify against Russian tanks. The men dug trenches and the women made "ropes" out of tree branches to hold the dirt in the trenches in place. There was a lot of disorganization. While he was in the camp, my father lost weight and teeth, due to the lack of food and poor nutrition.

In the winter of early 1945, they could hear the Russians coming. When the Russian tanks came, they drove right over these trenches. The guards fled and the prisoners, once they established that it was safe, followed their example. The prisoners tested the barbed wire fences and found that they were not electrified, so they fled. My father jumped on a freight train and collapsed for three days. The train traveled to Vienna, around Czechoslovakia, to avoid the Russians. There, his plan was to meet Ursula, who had fled the camp before him, and her half-sister and her half-sister's husband. When the Russians came to Vienna, they left again, and stole four bicycles, a cart, a typewriter, and official stationery. They would type letters that they were on official business and that the local mayor needed to give them food stamps, as it was still Nazi time. They traveled through the Alps, to Kaufbeuren im Allgäu, where they knew the Americans would come, and to Nesselwang, where they worked on a farm in the mountains, in exchange for food. At 5 a.m., they milked cows. There was one bowl on the table to serve the food. If they spent too much time talking, there wouldn't be any food left.

They eventually made their way to Augsburg, where my uncle Dieter and aunt Lucie, also a Mischling, met them. Dieter and Lucie had been sent to Erfurt after their work in the forced-labor camps, Trachtenburg, Waldenburg, and Schmiegröde, where there were between 800 and 1,000 people in the camps and no food. Uncle Dieter had an opportunity to work indoors doing office work in Schmiegröde. He was especially glad to get inside, as the winter of 1944–5 was brutally cold. The SS came and moved them further west in February of 1945. In Waldenburg, Dieter was back to digging trenches. It was very cold there. He was able to cleverly finagle himself into a position as a surveyor or engineer. He was an eighteen-year-old, head of a labor group of older men.

When the Russians came, they questioned Uncle Dieter. They wanted to know if he was part of the German military. He kept insisting he wasn't, that he was a prisoner. He was nevertheless beaten; his watch, a gift from his confirmation, was taken. They took him to a barn and threatened to kill him. Instead, they shot their guns into the air. He escaped, went to look for his and my father's family home in Breslau. No one was there. Everything was destroyed. The Russians and the Poles came, taking over property as an occupying force, appropriating people, making it impossible for people to live where they had lived before. At his gymnasium he had to identify a dead friend. There were 300 dead. He felt he had to leave, this was no longer his home.

From Breslau, Dieter was sent to Erfurt. He continued to Augsburg, where the Americans interviewed them. My father was able to work in the American military government, working on denazification in the identification control division. He also worked for the Americans in an artistic role. He helped them make determinations in theater and art with the denazification process and worked as a set designer. After some time, he was able to establish a storefront commercial art business. Given that this was a Catholic area of Germany, he was hired to draw a booklet of the twelve stations of the cross. This was not out of religious conviction but rather as a commercial enterprise. The drawing "Leid," (in English, "grief or sorrow") pictured in my film, comes from this job. I had always thought that he drew it to express his feelings during and after the war. This drawing hung near my piano. I would pour feelings into my playing of Chopin Nocturnes, and Rachmaninoff Preludes, thinking that I was somehow relating to his pain. I only learned recently that he was hired to draw it. It is a portrait of Mary, mother of Jesus, in her grief.

My father emigrated with Ursula to the United States in September 1947, arriving at Ellis Island, and made his home in New York City. The United Church World Services sponsored them, as the Jewish agencies were overwhelmed with survivors. He thought that the United States would be a good place to go, because he liked the American jazz that they were able to listen to in secret during the Nazi time.

As for my father, Horst, once safely in the United States, he had to start from scratch. Having a wife and baby, it was sink or swim. Residual traumas may have contributed to their marriage ending in divorce. My father, after a few years, met my mother Elaine Saunders, who was teaching in the elementary school on Long Island, NY, where my older half-sister was a student. They dated and married in 1953. My mother is from Philadelphia, a Presbyterian.[9]

During the early years of their marriage, they enjoyed socializing with their church group in Jackson Heights, Queens, NY. I was born in 1958, my parents' first child of four. I was baptized at the Methodist Church in Tenafly, New Jersey. My godfather, Harry Steinfeld, was a nonpracticing German Jew. My godmother, Rosemarie Lebek Steinfeld, was a Mischling; her mother, Marianne Sachs, was Jewish and her father, Erwin Lebek was a lapsed Catholic. In Germany, they were not very religious. In the United States, they attended the Protestant church regularly for over fifty years. My godmother liked it because of the music. She was a member of the choir for years.

My Godparents' Family History

Here, I would like to say a few words about my godparents' experience with the Nazis. Their story also influenced my interest in the Holocaust, German Jewry, and the Mischlinge. My godfather, Harry Steinfeld, who was born about ten years before my father, left Germany in 1933, soon after his brother was killed. He belonged to a Social Democrat party that was outlawed by the Nazis, Iron Front. He feared that the Nazis were after him. His brother Walter Steinfeld had been stabbed to death on February 5, 1933, on his way home from a political rally against the Nazi seizure of power. Walter may have been one of the first Jewish victims of the Nazis.[10] My godfather initially went to Cuba. From there he was able to emigrate to the United States in 1936. He became a sergeant in the US army, serving from 1942 to 1945, and went back to Germany to fight against the Third Reich. After surviving Normandy, he was wounded at the Battle of the Bulge.

My godmother, Rosemarie Steinfeld, née Lebek, was born in 1922, in Königstein, a suburb of Frankfurt. Her father, Erwin Lebek, studied and taught languages, Latin, Greek, and French. He fought in the First World War. In 1928, the family moved to Breslau. Rosemarie's mother, Marianne Sachs, was a child therapist. Rosemarie and her brother Klaus, my father's best friend, were baptized by their parents. Rosemarie's father was a lapsed Catholic and her mother was Jewish, although she did not feel connected to Judaism. They felt that the children should have some connection to religion.

One day Rosemarie received a letter that confused her. She didn't have any idea that she had a mixed heritage. Her mother explained their situation to her. At school, the non-Jewish girls stopped playing with her, the Jewish girls did as well. She was not Jewish and not Christian. She tried to hide that she was half-Jewish. For the other girls, there was the Hitler Youth. Rosemarie was not allowed to participate. She couldn't tell if her grades were connected to the antisemitism of her teachers.

On Easter 1937, her father was fired from teaching, for being in a mixed marriage. He tutored privately. He was a popular teacher. As a non-Aryan, her mother was not able to work after 1933. They taught the children Klaus and Rosemarie at home. Their classification of Mischlinge 1st Degree, Grade A, followed them in everything that they did. There were questionnaires that always asked, "What is the religion of your grandparents?"

The family started thinking about emigrating to America. Rosemarie's father was not allowed to leave, as he was considered an Aryan. Rosemarie's mother and the children needed guarantors and an affidavit from America to sponsor them. HIAS (Hebrew Immigrant Aid Society) didn't help Mischlinge, so they were not able to get an affidavit, even though Mischlinge were just as much endangered as Jews. However, there were organizations that helped Christians of Jewish backgrounds. I imagine that in the chaos of worldwide war, these agencies were overwhelmed. Communication channels were compromised and they would have been under surveillance.

On Kristallnacht, her grandfather, her mother's father, from Mannheim, was sent back from Dachau. He never thought of emigrating. He was a German. They thought, "Kristallnacht won't happen again." He was held in the gym. In October 1940, the first deportation of 6,500 people took place. No one knew where. It was done secretly. He was sent to Gurs concentration camp, in unoccupied France, where he died.

During the war, there were ration cards. Rosemarie's mother had a J stamped on her card. There was only one hour allowed to Jews for shopping and one hour for the rest of the family. They felt a slow degradation of their lifestyle.

Rosemarie's father Ernst was drafted in 1944. Aryans in mixed marriages were at least required to work in work camps. He was sent to Paris as he spoke French. Her mother, Marianne, was drafted to dig ditches and then to work in a factory to repair German uniforms. She lived at home. She was not allowed to use trains. Rosemarie had fled to Berlin. Her mother was finally able to travel to Berlin in January 1945, because she said that, in all the chaos, with the Russians coming, her identity papers were lost. After the war, Rosemarie went to Ireland as a domestic, and then finally to the United States. Her parents stayed in Germany after the war.

As a child, growing up, this history resounded around our dining room table: thick German accents, stories of Breslau (Wroclaw), before the war, how the educational system in Germany was superior to the one we were receiving in American suburbia, during the war, the restrictions, the lack of food, the loss of my godmother Rosemarie's brother Klaus, who had been my father's best friend. It must have been a comfort for my father and godparents to be able to be together in the present with their shared memories of their past.

The Effects

As Mischlinge my family and godparents felt like outsiders, which, in the long run contributed to their healthy pursuit of success, out of necessity and out of anxiety, I believe. My father used the monetary compensation for his forced-labor work to go to NYU for an undergraduate degree at night. The time in his life for university education had been stolen. He was awarded a number of honors, NYU Honors Society, Arch and Square Honor NYU School of Commerce, Alpha Phi Sigma, Editor-in-Chief of *The Night Owl Reporter*, for which he was very proud. Now, in the United States, as an adult with a family, he needed to make up for lost time. He pursued a master's degree at Pace College at the same time that my older sister was enrolled there as an undergraduate. He also studied at the Arts Student League in NYC. I feel for him, that he was not able to truly pursue his artistic talent.

At some point, my uncle Dieter traveled back to Breslau, today Wroclaw, Poland, to look for their mother's grave. It had been converted into a parking lot.

In 1974, when my father returned from Germany after the passing of his father, he brought home a notebook filled with family documents, many of them having Nazi seals and insignias stamped on them. This raised my curiosity and felt frightening. My father didn't talk about his war experiences very much. Seeing these documents was a shock.

In 1977, I was at Vassar College studying piano. I didn't like the piano teacher there. In the meantime, my piano teacher from high school landed a position at Molloy College, a small Catholic College on Long Island. I transferred to Molloy, to continue studying with my old teacher. Given that it is a Catholic college, they require nine credits of theology. One of the classes I took was an Introduction to Judaism. Judaism resonated for me. I met Rabbi Paul Joseph and started attending Reform services.

I identified myself as a Jew and was part of a Reform congregation for over twenty years. I went through a Reform conversion as well as an Orthodox conversion because someone once told me that I was not really Jewish after my Reform conversion (I had wanted a one-word answer, if asked what I was). To make sure that that could never be said of me, I went through an Orthodox conversion. At the time, I was also considering making Aliyah to Israel, and wanted to be able to be married and buried there (The Chief Rabbinate in Israel only recognizes Orthodox conversions). I have my one-word answer now, and my conversion cannot be questioned. I am Jewish.

While I was growing up, I didn't know very much about my father's experiences during the Holocaust. My godparents, the Steinfelds came over for dinner regularly. The table conversations were sprinkled with German and references to Breslau. There were thick German accents and a sense of feeling somehow more refined than typical Americans. My parents didn't have a lot of friends with whom they socialized. The friends that they did have, we called Aunt and Uncle. My mother is an only child. My father was an immigrant whose family was on the other side of the ocean. One of their friends and colleague of my dad's was "Uncle Coleman," a Hungarian Jew, who had many interesting stories, especially about his trip to Israel after the 1967 war. Sounds of the old European world peppered our lives.

I studied German in middle school, through high school and into college. I was not very good at it. My father and I rarely spoke German to each other. He worked long hours and came home late. I wrote letters in German to my grandfather in Germany, infrequently. My father was formal with us. He would give a handshake in a moment that someone else might have given a hug.

My father was consumed with work and providing for us. He had angry outbursts and I think some mild depression. I think he was frustrated with language to an extent, having to make his way in a foreign country. He worked for people that frustrated him. Being an outsider, he had his eyes open for doing things more efficiently and differently. He worked in commercial art, decorating windows, as he had in Breslau and then in quality control for a number of furniture distributors. He had applied for a job at the Metropolitan Museum of Art and was not hired. He concluded that his artwork was not the correct style for the United States, too Middle European. I think he was very disappointed not to work there. Eventually, after investing his retirement money in real estate, he was able to be independent. He frequently told us to work for ourselves rather than work for others. He was creative and a problem solver.

It is hard for me to know how his past affected him. He lost his mother at age seven, lived through the rise of Hitler and the Nazis, survived a forced-labor camp, emigrated to a new country, was divorced from his first wife, struggled financially, and had health issues. On the other hand, he was happily married to my mother, proud of his children while also being critical of us. After my piano recitals, he would say, "You made three mistakes," without giving any praise. He was a proud American, enjoyed attending performances, plays, operas, concerts, and visiting museums.

His discerning nature and attunement to the best and finest, in art, architecture, and music, certainly influenced my music making. I found a home filled with beauty and culture.

My siblings were also driven to work hard and pursue levels of perfection in their work and lives. One works in the film industry, one is a real estate developer, one is a biomedical engineer, and one was a professor of library science, retired now. Of my four siblings, two are Jewish, my brother and I, two are secular Americans, and one is a believing Christian.

During the time of my conversions, my father would, in every conversation we had, somehow tell me not to be Jewish. I argued, "What difference does it make if I go someplace on a Saturday morning or a Sunday morning?" He said, "Okay, then don't join, don't be on any list." He believed that the whole thing could happen again. He was afraid for my safety. I thought his fears were unfounded. After all, I grew up in Tenafly, New Jersey; no harm could come to me. On the day we heard about the Pittsburgh massacre at the Tree of Life Synagogue, I was in shock. It seems that my father was right. I have felt anxious ever since and no longer go to our local synagogue regularly. I am afraid. We have a guard with a gun in the building. Some of the congregants are carrying guns. I feel that it is safer to stay home out of harm's way. My father used to say, "All religions are political." Maybe he has a point.

My mother's reaction to my conversion was one of concern. As a believing Christian, she felt that I had put my after-life in peril.

Coming out of this unique background and history, I hope that I have put it to good use, with my *Mischlinge Exposé* project, to make people aware of the travails of the Mischlinge and to raise issues of identity and tolerance. The damage that was done to my family has inspired me to speak out, to share the story of the Mischlinge, which is not very well known, to add another layer to Holocaust education, and hopefully to empower the audience to feel more empowered in their own identities.

My Research

During my two trips back to Poland, I was able to track down and visit my father's homes in Breslau, and the Old Jewish Cemetery in Gleiwitz, where my great grandfather Ludwig Poppelauer and my great great uncle, Fritz Poppelauer are buried. In addition, I was able to visit every city that had been home to my forebears, Rybnik, Bytom, Ratibor, Racibórz, all in what had been the province of Silesia or Schlesien. My great great great grandfather Jakob Senig Poppelauer had been listed as a citizen in Rybnik. It was rare at the time for a Jew to be a citizen. I wonder what he did to distinguish himself? It is strange for me to refer to my Jewish forebears, having been raised as a Christian . . .

I was also able to go to Gross-Rosen concentration camp, where I saw the subcamps that my father had been in listed on a wall. This was the area that he had been sent to in 1944, from Breslau. I looked at the trees, wondering if those same trees had been there when my father was there . . . felt the angle of the sun, hoping to connect to his experience. To truly do so, I would have to return in the dead of bitter winter. The winter of 1944–5 was recorded to have been one of the coldest winters. What did my father do to keep warm?

Preparing for my trip to the cemetery in Gleiwitz, the genealogist that I've been working with was able to give me actual grave stone numbers for Ludwig and Fritz. Unfortunately the numbers have faded to a degree and the stones are in somewhat of a disarray. I wasn't able to locate their graves. To find someone to give us the key to get into the cemetery took some doing, especially because I don't know Polish, and Poles don't like to speak German. Through stubborn persistence and polite requests, we were able to accomplish our mission! To walk in the Jewish cemetery in Poland, of my great grandfather . . . profound.

On the second trip, I revisited the street of one of my father's homes. This time I was more certain of the house number and wanted to see it again, take pictures, share them with my siblings. There was a woman standing outside of the house. My friend and I parked the car, approached her, and asked her if she spoke some German. She did. We explained that my father had grown up in this house. Her first question was if I wanted to reclaim it. I said no, that it was an important family memory. She is in her eighties. She also asked, with some trepidation, if I wanted to go into the house. I said no, wanting to respect her privacy, although it would have meant a lot to me. She spoke to us for quite a while, telling us her wartime stories. She was from Ukraine, and had been sent to Auschwitz with her family. I assume that they were Orthodox Christians, deemed unwanted by the Nazis. She and her father were able to escape. Her mother and sister were killed. I don't know how they got to Breslau. Populations were moved, houses were filled with people from the east as borders changed and countries were reorganized postwar. She isn't Jewish. Maybe she's even anti-Semitic. She lost her family in Auschwitz next to mine. What for? When does it end . . . . Innocent people harmed, murdered . . . for what . . . survivors and their families bearing psychological issues that pass down through the generations . . . when does it stop? I am grateful to have met her and heard her story. Person to person, that's where I can feel, communicate, share, uplift, hope.

My Earliest Memories of Judaism

In Sunday school, when I was around nine, we were learning about the Last Supper, in preparation for Easter. We learned about the Hebrews' exodus from Egypt, their time in the desert, on the run, baking matzah on rocks in the sun. I lied when I told a story that we also baked matzah using the ancient methods, and had a Passover seder at home. I don't know why I would have concocted such a strange tale! Or how I would have connected to the Passover seder.

When I was in high school, my close friend Fran Levine invited me to her family's seder. The sound of her father chanting in Hebrew and singing the songs of the seder resonated deeply for me. For me, hearing Hebrew resonates as deeply and as familiar as the sound of Beethoven.

When my father returned from Germany with the notebook, with the many family documents, my life changed. I felt that there were things that I needed to know that weren't talked about. The silence around this history as I was growing up felt louder than the actual story. I felt that there were secrets (I may have been picking up on my father's first marriage). My radar was up.

My father finally did tell me his story when I was eighteen. I had come down from Poughkeepsie, where I was studying at Vassar, for a piano lesson with my teacher from high school. My father picked me up and in the car, started telling me his story. I hadn't asked. He must have felt that it was time for me to know. It was hard for me to listen and to actually hear what he was saying, as I had picked up the nonverbal message that this was information that I wasn't supposed to know. After he told me his story, over months and years, I had to ask him to repeat things, because I couldn't remember or couldn't retain, or couldn't hear clearly. . . . The feeling was as if my hands were covering my ears as he spoke. And yet, after seeing the notebook, this was what I wanted to hear. . . . I wanted, with every fiber, to hear his story.

Another Jewish influence for me was the Friday night service at Temple Emanu-El, NYC, broadcast on WQXR, the classical radio station in the New York area. I was already a regular listener. The Friday evening broadcast resonated and made me feel connected to Judaism.

Helen Epstein's book, *Children of the Holocaust: Conversations with Sons and Daughters of the Holocaust*, was the first book that I read about and by children of survivors. I felt very connected to the stories of other children in similar situations. Their words helped me feel validated, although the fact that my father was a Mischling somehow reduced my feeling as an "authentic" daughter of a survivor. My father was not in a death camp. How could I call him a survivor? I wasn't Jewish. How could this be about me? And yet, it felt familiar. The loud silence, the darkness, I felt it in my home also, maybe not to the same degree . . . but it was there.

Since then, I have attended and been a member of Second Generation groups for many years and regularly attend Yom HaShoah events commemorating the Holocaust. I feel a deep connection on the one hand and like an outsider on the other. My conversion helps a bit to root my identity, and I have come to own my family history and story as legitimate.

After my father's passing, in going through his papers, I have found that he had wanted to publish his experiences. He had contacted a publisher and met with his granddaughter, my niece, who spent days with him taking notes and listening to him recall the events. (This is fairly common, that survivors have an easier time sharing their experiences with their grandchildren than with their children. The wounds may be too fresh. They want to protect their children, they are busy surviving in a new country . . . with grandchildren, the intensity of their experiences may have started to diminish. I have heard this over and over in the second generation groups.)

Closing Thoughts

What I've come to understand is that the Mischlinge were neither here nor there, under the radar, with an outsider status, no matter where they were.

My dad had an upbeat attitude. He was so happy to be in the United States and very proud of his accomplishments, especially his children. His dogged pursuit for success has influenced all of us. We are hardworking, creative, and driven; one of the mixed blessings of feeling like an outsider.

My father had wanted to write of his experiences, and had even contacted a publisher. He didn't continue to completion. I wonder if he was not able to, in the end. The layers of his losses and his forward looking attitude made him a compassionate man, sensitive to the suffering and hardships of others, especially immigrants, a creative man, with an eye out for what was coming next, thinking out of the box, an emotional man, artistic, talented, moody, hurt, a loving father, whose greatest pride was his family, for whom he would move heaven and earth.

"Survival is actually a synthesis of winning and losing."

—*Mika Cloud*

Notes

1. Hanns Eisler is the only "Mischling" in the program; the rest are German-Jewish converts.
2. My grandfather had fought in the First World War as a member of the cavalry.

3. During Felix Mendelssohn's lifetime (one of the composers featured in my project), ideas floated around that Christianity and Judaism were soon to become one religion.

4. Nazi Germany was an unsafe place for them as well, having no religious liberty.

5. This is where I recently gave the European premiere of my multimedia project, "*The Mischlinge Exposé.*"

6. President Franklin D. Roosevelt called for a conference in Evian, France, in July 1938, to discuss the issue of German and Austrian Jewish refugees. Aside from the Dominican Republic, none of the thirty-two participating countries agreed to accept the Jewish refugees fleeing Nazi Europe.

7. Second Degree Mischlinge (people with one Jewish grandparent) were not discharged.

8. Ursula was also a Mischling Grade A. Her father was Jewish.

9. My mother's family had a long history in the United States, some of it dating back to the American Revolution.

10. Walter was a student at the Technical University and a member of Iron Front, a Social Democrat antifascist movement. My godfather claimed that he himself was the intended target of the attack by those early Nazis, but that they walked home separately, and tragically Walter was mistakenly killed instead. My godfather said that he was much more deeply involved in the Iron Front antifascist movement than his brother Walter.

EPILOGUE
Mordecai Paldiel

In this book, we covered a lot of ground dealing with various forms of women resisters against Nazism: those who were prompted to act due to ideological or political or ethical considerations, as well as from personal commitments to save either their loved ones in mixed marriages, who were targeted as a result of Nazi racism, or persons not known to the rescuers, but also singled out for persecution. As noted by Nathan Stoltzfus, the role of the protest of the women married to Jewish men, known as the Rosenstrasse Protest, forced the very anti-Semitic Joseph Goebbels, with Hitler's endorsement, to liberate the Jewish husbands, upsetting the earlier intentions to immediately do away with these men. The force of the protest by these "Aryan" women, on the streets of Berlin, soon after the terrible Stalingrad debacle, and a major allied bombing of Berlin, even prompted Hitler, for purely tactical reasons, to delay the deportation of these Nazi-styled "full Jews," and most of them eventually survived. That is quite an unforeseen achievement by these brave women.

Judy Baumel-Schwartz highlights the importance of women gender as a legitimate historical study of the Holocaust, and notes their role in acts of psychological subversion as against the preferred physical forms of sabotage response by men resisters. She exemplifies this by women in the clothing sorting area in Auschwitz, dubbed Kanada, who placed notes in pockets of coats of those sent to the gas chambers that read: "German women: know that you are wearing a fur coat that belonged to a Jewish woman gassed to death in Auschwitz." Contrasting this with men who removed the linings of the coats, to disqualify them for wearing in cold weather.

Other chapter contributors dealt with other forms of women resisters. Volker Berghahn emphasized the role of persons in communist and socialist movements in opposing the Nazi regime, a role also highlighted by Anne Nelson in her description of Suzanne Spaak and the women of the so-called Red Orchestra (*Rote Kapelle*), which operated in France and Germany, as well as Paula Schwartz's mention of women food protesters in occupied France, as also a form of women resistance with some positive results. Berghan also mentions the courage and heroism of Sophie Scholl and her university student friends of the White Rose circle, in Munich. She paid with her life in a most brutal way for publicly denouncing the wartime atrocities of the Nazi regime. Susanne Heim returns us to the Rosenstrasse women protesters and their memorialization in Germany. Gabrielle Nissim, who heads an institution in Italy hailing the role of rescuers in opposition to various instances of regime misdeeds, cautions us that rescuers are not necessarily paragons of virtue from the start and that their involvement may start from small acts that incrementally increase to larger and more widespread forms of altruistic help. As for Carolyn Enger and Ruth Wiseman, both of a Mischlinge background, they detail their return to Judaism, which may also have been psychologically prompted as a response to the Nazi attempt to murder all Jews.

My two chapters dealt with women, non-Jewish and Jewish, whose involvement in rescue operations was primarily the result of what Judy Baumel-Schwartz terms "resisting obliteration," that is, the physical disappearance of all Jews by the Nazi regime, by either forced emigration or mass extermination. Baumel-Schwartz also points out that Jewish women were often the first to realize the depth of Nazi antisemitism, a point also raised by Marion Kaplan, who notes in her study of Jewish life in Nazi Germany that "women usually saw the danger signals first."[1]

It is worth remembering that the Nazi targeting of Jews was in principle not based on any political, or economic, consideration, nor solely on account of racism, but simply on the assertion that Jews by their very existence endangered Germany and the entire world. It was not like the Nazi opposition to communists and socialists, who represented a direct threat to the Nazi regime, and were thus relentlessly persecuted until they were totally silenced, as pointed out by Nathan Stoltzfus and Volker Berghahn in the introduction. Nazi propaganda wrongly depicted the Jews, in Germany and elsewhere, as the fiendish enemies of Germany. In Hitler's mind, as already expressed in his 1925 book *Mein Kampf*, in his speeches, his wartime *Table Talks*, and his political testament, the Jews represented and stood for all that was wrong, not only in German society but throughout the world. They were the harbingers of communism, socialism, and democracy, ideas that challenged the racist principle of the division of the human species into superior and inferior races and the primacy of the so-called Aryan race.[2]

But here, the paradox. The Jews as the principal "enemies" of Germany existed only in the Nazi imagination. In fact, German Jews were known for their great love of Germany, at times above and beyond their Jewish loyalties, and this also applied to many Jews in other countries who hailed Germany as the beacon of civilized life. When Hitler came to power, some Jews, but only a few, did not contest the regime's legitimacy as did the communists and socialists, but some even tried to accommodate the so-called National Revolution (but were rejected).[3] Jews as diehard enemies of Germany existed only in the deranged minds of the Nazi leadership, but was strongly believed in, as also evident in the Joseph Goebbels diaries, to the point that the Nazi regime could not conceive of or tolerate the coexistence of Jews and Germans. The Jews had to disappear, to allow the opposing party to survive and prosper, and thus the Nazi justification of the Final Solution. The 1935 Nuremberg Laws also outlawed sexual intercourse between Jews and the so-called Aryans as a cardinal sin (*Rassenschande*), and consequently a foremost affront and challenge to one of the principal tenets of Nazi ideology.[4] So, whereas communists, socialists, and others who opposed and repudiated the Nazi ideology would be forgiven if they "repented" and renounced their earlier opposition, no such option was available to Jews of all political factions and affiliations, even those who had renounced Judaism and converted to another religion. The blood in their veins was like a cancer that had to be physically destroyed.

The women mentioned in mine and other chapters (such as Suzanne Spaak and the Rosenstrasse protesters) fought back, not necessarily in attempts to undo the regime by their mostly singlehandedly acts, as was the exceptional case of the military figures who plotted the assassination of Hitler when they realized that he was leading Germany to a doomsday scenario. These women fought back by preserving lives. This applies even more so to Jews in mixed marriages, where, as described by Nathan Stoltzfus, the non-Jewish women faced intense pressure to divorce their Jewish spouses, and underwent various regime-prompted social humiliations and ostracism while maintaining their marital bonds, and thus saved their Jewish spouses from deportation, as amply demonstrated in the Rosenstrasse women's protest.

In the rescue of Jews, some of the women rescuers acted alone or banded together to create clandestine organizations, such as the French-Jewish Madeleine Dreyfus and Andrée Salomon, of the children's *Oeuvre de Secours aux Enfants*, or the German-Jewish Reicha Freier, who created the first youth rescue network, later dubbed as Youth Aliyah. On the non-Jewish women side, while we have stories of women who saved persons they knew from before the war, we also have accounts of women who met their future wards during the war years, as well as those like Erna Härtel, who admitted into her home a woman who had fled from a death march. When speaking of the rescue of children, here too Jewish mothers are to be commended for their courage, in their painful decision to let go of their children, and turn them over into, sometimes, strange hands, without any advance information where the children would be taken, and in preparation for this separation, training their children to deny their true motherhood links. As told by Henriette Altman, a survivor of the Będzin ghetto, "every child in the ghetto was taught that a day may come when they will get a new name, a new 'mama,' and that in that event they shouldn't cry or talk about their real parents and never admit that they lived in the ghetto and are Jewish."[5] All this in order to at least assure the children's survival, in case they were never to see their parents again.

As mentioned in the chapters, some of these rescuers paid the ultimate price for trying to save the lives of innocent persons. On the Jewish side, apart from Gisi Fleischmann, we have Marianne Cohn, arrested and executed for trying to spirit Jewish children across the Franco-Swiss border.[6] Among the non-Jewish women rescuers who suffered retribution for trying to save Jewish lives, we mention here Jadwiga Deneko, imprisoned and shot by the Gestapo in Warsaw, as well as Sára Salkaházi, shot by the pro-Nazi Arrow Cross faction in Budapest, with her body dumped into the Danube River, and Suzanne Spaak, shot in Paris, on the eve of the city's liberation.[7] A further note also requiring mention here is the story of the Jewish Gisella Perl, who saved the lives of Jewish women in Auschwitz, at various stages of their pregnancy, by either helping abort their unborn children or helping deliver the children, but horrifyingly killing them immediately upon birth in order to prevent their crying voices from alerting the Nazi guards and thus endanger their mothers. That, too, required great courage. After the war, as a practicing gynecologist, she helped to deliver hundreds of children, to compensate, in her words, for the babies whose lives she had to end in the inhuman conditions of Auschwitz.[8]

There were also not many women of the caliber of the German Ilse Sonja Totzke, who openly claimed before her Gestapo interrogators that she was opposed to the 1935 Nuremberg Laws and later added, when she tried to flee from Germany to

Switzerland by taking along a Jewish woman, that she could no longer live in a Germany ruled by Hitler. For this she was sent to a concentration camp. Or another heroic woman like the French medical doctor Adelaïde Hautval, who, as a prisoner in Auschwitz, refused to participate in the pseudo-medical experiments on the bodies of Jewish women, and who, in response to the chief SS physician's claim of the existence of a difference between her and the Jewish prisoners, stated that the only difference that existed in her eyes was between herself and the SS officer facing her.[9] And, of course, not to forget the tragic Sophie Scholl and her student friends in the White Rose movement—a unique and exceptional story of student resisters in Nazi Germany at the height of the war.

The record at Yad Vashem suggests that women rescuers of Jews at the very least equaled and may even have totaled more than men rescuers. That has yet to be further studied, but there is no doubt that women played a major role in all rescue operations to save lives from obliteration by hiding them from the reach of their executioners. It is thus hoped that their legacy will serve as beacons of light for present and future generations that may face tyrannical regimes of even a lesser hideous nature than Nazism. The recent inclusion of the Rosenstrasse protesters among those honored in the Milan, Italy, Garden of the Righteous, created by Gabriele Nissim, is a positive step in that direction. This book, therefore, is in a certain sense a call for action to create a more just society, with women playing a significant role, as they so eminently displayed during the period of the Nazi regime and the Holocaust.

Notes

1. Marion Kaplan, *Between Dignity and Despair* (New York: Oxford University, 1999), 63.

2. In *Mein Kampf*, written in 1924, Hitler warned in apocalyptic terms of an end of all human life if the Jews, according to his psychotic mind, are allowed to dominate. He wrote, "if the Jew is victorious, his crown will be the funeral wreath of humanity and this planet will, as it did millions of years ago, move through the ether devoid of men." Adolf Hitler, *Mein Kampf* (Boston: Houghton Mifflin, 1971), 65.

3. Interestingly, Yehuda Bauer mentions that, hoping for a sort of an entente with the new regime, the orthodox Jewish community addressed a letter to Hitler, in October 1933, stating among other: "We have learned to love the German soil. . . . We have learned to love the Germans sun . . . and we have learned to love the German people. . . . We feel closely linked to its culture . . . . The German Jews will gladly take part in the task of reconstruction of the German Nation." No response was received to this letter. Yehuda Bauer, *A History of the Holocaust* (New York: Franklin Watts, 2001), 126. Earlier, in 1917, the British Balfour Declaration in favor of the establishment of Jewish National Home in Palestine was prompted in part to sway Jewish loyalties from Germany to the Allies. Howard Sachar, *A History of Israel* (New York: A.A. Knopf, 2001), 102.

4. In 1915 there were more mixed marriages in Germany than marriages between two Jewish partners. Walter Laqueur, *A History of Zionism* (New York: MJF Books, 1972), 25.

5. Genia Pająk file, Yad Vashem Archives M31.2/ 2349.

6. On these and other Jewish women rescuers, see: Mordecai Paldiel, *Saving One's Own* (Philadelphia: JPS, 2017).

7. Further information on the following rescuers can be had from the Yad Vashem Archives (YVA). Jadwiga Deneko (YVA 31.2/3575), Sára Salkaházi (YVA 31.2/495.1), Suzanne Spaak (YVA 31.2/62).

8. See her book, *I Was a doctor in Auschwitz* (International Universities, 1948).

9. For more on these two women, consult Ilse Sonja Totzke (YVA 31.2/6335), and Adelaïde Hautval (YVA 31.2/100).

APPENDIX I
UNPUBLISHED LETTER TO THE EDITOR FROM ROSENSTRASSE SURVIVOR

Following is a letter dated September 20, 2003, from Hans-Oskar Baron Löwenstein de Witt to the editors of the *Süddeutsche Zeitung*. Mr. Löwenstein de Witt was a survivor imprisoned with his father at Rosenstrasse 2–4 during the massive roundup that led to the Rosenstrasse Protest, as his mother and aunt protested with the crowd outside on the street. The last time I visited Mr. Löwenstein de Witt shortly before his death in 2004, he gave me a copy of the letter saying that after faxing it in, he had withdrawn it under pressure not to publish it, which raised questions for him about the objectivity of German historians and remembrance of the Holocaust. The letter was not published until 2005 in Antonia Leuger's Berlin, Rosenstrasse 2–4: Protest in der NS-Diktatur : neue Forschungen zum Frauenprotest in der Rosenstrasse 1943 (Ploeger), 244–5. We are obligated to Mr. Löwenstein de Witt to publish his letter here in translation.

Letterhead: Hans-Oskar Baron Lowenstein de Witt. 10748 Berlin. P.O. Box 301669
To: Fax: 21283-787; Editorial Staff, *Süddeutsche Zeitung*, Munich

Dear Editors!
In your feature section today (20./21.09. [20] 03), you publish an article on the Rosenstrasse War ( ) on the bottom of page 13, right hand side. Necessarily I must ask you to print the following reply as a refutation of statements from Prof. Wolfgang Benz [Director, Center for Antisemitic Research, Berlin]. In a long telephone conversation with Benz yesterday, I, Hans-Oskar Löwenstein de Witt, as one of the few remaining survivors of the big "Factory Action," most sharply expressed my rejection of his thesis that the demonstration of many Christian relatives did not result in our release. The newly-emerged thesis that we would have been released in any case is in my opinion absolutely illogical. If the Nazi regime had really wanted to release us without regard to these courageous demonstrations, why did it first excite such a complicated and unique scandal, the uprising in the Rosenstrasse? They could have simply sorted us out and sent us directly home from the many collection centers where [we were first brought] and where we spent one to three days [before being sent to Rosenstrasse 2–4]. Also, "evidence" that [the regime] wanted to exchange us for Jewish [workers] at the "Reich Association of Jews" or the Jewish Hospital, does not hold considering the fact that, indeed, many children and youth as well as persons totally untrained for such work were imprisoned at Rosenstrasse. Consider as well that the "protection" for intermarried Jews and Mischlinge only held, more or less, in five big cities; from Stralsund, Potsdam,

and very many small cities, even Mischlinge and Jews from privileged marriages were deported . . .

I thank you for printing this rebuttal as quickly as possible,

—Hans-Oskar Baron Löwenstein de Witt

See *Süddeutsche Zeitung* of September 20/21, 2003: "Rosenstrasse War: Benz defends himself against Trotta."

CONTRIBUTORS

Judy Baumel-Schwartz is Director of the Finkler Institute of Holocaust Research and Professor of Jewish History at Bar-Ilan University, Israel. She is the author of many books, including *Double Jeopardy* (1998), *Perfect Heroes* (2010), *Identity, Heroism and Religion in the Lives of Contemporary Jewish Women* (2013), *My Name Is Freida Sima* (2017), *A Very Special Life* (2017), and *For the Love of Shirley* (2020).

Volker Berghahn is Seth Low Emeritus Professor of history at Columbia University, USA. His many publications include *Modern Germany* (1982), *Imperial Germany* (1995), *America and the Intellectual Cold Wars in Europe* (2001), *Europe in the Era of Two World Wars* (2006), and *Journalists Between Hitler and Adenauer* (2018). Berghahn is also Fellow of the Royal Historical Society, UK.

Carolyn Enger is an internationally acclaimed concern pianist and filmmaker whose film *The Mischlinge Exposé* (2017) shines a light on the stories of Mischlinge (half-Jews) and German-Jewish Converts in Germany before, during, and after the Holocaust.

David Gill is a civil servant and politician. Since October 2017, Gill has served as German Consul General in New York, USA, and he has previously been Secretary of State and Head of the Office of the Federal President (2012–17).

Susanne Heim is Professor of history at Freiburg University, Germany. She is the project manager of the edition project "The Persecution and Murder of European Jews by National Socialist Germany 1933–1945" and is the author of *Architects of Annihilation: Auschwitz and the Logic of Destruction* (2003).

Anne Nelson is a Research Scholar at the Saltzman Institute of War and Peace Studies, and Adjunct Associate Professor at the Columbia School of International and Public Affairs. Her research focuses on human rights and media systems and she is the author of *Red Orchestra: The Story of the Berlin Underground and the Circle of Friends Who Resisted Hitler* (2009). She has also won various awards for her journalism, including the Livingston Award for international reporting.

Gabriele Nissim is Founder and President of the Garden of the Righteous Worldwide Committee (Gariwo), based in Milan, Italy. Gariwo is a not-for-profit organization which is guided by the idea that the memory of good is a powerful educational tool and can help prevent cases of genocide and crimes against humanity. Nissim has been the recipient of numerous awards, including most recently the Raoul Wallenberg medal (2020).

Chris Osmar is an independent scholar who achieved his PhD in 2018 from Florida State University, USA. His thesis, "Now I Am in Distant Germany, It Could Be that I Will Die: Colonial Precedent, Wartime Contingency, and Crisis Mentality in the Transition from Subjugation to Decimation of Foreign Workers," won the Martin-Vegue Dissertation Fellowship Award (2017).

Mordecai Paldiel is the former head of the Righteous Among the Nations Department at Yad Vashem. He is currently Adjunct Professor in Jewish history at Yeshiva University, USA. He is the author of eleven books, including *Saving One's Own* (2017) and *The Righteous Among the Nations* (2007).

Paula Schwartz is Lois B. Watson Professor of French and Francophone studies at Middlebury College, USA. Her teaching and research interests include twentieth-century France, the Second World War, the French Resistance, gender studies, and food and culture studies.

Nathan Stoltzfus is Rintels Professor of Holocaust studies and of history at Florida State University, USA. He is the author of *Hitler's Compromises* (2016) and *Resistance of the Heart* (1996), which was a co-recipient of the Institute of Contemporary History's Fraenkel Prize.

Ruth Wiseman is an independent scholar, and the daughter of Rita Kuhn, who was among the imprisoned at Rosenstrasse, Berlin, in February 1943. Ruth graduated from U.C. Davis in 1992 in International Relations and Russian, and is the author of *How the Moon Became Dim* (2017).

SELECT BIBLIOGRAPHY

Adler, Hans Günther. *Theresienstadt 1941–1945*, translated by Belinda Cooper. Cambridge: Cambridge University Press, 2017.

Andreas-Friedrich, Ruth. *Berlin Underground, 1938–1945*. New York: Henry Holt and Company, 1947.

Arendt, Hannah. *Responsibility and Judgement*, edited by Jerome Kohn. New York: Schocken Books, 2003.

Bauer, Yehuda. *Rethinking the Holocaust*. New Haven: Yale University Press, 2001.

Baumel, Judith Tydor. *Double Jeopardy: Gender and the Holocaust*. London: Vallentine, 1998.

Benshalom, Rafi. *We Struggled for Life*. Jerusalem, New York: Gefen Publishing, 2001.

Blau, Bruno. *Das Ausnahmerechte für die Juden in Deutschland 1933–1945*. Düsseldorf: Verlag Allgemeine Wochenzeitung der Juden in Deutschland, 1954.

Blau, Bruno. "Die Mischehe im Nazireich." *Judaica* 4 (1948): 46–57.

Blumenthal, W. Michael. *The Invisible Wall: Germans and Jews - A Personal Exploration*. Washington, DC: Counterpoint, 1998.

Browning, Christopher. *The Origins of the Final Solution: The Evolution of Nazi Jewish Policy, September 1939–March 1942*. With Contributions by Jürgen Matthäus. Lincoln: University of Nebraska Press, 2004.

Campion, Joan. *In the Lion's Mouth: Gisi Fleischmann and the Jewish Fight for Survival*. New York: to Excel, 1987.

Carlebach, Elisheva. *Divided Souls: Converts from Judaism in Germany, 1500–1750*. New Haven and London: Yale University Press, 2001.

Clementi, Federica K. *Holocaust Mothers and Daughters: Family, History and Trauma*, Waltham: Brandeis University Press, 2013.

Dallin, Alexander. *German Rule in Russia 1941–1945. A Study of Occupation Policies*. London: MacMillan, 1957.

Debré, Jean-Louis. *Les Femmes qui ont reveillé la France*. Paris: Fayard, 2013.

Demant, Froukje. "The Many Shades of Bystanding. On Social Dilemmas and Passive Participation." In *Probing the Limits of Categorization: The Bystander in Holocaust History*, edited by Christina Morina and Krijn Thijs, 90–106. New York, Oxford: Berghahn, 2019.

Dror, Tamar. *A Green Parrot*. Sydney: Book House, 1999.

Epstein, Helen. *Children of the Holocaust: Conversations with Sons and Daughters of Survivors*. New York: Penguin Books, 1979.

Fatran, Gila. "The Working Group." *Holocaust and Genocide Studies* 8, no. 2 (Fall 1994): 164–201.

Fischer, Erica. *Aimée and Jaguar: A Love Story, Berlin 1943*. New York: Perennial, 2015.

Freier, Recha. *Let the Children Come: The Early History of Youth Aliyah*. London: Weidenfeld and Nicolson, 1961.

Friedenson, Joseph and David Kranzler. *Heroine of Rescue: The Incredible Story of Recha Sternbuch*. Brooklyn: Mesorah Publications, 1984.

Fuchs, Esther (ed.). *Women and the Holocaust: Narrative and Representation: Studies in the Shoah*, Vol. 22. Lanham, New York, Oxford: University Press of America, 1999.

Goebbels, Joseph. *Die Tagebücher von Joseph Goebbels, Part II*, Vol. 7. Munich: K.G. Saur, 1993.

Gruchmann, Lothar. *Justiz im Dritten Reich 1933–1940 - Anpassung und Unterwerfung in der Ära Gürtner*. Berlin: Oldenbourg Wissenschaftsverlag, 2009.

Select Bibliography

Gruner, Wolf. *Widerstand in der Rosenstraße. Die Fabrik-Aktion und die Verfolgung der "Mischehen" 1943*. Frankfurt a. M.: Fischer Taschenbuch Verlag, 2005.

Hackel, Sergei. *Pearl of Great Price*. London: Darton, Longman Todd, 1981.

Hautval, Adelaide and Hallam Tennyson. "Who Shall Live, Who Shall Die?" *Intellectual Digest*, 2 no. 7 (March 1972): 52–4.

Havel, Vaclav. *The Power of the Powerless*. London: Vintage Classics, 2018.

Hertzog, Esther (ed.). *Life, Death and Sacrifice: Women and Family in the Holocaust*. Jerusalem: Gefen, 2008.

Hilberg, Raul. *Destruction of the European Jews*, Vol. 2. New York: Octagon Books, 1978.

Jacoby, Susan. *Half-Jew: A Daughter's Search for Her Family's Buried Past*. New York: Scribner, 2000.

Kaplan, Marion A. *Between Dignity and Despair: Jewish Life in Nazi Germany*. New York and Oxford: Oxford University Press, 1998.

Kershaw, Ian. *The Hitler "Myth". Image and Reality in the Third Reich*. Oxford: Oxford University Press, 1987.

Kuhn, Rita. *Broken Glass, Broken Lives: A Jewish Girl's Survival Story in Berlin, 1933–1945*. Oakland: Barany, 2012.

Kwiet, Konrad. "Without Neighbors: Daily Living in Judenhäuser." In *Jewish Life in Nazi Germany. Dilemmas and Responses*, edited by Francis R. Nicosia and David Scrase. New York: Berghahn Books, 2010.

Laska, Vera (ed.). *Women in the Resistance and in the Holocaust: The Voices of Eyewitnesses*. Westport: Praeger, 1983.

Latour, Anny. *The Jewish Resistance in France (1940–1944)*. New York: Holocaust Library, 1981.

Lazare, Lucien. *Rescue as Resistance: How Jewish Organizations Fought the Holocaust in France*. New York: Columbia University, 1996.

Leugers, Antonia. "Widerstand gegen die Rosenstraße. Kritische Anmerkungen zu einer Neuerscheinung von Wolf Gruner." *theologie. geschichte* 1 (2006): 131–205.

L'Union des Femmes Françaises. *Les Femmes dans la Résistance*. Paris: Éditions du Rocher, 1977.

Meding, Dorothee von. *Courageous Hearts: Women and the Anti-Hitler Plot of 1944*. New York: Berghahn Books, 1997.

Meed, Vladka. *On Both Sides of the Wall*. New York: Holocaust Library, 1993.

Meierhenrich, Jens. *The Remnants of the Rechtsstaat: An Ethnography of Nazi Law*. Oxford: Oxford University Press, 2018.

Mieszkowska, Anna. *Irena Sendler: Mother of the Children of the Holocaust*. Santa Barbara: Praeger, 2011.

Mommsen, Hans. "Cumulative Radicalization and Progressive Self-Destruction as Structural Determinants of the Nazi Dictatorship." In *Stalinism and Nazism: Dictatorships in Comparison*, edited by Kershaw Ian and Lewin Moshe. Cambridge: Cambridge University Press, 1997.

Nelson, Anne. *Red Orchestra: The Story of the Berlin Underground and the Circle of Friends Who Resisted Hitler*. New York: Random House, 2009.

Nelson, Anne. *Suzanne's Children: A Daring Rescue in Nazi Paris*. New York: Simon & Schuster, 2017.

Nissim, Gabriele. *Il tribunale del bene. La storia di Moshe Bejski l'uomo che creò il Giardino dei Giusti*. Milan: Mondadori, 2004.

Ofer, Dalia and Lenore J. Weitzman (ed.), *Women in the Holocaust*. New Haven: Yale University, 1998.

Paldiel, Mordecai. *The Righteous Among the Nations*. New York: HarperCollins, 2007.

Paldiel, Mordecai. *Saving One's Own: Jewish Rescuers During the Holocaust*. Philadelphia: Jewish Publishing Society, 2017.

Peleg-Mariańska, Miriam and Mordecai Peleg. *Witnesses: Life in Occupied Kraków*. London, New York: Routledge, 1991.

Proctor, Robert N. *Racial Hygiene: Medicine Under the Nazis*. Cambridge, MA and London: Harvard University Press, 1988.

Roloff, Stefan and Mario Vigl. *Die Rote Kapelle*. Berlin: Ullstein, 2002. (See also companion documentary in English, "The Red Orchestra," 2002, by Stefan Roloff.)

Rosensaft, Hadassah. *Yesterday: My Story*. New York, Jerusalem: American Society for Yad Vashem & YadVashem, 2004.

Samuel, Vivette. *Rescuing the Children*. Madison: University of Wisconsin, 2002.

Schneider, Peter. "Saving Konrad Latte." *The New York Times Magazine*, February 13, 2000, 52–95.

Schulle, Diana. "The Rosenstrasse Protest." In *Jews in Nazi Berlin: From Kristallnacht to Liberation*, edited by Beate Meyer, Hermann Simon and Chana Schütz, 159–70. Chicago, London: University of Chicago Press, 2009.

Sokolow, Reha and Al. *Defying the Tide*. Jerusalem, New York: Devora, 2003.

Speer, Albert. *Inside the Third Reich*. New York: Macmillan, 1970.

Sterno, Ida. "Hiding of Jewish Children in Belgium." *Yad Vashem Archives* 02/571, 1–3.

Stoltzfus, Nathan. *Hitler's Compromises: Coercion and Consensus in Nazi Germany*. Yale: Yale University Press, 2016.

Stoltzfus, Nathan. *Resistance of the Heart: Intermarriage and the Rosenstrasse Protest in Nazi Germany*. New York, London: W.W. Norton & Company, 1996.

Stoltzfus, Nathan and Birgit Katkin-Maier (eds.). *Protest in Hitler's "National Community": Social Unrest and the Nazi Response*. New York: Berghahn, 2015.

Ten Boom, Corrie. *The Hiding Place*. London: Hodder & Stoughton, 1971.

Thomas, Gordon and Greg Lewis. *Defying Hitler: The Germans Who Resisted Nazi Rule*. New York: Dutton Caliber, 2019.

Todorov, Tzvetan. *The Fragility of Goodness: Why Bulgaria's Jews Survived the Holocaust*. Princeton: Princeton University Press, 2001.

Weber, Thomas. *Becoming Hitler: The Making of a Nazi*. New York: Basic Books, 2015.

Wickert, Christi (ed.). *Frauen gegen die Diktatur: Widerstand und Verfolgung im nationalsozialistischen Deutschland 1933–1945*. Berlin: Gedenkstätte Deutscher Widerstand, 1995.

INDEX

Index